The Power of News

The Power of News

Michael Schudson

Harvard University Press
Cambridge, Massachusetts
London, England
1995

Library of Congress Cataloging-in-Publication Data

Schudson, Michael.
    The power of news / Michael Schudson.
      p. cm.
    A collection of the author's essays and research articles previously published between 1982 and the present; the extensive introductory chapter is published here for the first time.
    Includes bibliographical references and index.
    Contents: Introduction : News as public knowledge — Three hundred years of the American newspaper — The politics of narrative form — Question authority : a history of the news interview — What is a reporter? — Trout or hamburger : politics and telemythology — The illusion of Ronald Reagan's popularity — Watergate and the press — National news culture and the informational citizen — Was there ever a public sphere? — The news media and the democratic process.
    ISBN 0-674-69586-0
    1. Television broadcasting of news—United States. 2. American newspapers.
    3. Reporters and reporting—United States. I. Title.
PN4888.T4S38   1995
070.1'95—dc20
94-36194

Acknowledgments

This volume collects essays and research articles published between 1982 and the present. Even the earliest pieces (Chapters 2 and 10) strongly share theme and orientation with the latest. The introductory chapter, which refashions and extends the viewpoint of all the others, is published here for the first time.

I am grateful to Michael Aronson for helping me to see this was a book, and to the outside reviewers at Harvard University Press for encouraging me to write a substantial introduction, which nearly became a book in itself. I am obliged to Herbert Gans, Todd Gitlin, Daniel Hallin, Michael Janeway, Robert Manoff, Jay Rosen, and Barbie Zelizer for their critical readings of the introduction. I thank Mary Ellen Geer at Harvard University Press for her marvelously skillful editing.

Contents

The Power of News

Introduction: News as Public Knowledge

Imagine a world, one easily conceivable today, where governments, businesses, lobbyists, candidates, churches, and social movements deliver information directly to citizens on home computers. Journalism is momentarily abolished. Citizens tap into any information source they want on computer networks. They also send their own information and their own commentary; they are as easily disseminators as recipients of news. The Audubon Society and the Ku Klux Klan, criminals in prison, children at summer camp, elderly people in rest homes, the urban homeless and the rural recluse send and receive messages. Each of us our own journalist.

What would happen? At first, I expect, citizens would tend to rely on the most legitimate public officials for news, trusting especially to what the White House sent their way. The President, as the single most symbolically potent and legitimate source of authority, would gain greater power to set the national agenda than he has even today. Beyond a few obvious and highly legitimate sources like the President and the Chief Justice of the Supreme Court, people would tend to rely on local sources whose credibility on the information superhighway could be vouched for by their accessibility in person. Congregants would turn to their ministers, young athletes to their coaches, husbands and wives to each other. Other sources would be too difficult to evaluate. Congress, for instance, would be more cacophonous than ever. Lines of authority that today give congressional leaders more of a place in the public eye than congressional neophytes would erode.

At that point, even social critics who now long for more

public dialogue, more democratic discourse, more voices in the public sphere would have had enough. People would want ways to sort through the endless information available. What is most important? What is most relevant? What is most interesting? People would want help interpreting and explaining events. It is all very well to be able to call up at will the latest Supreme Court decisions, but who among us is competent to identify the key paragraphs and put them in context? A demand would arise not only for indexers and abstracters but for interpreters, reporters, editors. Some people would seek partisan abstracts and analysis, but others, less confident that any existing parties, cults, or sects represent their own views, would want independent observers, people wise to the ways of politics but without strong commitments to party, people able to read politicians well, to know them intimately, to see them and see through them.

Journalism—of some sort—would be reinvented. A professional press corps would reappear. With strong enough market incentives, it would be organized by commercial publishers. In the unlikely event that American political parties became unified enough to offer coherent perspectives on the news, a party press might surface. If government leadership itself were not satisfied with these alternatives, a government mouthpiece might find a spot, as it did up to the Civil War. It is hard to picture the contemporary world, even in the face of a technology that makes each of us potentially equal senders and receivers of information, without a specialized institution of journalism.

But why? Why do people feel a need for journalism? Why do people long to hear the news—not just gossip, not just information about people and places they know, not just a record of mysteries and marvels worldwide, not just practical bits of advice and useful notices, but a composite, shared, ordered, and edited product? What is the place of journalism in modern culture? What is it about news that makes it so much an element of modern public consciousness?

To understand journalism as a part of contemporary culture requires seeing how it works as both a set of concrete social institutions and a repertoire of historically fashioned literary practices. It requires, further, seeing how these institutions and practices are set within and in orientation to political democracy. This is no easy matter. Historians have neglected the topic of communication. Although some political scientists have recently renewed the study of political communication that briefly flourished in the 1950s and early 1960s, the media remain at the outskirts of academic studies of government, even if they are close to downtown for practicing politicians.[1] As a result, we have surprisingly little evidence about even fundamental questions. Is one kind of free press any better than the next at fostering democracy? Is it better for the media to be affiliated with parties or independent? Is a national commitment to public service broadcasting essential, as many European thinkers contend, or can market mechanisms suffice?

Do we even know what we would like the media to do? To provide information fully and fairly? To uncover wrongdoing and protect the people from political corruption? To excite and energize the public? Even if you or I knew our own preferences, we would not know which institutional arrangement for journalism would best serve them.

Be that as it may, journalists, politicians, academics, and the men and women in the street have a great deal of advice for the news media. Everyone in a democracy is a certified media critic, which is as it should be. Still, most criticism misfires because it misunderstands the character of contemporary journalism. What I want to suggest here, and what I hope many of the chapters that follow illustrate, is that we can understand the news media better if we recognize that what they produce—news—is a form of culture. This is to assert that news is related to, but is not the same as, ideology; it is related to, but is not the same as, information; and it is potentially, but only indirectly, a social force. What produces the news in this country—exchanges between sources and journalists within the structure of representative government and private news-gathering enterprises—is a strategic ballet, a form of political action in itself. But the news as such is a cultural product, not a political action; what connection it has to the political action of readers or viewers or to further political acts of government officials or other elites is rarely clear. News is a form of culture I will call here "public knowledge." This book explores the sociology and history of the American version of news, this modern, omnipresent brand of shared knowing.

News as Social Institution and Cultural Form

After the Eastern European revolutions of 1989, American journalists and media experts invaded the newly liberated societies with all kinds of advice on a free press, with a presumption of innocence unbecoming to a media system with faults as severe as our own. The absence of serious local broadcast news, the tabloidization of network magazine news shows, the cutbacks in national network news divisions, the resistance to news that does not fit professional consensus (remember that the *Washington Post* pursued the Watergate story for months largely on its own)—these are matters that might have been grounds for at least a bit of self-deprecation.[2]

There are serious defects in American journalism, and many of them can be traced to the profit motive. No one can blithely assume that the press will be free when patently it is run by a specific segment of the society with its own limited vision. This poses a problem for anyone who seeks to defend a capitalist press as a free press. There is no free lunchtime reading.

Of course, this observation is only a partial explanation of American journalism, as most leading thinkers on the left understand. But a sophomoric, populist vision persists that sees capitalist self-interest at every turn; each cover of *Time,* each "60 Minutes" investigation, and every *New York Times* front page designed with unfailing prescience to shore up a capitalist system; every apparent sign of debate or controversy merely a cover for a deeper uniformity of views.

For Noam Chomsky and Edward Herman, the whole matter is just that simple: the *New York Times* is *Pravda* (and the state apparently little more than a front for the ruling class).[3] Everything else is eyewash. This is misleading and mischievous, and it is worth taking a moment to say why. First, the *New York Times* has never intended to be anything like the late, unlamented *Pravda. Pravda* journalists understood their primary aim to be supporting the revolutionary socialist agenda as interpreted by the Communist Party of the Soviet Union. The *New York Times* journalists, although they may indeed be American patriots, see their day-to-day task as reporting the news, not elucidating a party line. They believe in fair and objective reporting. They almost always have strong views of professional ethics, but it is the unusual reporter who will have a strong political framework within which to see events of the day. Media owners, obedient to market demands or at least their sense of what the market demands, set limits on news coverage—notably, by setting budgets. But today they rarely seek to use the press as a soapbox for their own political views or the views of whatever political orthodoxy they subscribe to—if they subscribe to any.

Second, there is a vital arena of acceptable controversy in the United States. The grounds of difference between the leading political parties constitute a field of legitimate disagreement where the contemporary news media seek to represent both sides fairly. Neither George Bush nor Michael Dukakis questioned capitalism, neither Bill Clinton nor Bush questioned economic growth, and yet the differences between them are real and consequential—say, for gays in the military, women seeking abortions, men and women requiring welfare, poor people needing medical care, businessmen looking for tax breaks, manufacturers feeling oppressed by regulation. The differences make a difference, and it seems to me a stunning display of ideological blindness to suggest otherwise. Only if one can look in the eye the young gay man seeking a military career, the woman seeking a safe and legal abortion, the people whose "pre-existing conditions" keep them from obtaining health insurance and tell them all that their desires and hopes mean nothing in the greater scheme of things could one seriously hold such a view.

Third, there are multiple voices in the American news media. The American media do not have a wide-screen view of the range of possible political positions. Compared to the press in most liberal democracies, they foreshorten the representation of views on the left, as does the American political system generally. But these tendencies stop far short of uniformity. If competition often pushes the media toward the least common denominator of news reporting, other competitive pressures push news institutions not to miss a hot story—at least, not when it has reached a certain level of notice and notoriety. And a "hot story" is not necessarily one that pleases the powers-that-be. It may turn out to be My Lai or the Pinto or an oil spill or Watergate or Iran-Contra. The American press is unusually aggressive among Western news institutions in pursuing scandal.[4]

Moreover, the complexity of the American population and of its media industry means there are a variety of institutions and audiences whose interests do not line up neatly. Since *Sports Illustrated* numbers among its readers many boating and fishing enthusiasts, it published an early story on acid rain. Some powerful interests may have a stake in serving the masses— thus E. W. Scripps, Joseph Pulitzer, and William Randolph Hearst, media moguls whose papers sought a working-class clientele, endorsed policies and political causes that working people believed in. Whether their sympathy for the masses was sincere or not, sponsoring the cause of the relatively powerless served their interests.

Finally, the media are obligated not only to make profits but to maintain their credibility in the eyes of readers as they do so.[5] "The most valuable asset a paper has is its credibility," a *Baltimore Sun* editor has observed. "If people think we don't cover stories because they involve us, people will start wondering what else we don't cover."[6] The media must retain credibility not only with the population at large but with expert and often critical subgroups in the population (particularly in Washington). So long as there is heterogeneity among those subgroups, there will be pressure for fairness in the press.

While the *New York Times* is not *Pravda,* some of the more carefully directed darts and arrows of the critics on the left hit home. Certainly the claim that the media are, generally speaking, "statist" and deeply nationalist can be demonstrated.[7] Certainly we can recognize the pleasure journalists take and the rewards they garner in being insiders rather than gadflies; the corporate media do not make life comfortable for the likes of Edward R. Murrow, Daniel Schorr, Bill Moyers, Sydney Schanberg, or Bill Greider. Certainly the press more often follows than leads; it reinforces more than it challenges conventional wisdom.[8] Views at the margins get little coverage, not because they lack validity or interest but because they lack official sponsorship. If the corporate structure of the media does not in itself determine news content, it still tends to marginalize some news and some ways of telling the news. It still tends to subordinate news values to commercial values, and critics from various political persuasions rightly worry over what CBS news anchor Dan Rather termed the "showbizification" of news.[9] But to conclude from this only that "in all press systems, the news media are agents of those who exercise political and economic power" and that "the content of the news media always reflects the interests of those who finance the press," as one journalism scholar does, overrides every important distinction, every precious way in which the press in liberal societies differs from the press in state-run, one-party systems.[10]

The press has prominent critics on the right as well as the left. Right-critics cannot point to media *structures* as biased against their views; the left-critics win hands down on this point. But the right-critics argue that reporters and editors at leading national news institutions have a predominantly liberal outlook. They argue that news has a liberal bias because writers and editors of news are recruited from left-liberal circles. If corporate organization tilts unmistakably rightward, patterns of occupational recruitment veer just as sharply the other way. Those influential media analysts Richard Nixon, Patrick Buchanan, and Spiro Agnew made this case in 1969. There was—and is—a point here. In surveys conducted by Robert and Linda Lichter and Stanley Rothman, 54 percent of journalists at the prestige national news outlets identified themselves as liberals, 17 percent as conservatives, and the remainder as "middle of the road." While this does not justify the authors' broad conclusion that national journalists are "homogeneously" liberal, and while the survey's methodology has been sharply called into question, it reinforces the more casual observations of many observers.[11]

The political views of American journalists as a whole, in contrast to the Washington and New York–based news elite, are closer to those of Americans in general.[12] Even with national journalists, however, the Lichters and Rothman found a very *thin* liberalism. The journalists turned out to be liberal socially (53 percent think adultery is not wrong) but plain vanilla on economic issues (only 13 percent think government should own big corporations). Even the bare majority (54 percent) of journalists who declared themselves liberal, in other words, fully accepted the framework of capitalism although they wished for it a human face.

The right-critics, moreover, never satisfactorily deal with the question of whether journalists are effective at putting professional norms of objectivity ahead of their personal views. Liberal-leaning though a majority of the surveyed national journalists may be, close observers find that they are not highly political or politicized; journalists see themselves as professionals rather than partisans. They act to uphold professional tenets rather than to satisfy political passions.[13]

Still, critics on the right have usefully called attention to who writes as well as who owns the news. And it does make a difference, if not always in the direction the right-critics presume. Indeed, what may influence national journalists much more than their professed political views are their increasingly affluent personal situations, in which case the left has more cause for complaint than the right. The journalist William Greider laments that working-class reporters have been replaced by "the well-educated."[14] Howard Kurtz of the *Washington Post* writes of the isolation of reporters who drive in from the suburbs and report "by phone and fax." How could such reporters cover poverty or other problems of the inner city? "The plain fact is that newspapers reflect the mood and values of white, middle-class society, and that society, by the early '90s, had simply grown tired of the intractable problems of the urban underclass."[15]

But it is more than a matter of boredom or weariness. Journalists, like other human beings, more readily recognize and more eagerly pursue problems and issues when they concern people like themselves rather than "others" beyond their social circles. Two examples may illustrate the point. When the "Zoe Baird problem" arose in the 1992 controversy over President Bill Clinton's nomination of Zoe Baird to be Attorney General, news media coverage was uniform in a way that escaped notice. Zoe Baird and her husband had hired two people to care for their children in their home. Like most Americans in the same situation, they failed to pay social security taxes, as required by law, for the domestic employees; the revelation of this fact doomed Baird's appointment as chief law enforcement officer of the land. News coverage in almost all cases examined the legal, moral, and political issues raised by this incident—from the viewpoint of Zoe Baird or other people in similar circumstances.

But what of legal and moral implications *from the point of view of the domestic workers?* Barely a mention, let alone careful analysis. One exception was Univision, the Spanish-language television network, which profiled the domestics and did an extended story on child care from the viewpoint of underpaid and overworked immigrant care providers. Journalists at Univision, just as committed to professional norms as other journalists, educated in the same schools, participating in the same broader journalistic culture, nevertheless could identify not only with Zoe Baird, as a hard-working professional, but with the Latino domestic workers she hired.[16] The consensus in the mainstream press arose not from journalistic routines or patterns of ownership but from the broad class and racial bias in American society as a whole and the taken-for-granted angle of vision of mainstream journalism.

Or take the remark of the late Randy Shilts, the writer and *San Francisco Chronicle* reporter who covered AIDS full-time for his paper. When his book on AIDS, *And the Band Played On,* was published in 1987, he said in an interview, "Any good reporter could have done this story, but I think the reason I did it, and no one else did, is because I am gay. It was happening to people I cared about and loved."[17] Shilts's remark is simple and obvious—yet generally neglected in most analysis of journalism. Of course a woman reporter is more likely than a man, other things being equal, to see rape as a newsworthy issue. Of course an African American reporter rather than a white reporter, other things being equal, will find issues in the African American community newsworthy.

Empathy, fortunately for us all, is not beyond human capacity; good journalism often is the means by which empathy is evoked. But who writes the story matters. When minorities and women and people who have known poverty or misfortune first-hand are authors of news as well as its readers, the social world represented in the news expands and changes.

* * *

Critics from the right and critics from the left compose variations on the same theme—that the media are politically biased. An alternative view is that the media are not politically but professionally biased. Critics of political bias ordinarily presume that the journalist should be a professional who tells the truth. But for other critics, professionalism is the disease and not the cure.

Whether part of the problem or part of the solution, professionalism is the hallmark of the contemporary American press. In historical perspective there is nothing more striking than the transformation of journalism from the nineteenth-century partisan press to the twentieth-century commercial-professional press.[18] Comparing any leading metropolitan paper of 1995 to any of 1895 demonstrates instantly that today's news is shaped much more by a professional patina and is much less inflected by partisan hopes or fears than a truly political press. Reporters are far freer from marching in step behind an editorial line set by the publisher than they once were.

Analyzing the anti-political, anti-partisan perspective of professionalism is essential to understanding the contemporary press. But what follows from a view of the press as "professional"? Beginning in the early 1970s, sociologists and political scientists conducted studies, usually based on ethnographic observation of newsroom practices, that showed how media bias derives not from intentional ideological perversion but from professional achievement under the constraints of organizational routines and pressures. For these researchers, news organizations and news routines produce bias regardless of media ownership on the one hand or the outlook of individual reporters on the other. The quest for objectivity itself, in this view, is a source of bias.[19]

Four kinds of bias are frequently cited: news is said to be typically negative, detached, technical, and official. First, news tends to be bad news. Michael Robinson and Margaret Sheehan found that television news covering the 1980 presidential campaign was neutral or ambiguous in its evaluation of candidates most of the time. But in the one story out of five that could be judged "positive" or "negative," coverage (CBS) was negative 70 percent of the time (while the wire service, UPI, was more even-handed).[20] In 1992, television coverage of the three leading presidential contenders proved more negative than positive in every case, not because journalists are "adversarial" or nihilistic, but because they are professional.[21] News tends to emphasize conflict, dissension, and battle; out of a journalistic convention that there are two sides to any story, news heightens the appearance of conflict even in instances of relative consensus. Reporters increasingly try to "see through" rather than observe politics. While this keeps them from being bamboozled by the politicians they cover, it strips political leaders down to their worst stereotypes, people possessing no motive but political advantage.

Second, news tends to be detached. Increasingly, journalists take a distanced, even ironic stance toward political life—in fact, they are enjoined to do so by both the tenets of their professionalism and the cynical culture of the newsroom. Obviously, this does not apply to the sports story that takes partisanship for granted, or the human interest feature that depends on human sympathy in the reporter's and reader's hearts, or investigative reporting that presumes a capacity for moral indignation. But in election campaign news, for instance, detachment tutors readers in the cool and professional gaze that sees through policy pronouncements and rhetorical appeals to the strategies and tactics of the political trade. The "implied reader" of election news is a consumer in the political supermarket, someone with the time, interest, and attention to comparison-shop, to read the lists of ingredients on each package, to check the store's information on unit pricing, to attend to advertising as a form of information while learning to discount it as a type of propaganda. This ideal political consumer will then develop a reasonably rational preference for one candidate or the other. The trouble is that he or she will not have any incentive for actually turning that preference into a vote by going to the polls. The careful reader and watcher of the news might well be moved to stay at home, taking the lesson of contemporary campaign reporting to be "a pox on both your houses."

This relates to a third tendency in American journalism: an emphasis on strategy and tactics, political technique rather than policy outcome, the mechanical rather than the ideological. Focusing on the technical enables the journalist to be professional, because then he or she can remain apart from "the conflicts of interest, perspective, and value that are the dangerous stuff of political life."[22] Political reporters tend to be politics-wonks rather than policy-wonks, absorbed in "inside baseball" analysis rather than fascinated by the question of how government should run the country.

If you start with news professionalism in contemporary political culture, news that is negative, detached, and strategic naturally follows. Take the time when President Ronald Reagan, after vacationing in California, flew back to Washington but stopped en route in flood-ravaged Louisiana. There he made a brief radio broadcast from a flooded town, encouraging local citizens and promising federal aid. An

AP photo, accompanying the *New York Times*'s coverage, showed the President with a shovel helping to fill sandbags. The *Los Angeles Times* headlined its story, "Reagan Pitches In to Help Flood Victims." The *New York Times* played the story straight, but the *Los Angeles Times*, in the sixth paragraph, noted that this was just "the type of event Reagan's advisers constantly are on the lookout for." It was a chance to show the President "in a highly photogenic setting expressing concern for those in distress," and it came at "an opportune time for White House strategists" by drawing attention away from the "holiday with wealthy friends in Palm Springs." The report even noted that thirty-five telephone company workers were called away from flood duty to install cable for the radio broadcast facility for the President. The only hint of this critical analysis in the *New York Times* was a mention in the eleventh paragraph that "at one point, Mr. Reagan waited while a group of cameramen was ferried across a flooded area to the radio station so they could film him arriving there by Jeep."[23]

Was the *New York Times* derelict in failing to provide the strategic and political context that the *Los Angeles Times* offered its readers? Or was the *Los Angeles Times* unduly cynical? Was this a case where the show-biz President, struggling in the polls in a weak economy early in 1983, could help himself while genuinely helping the community? Can we be sure, as the *Los Angeles Times* report implies, that the radio broadcast stood in the way of genuine relief by removing the workers from flood duty? Or might it be that, for local morale, such a sacrifice was well worth it? Perhaps the *Los Angeles Times* went too far, but it is easy to recognize the grounds on which its story can be judged superior to that in the *New York Times*.[24]

Both stories illustrate the fourth tendency in the news: it is official, dependent on legitimate public sources, usually highly placed government officials and a relatively small number of reliable experts. News is as much a product of sources as of journalists; indeed, most analysts agree that sources have the upper hand.[25] Does this contradict the observation that professionalism leads to negative news? Not really. We can distinguish between routine news from official sources that occupies most of the paper most of the time and the more occasional news in which official pronouncements are questioned or undermined by accidents, scandals, leaks (from other officials), or the ironic reservations of the journalists themselves. In any event, officials remain the subject of news as well as its source, even though news often entangles them in negative coverage.[26]

Negative, detached, technical, and official—in this view, the problem with the press is professionalism, not its absence. Professionalism produces its own characteristic angle of vision, one which in the coverage of government may create a news product that helps reinforce in citizens a view of politics as a spectator sport.

To focus on media professionalism in understanding the news courts the danger of seeing journalism as journalists themselves do. When journalists portray themselves as hard-working, well-informed professionals whose idealistic streak and dedication to truth are dimmed only by competitive pressures, deadlines, conservative owners, and allegiance to official rules, they bask in their integrity as professionals. This represents their own subjective experience, but at the same time it misunderstands journalism as a whole. Journalism is not the sum of the individual subjective experiences of reporters and editors but the source or structure that gives rise to them. It is the matrix of institutions and outlooks that produce people who understand their situations in these terms.

This point requires illustration. The self-understandings of journalists do not go far enough. Take, for instance, this one: "We ran the story this way because the publisher/editor/producer has to keep his/her eye on the bottom line." The "bottom line" is one of the most elastic cultural constructs in the modern world. Not that there aren't financial constraints—businesses do regularly fail. But accounting is more art than science. This is especially true for news institutions, which normally operate with high profit margins and a high degree of organizational "slack," so that cutting costs or watching a budget is hardly ever a sufficient, or even genuine, explanation for why news is handled the way it is.

Or consider this sort of explanation: "We did not cover X or Y better because we were under deadline pressure." For more than thirty years print journalists have been saying that they can't compete with television as a "headline service." And for thirty years they still defend shoddy work by deadline pressure. The *Wall Street Journal* doesn't publish on Saturday or Sunday. Why does everyone else? Deadline pressure, like economic constraint, exists, but it is socially constructed, manipulable, revisable.

Journalists misunderstand themselves (to be fair, so do all other occupational groups, including professors). Caught up in the heat of office politics and personalities, inclined to explain the vicissitudes of news coverage by economic pressures, personal motives and biases, or the imprint of powerful individuals, they see the differences that surface and often fail to notice the common ground on which they stand. Not only do journalists work in particular kinds of organizations, but their work draws on and depends on particular cultural traditions. These traditions concern, among other things, how to know what is interesting or unusual, how to validate a claim, how to demonstrate one's own authorial legitimacy, how to write an arresting lead, how to win a journalistic prize, how to construct a news story as an acceptable moral tale.[27] The cultural traditions, often unspoken, often taken to be instinctual ("a nose for news") or acquired only by long experience in the field ("news judgment"), are the literary, intellectual, and cultural scaffolding on which the news is built.

Journalists, well aware of the formal and informal norms of professional practice, are less cognizant of the cultural traditions that specify when or how professional norms are called into play. Daniel Hallin writes of three domains of reporting, each operating by different journalistic rules.[28] In the zone of "legitimate controversy," recognition of a culturally sanctioned conflict (like anything on which the two leading political parties differ) guarantees a professionalism dedicated to presenting both sides. In the zone of deviance, there is coverage of issues, topics, or groups beyond the reach of normal reportorial obligations of balance and fairness. These can be ridiculed, marginalized, or trivialized without giving a hearing to "both sides" because reporters instinctively realize they are beyond the pale—like the women's movement in its earliest years.

The third zone is reporting on topics in which values are shared. It includes most feature writing, human interest reporting, much sports reporting, and occasional hard news reporting that can trust in a taken-for-granted human sympathy between reporter and reader. For instance, it is in theory conceivable that when expensive houses perched on the edge of canyons are destroyed by mudslides in California or when elegant vacation homes nestled in a flood plain are wiped out, a reporter would inquire of the devastated homeowners why they had been so stupid as to build there in the first place (or alternatively, they might ask the local zoning authority why they had allowed it). But by unspoken understanding, there are not two sides to human tragedies. Nor would a private citizen ever be interrogated with the kind of aggressive questioning a public official routinely receives. No one teaches this at a journalism school, but everyone knows it. It is part of the culture of news gathering, part of the etiquette of the profession.

Another crucial cultural distinction in journalism separates news into departments—local, national, and foreign; or general news, business, sports, and features. These are very powerful and consequential ways of dividing the field covered by news reporting. Take the distinction between general news reporting, centering on politics, and business reporting. Executives of large corporations who may often have more influence on the daily lives of citizens than government officials are invariably less visible in general news. Their names may be found on the business pages—but there the way they are covered is radically different. On the front page, journalists write in anticipation of readers who ask, "What is happening in the world today that I should know about *as a citizen* of my community, nation, and world?" On the business page, journalists presume readers who ask, "What is happening in the world today that I should know about *as an investor* to protect or advance my financial interests?"[29] The reporter may be scrupulously professional in both cases, but it is the conventions of the genre, not the competence of the reporter, that determine what can or cannot become a story, what angle will or will not make sense.

The news, then, is produced by people who operate, often unwittingly, within a cultural system, a reservoir of stored cultural meanings and patterns of discourse. It is organized by conventions of sourcing—who is a legitimate source or speaker or conveyer of information to a journalist. It lives by unspoken preconceptions about the audience—less a matter of who the audience actually may be than a projection by journalists of their own social worlds. News as a form of culture incorporates assumptions about what matters, what makes sense, what time and place we live in, what range of considerations we should take seriously. A news story is supposed to answer the questions "who," "what," "when," "where," and "why" about its subject, but understanding news as culture requires asking of news writing what categories of people count as "who," what kinds of things pass for facts or "whats," what geography and sense of time are inscribed as "where" and "when," and what counts as an explanation of "why." James Carey has argued brilliantly that news incorporates certain modes of explanation—and rejects, or makes subsidiary, others. For most news, the primary mode of explanation is "motives." Acts have agents, agents have intentions, intentions explain acts. In the coverage of politics, the agent is ordinarily a politician or candidate, the motive is ordinarily political advantage or political power. If this mode of explanation seems insufficient to understand a given act or event, reporters may look also to "causes," broader social or institutional forces at work. The unspoken convention is that reporters may ascribe motives on their own authority, but if they have recourse to "causes" they must find "experts" to make the case.[30]

The "what" of news is equally a product of cultural presuppositions. Metropolitan newspapers are increasingly dependent on their suburban readers and sometimes cater directly to their presumed needs and interests. But, as Phyllis Kaniss has observed in an important study of local news in Philadelphia, the central city remains the heart of local news coverage. Although a majority of readers do not live or work in the city or vote there, "news of the city government and city institutions . . . takes premier position over policy issues facing suburban communities." The development of suburban industrial parks is barely noticed, while downtown development or the renovation of the old train station wins continuous coverage. "These projects are given a place of prominence in the local news media not because of their importance to the regional audience, but because of their symbolic capital."[31] The mass media carry a great deal of symbolic freight in urban and regional identity, more than they know, certainly more than they self-consciously engineer. They help to establish in the imagination of a people a psychologically potent entity—a "community"—that can be located nowhere on the ground. News, in this sense, is more the pawn of shared presuppositions than the purveyor of self-conscious messages.

By advancing a notion of news as culture, I do not replace the determinisms of political economy or sociology for an equally rigid "culturology" that takes journalists to be cogs in a machine for the reproduction of an unvarying symbolic logic. On the contrary, I see political economy, geography, social systems, and culture interacting in the usual complex ways that only the best narrative history seems able to capture.

The interaction, of course, takes place *over time*. The culture of American journalism changes. It has been transformed in the past hundred years in several startling ways, two of which I describe in later chapters. The summary lead (see Chapter 2) and the news interview, as both a social and a literary practice (Chapter 3), are fundamental practices of news work today that no American editor or reporter before the Civil War would have recognized. Both the social practices and literary conventions of journalism are historical precipitates. Cultural forms did not creep out of the primordial ooze but emerged historically. They reflect, incorporate, and reinforce structures and values of a particular social world in ways that testify both to the structure and values of journalism and to the "world" it presumes to cover.

Journalism as a cultural system is not seamless. If there is danger in standing too close to the journalist, there is also risk in standing too far away. Individual journalists have individual voices, something I have tried to recognize in "What Is a Reporter?" (Chapter 4). Journalistic culture varies across different departments of a paper, across different media, across different news organizations. Publishers can make an enormous difference. "You show me a good editor and I'll show you a good publisher," former *Washington Post* editor Ben Bradlee said, "an owner who has encouraged that editor and given that editor the tools."[32] Different newspapers establish different historical traditions. The *New York Times* is known as an editor's paper, the *Washington Post* as a writer's paper; different firms have distinctive corporate cultures. Even a single news institution harbors many cultures, and they may be cultures at war—across different generations everywhere, across Jew and gentile, City College and Ivy League at the *New York Times,* or elitist and populist at the *Boston Globe.*

Journalism varies also across genre—even thinking only of political news, it varies from the breaking story to the reflective news analysis to the investigative series that takes three days to run, to the magazine essay, to the full-length book that is often a second look at material the writer first wrote as hard news. Even within a single story there is variation, from the headline and lead, which in the prestige press tend to defer to official sources, to the body of the story, in which alternative interpretations may appear and in which (as in the *Los Angeles Times* story on Reagan in Louisiana) an account may emerge that directly undermines the official version.

It is not enough, then, but it is at least the beginning, to recognize news as a social and cultural institution far more complicated than anything one could reduce to an articulate political ideology. News is a form of culture; but its particular features—what I call "public knowledge"—have still to be discussed.

Do the Media Cause Anything?

News is part of the background through which and with which people think. It is also one of the things—news or "the media" in general (in addition to the content of a particular news story)—that people think about. In Part II of this book I examine some of the beliefs people have about the news media—beliefs, I argue, that are quite wrong. I claim (in Chapter 5) that the visuality of television is much overrated as a source of its power. In Chapter 6, Elliot King and I argue that the press consistently exaggerated Ronald Reagan's popularity in his first years in office in part because of an ardent, if cynical, belief among Washington insiders that anyone who looked and sounded as good on television as Reagan did *must* be popular. And finally I look at the legacy of Watergate in journalism (Chapter 7), noting its importance for the culture of journalism but observing at the same time that both the Nixon administration and media professionals exaggerated the influence of the press in bringing down a president.

Together these three chapters emphasize that the media are a central topic in our cultural and political life and that estimates of their power are frequently exaggerated. Critics look at the press and see Superman when it's really just Clark Kent. This misperception, sadly, is not innocent. ABC news commentator Jeff Greenfield warns that if citizens believe the "myth" of media power (especially television power) to be true, "then it will become true sooner or later by default because it will disengage the citizens from the political process." It is not media power that disengages people but their belief in it, and the conviction of their own impotence in the face of it.[33] That belief is equally corrosive among elites. People drinking up the dominant culture of Washington, *New York Times* reporter Michael Kelly has suggested, "believe in polls. They believe in television; they believe in talk; they believe, most profoundly, in talk television. They believe in irony. They believe that nothing a politician does in public can be taken at face value, but that everything he does is a metaphor for something he is hiding . . . Above all, they believe in the power of what they have created, in the subjectivity of reality and the reality of perceptions, in image."[34]

The media are not nearly as important as the media, media culture, the talk show culture, and popular reflexes suggest.[35] (How is it that half of the American people believe in devils when there's not a trace of the devil to be found in the relentlessly secular mainstream media?)[36] They are not more important influences on the fabric of society than, say, the family, the schools, the criminal justice system, or—to choose two institutions that are not cultural objects in the popular culture or media culture at all—state governments or federal regulatory agencies.

Can I really mean that? I really do. There is little a television program or news story has ever done that produces as much direct, manifest, lacerating cruelty as parental acts, school policies, and government agency regulations regularly inflict on people.

News institutions, as social and economic actors, do have enormous impact on the well-being of their own employees. They or their representatives may also be significant political actors. In presidential primaries, for instance, reporters may seek to enhance or torpedo the prospects of particular candidates as they talk among themselves; newspaper endorsements in local elections where voters often know little or nothing about candidates may be very powerful.[37] But the primary, day-to-day contribution the news media make to the wider society they make as *cultural* actors, that is, as producers—and messengers—of meanings, symbols, messages. Culture, as Clifford Geertz observed, is not itself "a power, something to which social events, behaviors, institutions, or processes can be causally attributed," but instead "a context, something within which they can be intelligibly . . . described."[38]

I endorse this view, up to a point. I do not think the role of meaning in making lives will ever submit to tight causal analysis. Culture is the language in which action is constituted rather than the cause that generates action. So it should be no surprise that there is no handy theory of how culture influences action. Media scholars are all over the map on this. Some thinkers, assuming the overweening influence of "discursive structures" in constituting self and society, elaborating various poststructuralist reweavings of "hegemony theory," find in advertisements, news stories, or popular song lyrics the ideological reproduction of subtle racist, sexist, and other -ist traces of American or capitalist or Western ideology. They suggest that these cultural forms not only express but sustain racist, sexist, and other behavior. Others, portraying themselves as social psychological realists, point to the extraordinary capacity of individuals to reinterpret, resist, or subvert media messages, no matter how ideologically nasty or subtly encoded they may be. They weigh in with data or anecdote on how children subvert "Barney" by singing parodies, how women find grounds for independence in the very process of gobbling up romance novels that portray women as subordinate, or how prejudiced people read racially loaded sitcom humor one way and tolerant people take the same jokes to have the opposite meaning. Academic battle is joined between interpretative moralists who have made of textual analysis a performance art, and self-proclaimed defenders of individual freedom wielding social science in the name of humanism.

Who is right? I think of the Yiddish story about the two women who bring their dispute before the rabbi. The first one tells her side of the story. "You are right," says the rabbi. The second one tells her side. The rabbi is again persuaded and declares, "You are right." The rabbi's wife, listening to all of this, asks, "How can they both be right?" Unperturbed, the rabbi replies, "You are right, too."[39]

But the question of causality refuses to be set aside. Do the media "cause" anything? Does television lead to a more violent or a more fearful society? Do romance novels buy off potential feminist unrest? Does advertising make people materialistic? Did Harriet Beecher Stowe help start the Civil War? Did Wagner give aid and comfort to the rise of Fascism? These questions may be naive, but they are recurrent and unavoidable, and they even become questions of public policy. Should advertisements on children's television programs be banned? Should pornography be forbidden? Do sex education classes initiate young people in sexual practices, or do they serve to help young people who will engage in sex anyway to do it more wisely? What is the impact of cigarette advertising? Or warning labels on cigarette packages? Or instructional leaflets in medicine packages?[40]

The media *are* a "cause." Distributing information has visible and measurable consequences. There are copycat crimes that could not have happened without the media. Alleged criminals are apprehended because citizens recognized them from "America's Most Wanted."[41] People go for cancer screenings (by the millions) after news that the President has had a cancer operation.[42] People advertise their garage sales or businesses their liquidation sales in the local paper and customers are on their doorstep in the morning. People read the business page and call their brokers to buy or sell. People watch coverage of hurricanes in Florida and change their travel plans. Ploddingly dull as it may be to admit, transmitting useful information makes a difference. The message is the message. The "value added" by the ways in which the media inflect the information they pass on—and this is where almost all the attention of critics is focused—is a fractional increase to the sheer force of the mass distribution of information. News media, the sociologist Herbert Gans has argued, "remain primarily messengers . . . If they report news about rising unemployment, for example, the effects they produce stem from the unemployment, not of their reporting it." They are messengers of their major sources more than they are autonomous setters of the political agenda.[43]

But the media do add something to every story they run. When the media offer the public an item of news, they confer upon it public legitimacy. They bring it into a common public forum where it can be discussed by a general audience. They not only distribute the report of an event or announcement to a large group, they amplify it. An event or speech or document in one location becomes within a day, or within hours, or instantaneously, available to millions of people all over a region or country or the world. This has enormous effects.

One effect is the stimulation of social interaction on a different scale. In the early nineteenth century, amplification through the media brought rural Americans in contact with their local communities and a wider world as nothing else in their lives could. In the late nineteenth century, amplification enabled the growth of downtown department stores and central business districts. Department store ads helped the newspapers to prosper and the availability of the newspaper for advertising made it possible for the downtown store to thrive, altering patterns of marketing and residence in urban areas.

Public amplification also provides a certification of importance. I can remember how my older brother grew in stature, in my eyes, when the daily paper carried the box score of the high school basketball team he played on. Much later I remember that faculty and students at the University of Chicago walked taller when the university's new president, Hannah Gray, was interviewed on national television by Dick Cavett. These are small matters, but the same kind of phenomenon may loom much larger. Alice Walker recalls growing up in the South during the civil rights movement. When, in 1960, her family first owned a TV, "The face of Dr. Martin Luther King, Jr. was the first black face I saw on our new television screen. And, as in a fairy tale, my soul was stirred by the meaning for me of his mission . . . I saw in him the hero for whom I had waited so long."[44]

In a political democracy, the media are a vital force in keeping the concerns of the many in the field of vision of the governing few. "No substantial famine," observes Amartya Sen, an economist who writes extensively about famines, "has ever occurred in a country with a democratic form of government and a relatively free press." This is an extraordinary remark. And Sen adds that this is so even for poor democracies beset by crop failures. Electoral democracy, with the support of the news media, prevents famines.[45] When the audience for news is expanded, the shape of politics changes.

This is amplification but something more; it is a kind of moral amplification and moral organization. News on television, radio, or in print, produced by journalists, is different from messages that a government official or corporate executive might deliver straight to the public on the Internet or by a direct mail circular. The difference is not only that the journalist has the opportunity, indeed the professional obligation, to frame the message. It is also that the newspaper story or television broadcast transforms an event or statement into the cultural form called news. A news story is an announcement of special interest and importance. It is a declaration by a familiar private (or sometimes public) and usually professional (but occasionally political) entity in a public place that an event is noteworthy. It suggests that what is published has a call on public attention. Placement on the page or in the broadcast indicates *how* noteworthy; readers and viewers understand the hierarchy of importance this creates. It is a hierarchy of moral salience. It is no wonder that the sacred center of the working day on a metropolitan newspaper is the editorial conference to decide what stories will make page one, and where on the page they will go.

The news gains power not in its direct impact on audiences but in the belief, justified in viable democracies, that the knowledge of citizens can from time to time be effective. The power of the press grows in a political culture characterized by this belief.

Thus, as distributors and packagers of news, and as moral amplifiers and organizers, the mass media are a central institution of modern life. But acknowledging this does little to help determine the influence of the slant of news to left or to right, the organization of news by partisan or by professional norms, the "agenda setting" of news by choices of the journalistic fraternity.

Take the much admired experimental research by Donald Kinder and Shanto Iyengar. It shows that people in laboratory settings respond to information. If people see more stories about unemployment on television, they then judge unemployment to be a more pressing national problem. There are statistically significant and relatively persistent effects (by the standards of social psychology—the effects were present when subjects were tested *one week* later) of television on attitudes with a relatively small increment in the number of stories on a given subject. Almost all critics have found these results impressive.[46]

But is this either surprising or distressing? Aren't people quite right to take cues like this from television news? How much are the cues they take even a function of the media presentation? The news reporting on Three Mile Island galvanized the American anti-nuclear movement in 1979. But was this a media effect or a Three Mile Island effect? Iyengar and Kinder further demonstrate that television news may have a "priming" effect, influencing not what people think of a candidate for office but by what criteria that candidate should be judged. Is this wrong? And, again, is it an effect of the media or of events as national elites interpret them?[47]

If the phenomenon to be explained is large enough and pervasive enough, then the media can be found responsible for it *no matter what the features of the media are.* If, for instance, we want to explain the political indifference of Americans (a phenomenon social critics have complained about in some form for two hundred years), any feature of the media may be judged a contributing factor. Are the media aggressive investigators and critics in the public interest? Then the news is negative and disillusions the citizenry. Are the media compliant and complicit with the powers that be? Then the public is lulled into complacency or boredom. Are the media skeptical, ironic, or detached? Then they encourage the public's detachment. Are they too full of praise and glad tidings? Then that's the feel-good sedative of happy-talk local broadcast news. Are they sensational? Then they distract audiences from political and community concerns altogether.

Is there any imaginable form of journalism short of tracts for revolutionary parties that cannot be read as contributing to political disaffection? (All of these familiar arguments, of course, assume that the United States has an unusually high level of political alienation. Survey results that ask about people's "trust in government" suggest that this is not so.)[48]

What must astonish people with casual beliefs in the vast power of the media is how difficult it is to measure media influence. Even in areas where substantial monetary incentives should by now have produced authoritative knowledge of cultural effects—say, concerning techniques of advocacy in trial law or methods of persuasion in advertising, reliable instruction that goes much beyond common sense (take your audience into account, be clear and simple) is hard to come by.[49] The omnipresent political consultants all claim to be experts but offer conflicting advice and alter their counsel from one election to the next. "We are still artists, trying to develop a dramatic way of capturing the attention and then inspiring resolve," one consultant has said. "But we really don't know a great deal. If we knew more we would be dangerous."[50]

Many instances of presumed media effects fade or disappear on close examination. In the late 1960s and early 1970s, no one seemed to doubt that television coverage of the horrors of the Vietnam war turned the American people against the war, strengthened the antiwar movement, impressed upon Washington that this was an unpopular war, and so forced the United States out. This was proclaimed everywhere. Only there was not a shred of evidence to support it. Television news coverage was overwhelmingly favorable toward the American war effort up to Tet in 1968. Far from demonstrating the horrors of war, television sanitized the conflict, and the networks were particularly loath to show American soldiers who had been killed or wounded.[51]

Yet well before Tet, there was substantial public dissatisfaction with the war effort. A 1967 poll found that 50 percent of Americans be-lieved involvement in Vietnam was a mistake. When television and other news outlets grew more critical of the war after Tet, polls actually found a temporary increase in support for the war, a rallying around the flag at a time of trouble. By the time Walter Cronkite declared (on February 27, 1968) that the war was a stalemate, he was only coming around to the views of middle America. It is hard to disagree with George Moss when he writes that public opinion influenced television coverage of the war more than television influenced public opinion. Moss concludes that the role of the media in determining the outcome of the war was "peripheral, minor, trivial, in fact, so inconsequential it is unmeasurable."[52]

Many "effects" once attributed to the powerful media turn out to be explained more simply by other factors. Did the yellow press lead America into the Spanish-American War? The press in fact was di-vided on the issue. There is little indication that the much denigrated mass-circulation New York papers had special influence on Congress or the President. When historians point to deep-seated expansionist tendencies in American foreign policy and the strong sense of political leaders stemming from the Monroe Doctrine that Latin America lay within the sphere of influence of the United States, it is hardly nec-essary to posit media-driven jingoism to explain the war with Spain. Early accounts of the war make no special mention of the yellow press. Historians in the 1920s and 1930s, however, shocked by World War I and convinced that British propagandists had helped drag the United States into a war where it had no real stake, read their analysis of the world war back into the Spanish-American one.[53]

They were wrong twice over. Each British propaganda effort in the United States in World War I was matched by a very skillful German one; the emphasis on "propaganda" does nothing to explain American intervention.[54] The revisionists of the thirties have long since passed from favor, but the legend they sowed of the yellow press still lives, and breathless accounts of media power go on and on. The present culprit is, of course, television. There is no doubt that television has had a significant influence on American politics and culture. It has certainly altered the character and style of political campaigning, for example, but this may have had little impact on voters' decision making. Despite the endless analysis of the political ills brought on by television's visuality and its short sound bites, all the problems wrought by the short attention span of television journalism, all the faults of horse-race coverage, and on and on, one political scientist who has reviewed the relevant studies of these changes concludes, "I have not . . . found any evidence that these changes have affected the quality of American democracy in any significant way."[55]

Now, it may be fair to respond, what counts as evidence of the quality of American democracy? But the question needs to be addressed by those who insist on the power of the media as well as those who deny it. I would at least propose what does not count as evidence: complaints about the media by losing candidates. Loss precipitates a search for scapegoats, and the media are a popular choice. Losing candidates in elections have been blaming their defeats on the weak-willed or misled public since colonial days, when losers regularly complained about "the declining state of republican virtue."[56] The modern version is to blame television for debasing the political coin and misleading or misinforming voters. Walter Mondale, losing the foreordained election of 1984 to Ronald Reagan, a peace-time president riding high in the polls on a wave of renewed prosperity after the 1981–82 recession, blamed his loss on television: "I've never really warmed up to television. And, in fairness to television, it has never really warmed up to me."[57] Michael Dukakis, after losing the 1988 race for president, attacked "the increasingly shallow nature of electoral campaigns that trivialize important issues in the service of image making." The election, he held, turned out to be "about phraseology. It was about ten-second sound bites. And made-for-TV backdrops. And going negative." His biggest mistake, he felt, was a failure to understand television news.[58]

Election *winners,* of course, do not attribute their victories to the same forces that the losers tell us caused their defeats. People frequently believe that their successes derive from their own capacities while their failures are the products of an external force.[59] There should be a moratorium on commentators' taking too seriously any of the remarks by winning or losing candidates.

Current preoccupation with the media mistakes the public parlor of loquaciousness for the heart of society. The life of a house is more often to be found in the kitchen or the bedroom. Still, we judge ourselves and are judged by others on the quality and character of talk in the public parlor. The parlor is the family's face to the world, the intersection of private and public. People rarely occupy it, but it is where they face outsiders; it is their symbolic self-portrait for the wider world.

Visibility is important in itself. The greatest media effects may not be measurable influences on attitudes or beliefs produced by media slant but the range of information the media make available to individual human minds, the range of connections they bring to light, the particular social practices and collective rituals by which they organize our days and ways. The media, I think, are more important, not less important, than popular opinion would have it, but rarely in the ways that popular views assume. The media organize not just information but audiences. They legitimize not just events and the sources that report them but readers and views. Their capacity *to publicly include* is perhaps their most important feature. That you and I read the same front page or see the same television news as the President of the United States and the chair of IBM is empowering; the impression it promotes of equality and commonality, illusion though it is, sustains a hope of democratic life. Moreover, visibility—public visibility—is of enormous importance even if few people bother to read or watch the news. So long as information is publicly available, political actors have to behave *as if* someone in the public is paying attention. If the news media are the messenger services for political elites, they are not private messenger services, and this is an essential element of the messages conveyed. (In contrast, in Chinese journalism two systems of reporting coexist, the public news printed daily in the papers and a second system of internal memos journalists write when the news might be embarrassing to the Communist Party or its key members if published.)[60] Contemporary American journalism presumes that the public is eavesdropping; even if the public is absent, the assumption of the public presence makes all the difference.

News as Public Knowledge

Suppose we ask why the public has vanished (if that is so)? Why an active citizenry has disintegrated (if that is so)? As I suggest in Chapter 9, I do not think these questions are fairly posed. But they are familiar questions in contemporary social criticism. And if we provisionally accept their premises, how do we explain the low level of active citizenship today?

The first half-dozen reasons, in order of importance, have little to do with the news media. For starters, there is the shift from a Congress-centered to an executive-centered government beginning early in this century; from a domestic-centered national government to one where military matters have dominated and a "national security state" has powered our political life, dating from the 1940s; the shift from a society of "island communities" where local politics was of substantial importance and the federal government only remotely and episodically relevant to everyday life to a world where the likes of an income tax (1913), social security and other welfare programs (1930s), direct grants to higher education and to students in higher education (1944), active federal intervention in state and local affairs to enforce the Fourteenth Amendment (1950s), and permanent federal responsibility for employment policy (1930s and after) have irretrievably national-ized the experience of being American. Add to this that the democ-ratization of political parties through primary elections has weakened their power and paradoxically reduced the participatory strength of local party organizations; that electoral reforms like the secret ballot and voter registration depressed voter turnout and removed the party's fingers from the ballot; that affluence and mobility have made family life more private—with fewer openings to the local bar, park, or neigh-borhood store, and more connections to persons and institutions far from local, geography-based political units. All this has more to do with the character of the public, the public sphere, and the possibil-ities of citizenship than the bias, ownership concentration, or intel-lectual quality of the news media.

I do not deny the news media their due; I want to know what that due is by seeing the media in the context of other social and political forces as part of a broad ecology of public communication. Too often debate about the role of the news media in democracy takes place in isolation, as if all democracy required were that the press transmit the best possible information from the expert journalists who can judge it to the masses of readers who can make use of it. Of course, political reporting should keep citizens informed. Without accurate information about the views and values of candidates for office, a citizenry cannot cast intelligent ballots; without adequate coverage of the operation of government between elections, the attentive populace cannot effec-tively monitor the performance of their chosen representatives.

But what can a citizenry do if it *does* have information? What would happen if professional journalists were free to provide the best infor-mation they could, undistorted by competitive feeding frenzies that center on matters irrelevant to the public good, unaffected by com-mercial requirements that displace political news for advertising, sports, and recipes, uncensored by the fear that writing in depth about real politics will bore the public and doom the stories to go unread? If journalists could write what they wanted according to the highest ideals of the press, would democracy be saved?

To ask the question is to recognize the answer: of course not. A public with information available to it is not an informed public. Even a public with information in its head is not necessarily a public with the motivation or frame of reference or capacity to act in a democracy. As I suggest in Chapter 8, there is a difference between the "informational citizen," saturated with bits and bytes of information, and the informed citizen, the person who has not only information but a point of view and preferences with which to make sense of it.

Indeed, one can make the perverse argument that the better and the more information journalism provides, the more anemic political society grows. Michael Robinson has argued that "any increase in available political information within a society, especially a libertarian society, will probably increase, to some degree, the level of political frustration or disaffection."[61] Robinson suggested that the more aggressive and critical journalism becomes, the more certain it is that regular news consumers will find politics leaving a bad taste in their mouths. Others have argued that the more news becomes objective, the more surely will readers and viewers reject politics as incomprehensible. At best, they will learn to judge politics from a distance, as expert critics rather than active participants.

Well, interesting if true.[62] But it is unlikely that such effects, if they exist, are very strong. There is a great distance between news and political action. The effect of the former on the latter will always be difficult to measure because news is not autonomous. It does not constitute political discourse but relays, refines, and reuses it. As news became both more negative and more professional over the past generation, the American right became more politicized on a mass base through the pro-life movement than perhaps ever before in this century. This is hardly the consequence media critics would predict. They see news making American politics conservative by demobilizing the left, not activating the right!

Meanwhile, citizens have elected substantial numbers of black politicians to office for the first time since Reconstruction. Women have become a political force and have been elected to political office in unprecedented numbers. A large and politically astute environmental movement has emerged. None of this was prevented by the demobilizing powers of the media. Could this political activity have been greater with better news? Perhaps, but I don't think any observer of these movements attributes their setbacks or their triumphs primarily to the media. Political activity leads people to follow the news. News does not ordinarily lead people to political activity.

The best study of the media and social movements, Todd Gitlin's book on SDS in the media spotlight, is equivocal. On the one hand, *New York Times* coverage of early SDS contributed significantly to the rapid growth of the organization. This was the power of amplification— the wide distribution of the news that the organization existed made the phone ring off the hook at SDS headquarters. But how much did the character of media coverage later, coverage that trivialized and marginalized the efforts of SDS, contribute to the breakdown of a rel- atively resource-poor, student-based movement buffeted by the growth of richer and more "legitimate" protest efforts of conventional liberals coming to oppose the Vietnam war, and torn by ideological struggles of the sort left-wing organizations have long been famous for? Gitlin suggests that media coverage contributed to the disintegration of SDS, and he may be right. But it is easier to see how the early, sympathetic coverage hurt SDS than the later critical coverage did. The early cov- erage was an advertisement for SDS that helped bring in new members. These "Prairie Power" members displaced the "Old Guard," shifting the orientation of SDS from an agency of the organized Left to a co- ordinating center for a mass student movement. New members were more volatile, more impatient, and the shift in leadership "fractured" the organization. It is not hard to argue that the influence of new members inside SDS rather than later condescending or dismissive news coverage outside made the largest difference in the implosion of SDS. Gitlin's analysis is compelling for what it says about the con- ventional or "hegemonic" political framework of the mainstream news media, but not for what it implies about the news as a social force in general.[63]

This is not to say that the press does not influence democracy; democracy in the contemporary world is scarcely conceivable, scarcely definable without it. But can the media do better in serving democ- racy?

Better at exactly what, we might ask. I can imagine at least seven not altogether compatible goals a media system dedicated to democ- racy might aspire to:

1. The news media should provide citizens fair and full information so that they can make sound decisions as citizens. (In other words, the media should do just what most journalists say they try to do—with the unhappy effect, according to some critics, of boring or confusing people, and turning them away from politics.)[64]

2. The news media should provide coherent frameworks to help citizens comprehend the complex political universe. They should

analyze and interpret politics in ways that enable citizens to understand and to act. (In other words, the media should do exactly what the professional goal of objectivity swears they should not do: interpret the news.)

3. The media should serve as common carriers of the perspectives of the varied groups in society; they should be, in the words of Herbert Gans, "multiperspectival."[65] (In other words, the media should not provide an overarching coherence to the news, exactly the contrary of goal 2.)

4. The news media should provide the quantity and quality of news that people want; that is, the market should be the criterion for the production of news. (In other words, the news media should adhere to the rule that many critics insist drives the press toward the sensational, the prurient, and the trivial.)

5. The media should represent the public and speak for and to the public interest in order to hold government accountable.

6. The news media should evoke empathy and provide deep understanding so that citizens at large can appreciate the situation of other human beings in the world and so elites can come to know and understand the situation of other human beings, notably nonelites, and learn compassion for them. (In other words, the news media should do exactly what diplomats who distrust compassion as a basis for foreign policy have roundly criticized them for doing in displaying the human plight of the people of Sarajevo and Somalia.)[66]

7. The news media should provide a forum for dialogue among citizens that not only informs democratic decision making but is, as a process, an element in it.

The news media collectively do all these things today. In fact, a single news institution may attempt all seven impossible things before breakfast. But note that one objective may contradict the next. And note as well that providing fair and accurate information, the measure by which the press is most often judged, is only one of many goals the press may hold out for itself. We are a long way from a coherent normative theory of journalism. And there is little to push news institutions to change this. Unlike the automobile industry or microelectronics, American journalism is not challenged from abroad. Unlike higher education, it is not stimulated by a diversity of models of excellence within. Diversity is not much admired inside journalism. The underground press, the partisan press, the alternative papers exist but are generally ignored. News stories trickle down from elite outlets to others, but the "trickle up" of significant stories is rare enough to excite comment or even a Pulitzer Prize.[67] Journalism seems to ignore or denigrate what could be its most valuable seeds of change. Small may be beautiful in Amish quiltmaking or in the start-up of software companies—but not in journalism. Journalism, even at its research centers and with its foundation supporters, seems overcome with the charms of celebrity, commercial success, and national reach.

Although in other spheres, from medicine to welfare to social work to education, a focus on the formulation of public policy sharpens thought, most policy concerns in the news media are entirely libertarian—just keep the government out. It is easy to have sympathy with that. But what follows is that the media do not have to think about themselves the way most other institutions do—as subject to public review and regulative public policies. Journalists' reflections on their own business are not tested in the discipline of actually having to influence institutional policy. In contrast, even a rube academic, working out the freshman general education course or revising admissions requirements or preparing a report for an accreditation committee, has more firsthand experience in policymaking than many experienced journalists who write about it.

The American news media may be the best in the world—although I doubt that political systems and cultures are comparable enough to make that a meaningful statement. American journalism may be better today than ever before—I believe this is so. But whether it serves democracy as well as it might is another matter, about which the press speaks in pragmatic terms very little and acts on still less. This may change. Within journalism, there is a fledgling movement for "public journalism" that seeks to institutionalize ways in which the general public, rather than journalists or government officials, could help set the news agenda.[68] There is now serious discussion of what to do when the First Amendment undermines rather than assures democracy. Cass Sunstein is among the constitutional scholars who argue that a "free market" view of free speech and press can stand in the way of promoting deliberative democracy. He points to policy options consistent with democracy that might be tried out: mandating by law a right of reply in newspapers, for instance, or even establishing content-neutral government subsidies to newspapers that provide in-depth coverage of political issues.[69]

These are encouraging developments. If they can be faulted, it is only that they still tend to treat news as information. That may be as mistaken in the long run as to take news as ideology. News is culture. To develop this notion consistently, the question would be not whether we have more or less news but what kind of news it is we have. And it is not a matter of deciding the impact of news on democracy (or democracy on news) but the mutually constitutive character of both.

Consider the implications of this for understanding the norms and routines of professional journalism. Media professionalism is defined not in relation to some abstract measure of professional integrity but in relation to concrete political structures and the political culture of a given society. Italian television news, in contrast to American, presents politics as party activity rather than as government or as presidential electioneering. That is, in this country, normal political news is the story of the President trying to govern, or trying to govern in a way to maximize his chances for reelection, aided or vexed by the Congress, buoyed or undermined by world events, his way eased or made precarious by economic forces largely beyond his control. Journalists are authorized to interpret the President's efforts, so long as they do so in terms of political motives rather than underlying social causes. In contrast, Italian television news regularly cites the positions of leading political parties on most major events of the day. The journalists act as mediators more than interpreters; by ceding to party spokesmen the responsibility for interpretation, they reinforce the priority of party politics as the acceptable framework for understanding political events. To take a third case, Japanese television portrays government as bureaucratic policymaking rather than as party politics or the individual heroics of leadership.[70] In all three cases, journalists adhere to professional standards, but they do so within different political cultures. What they produce and reproduce is not information— if there is such a thing; it is what is recognized or accepted as public knowledge given certain political structures and traditions.

In comparative perspective, what Americans get in their news is not so much the idiosyncratic interpretation of an individual journalist or newspaper but a more or less consensual interpretation springing from the common vantage of regular political correspondents who step into a public arena where political parties do not provide comprehensive viewpoints themselves. American television news—but also print news—credits the idea, in Paul Weaver's words, "that there exists in America a single coherent national agenda which can be perceived as such by any reasonable and well-intentioned person."[71] In Italy, news coverage gives parties their voices; in the United States, news coverage responds to the weakness of parties—and then adds to it.

The question is not how to inform or engage the public but what sort of public it is that in this time and this place might be informed or engaged. Media criticism that yearns for an active public needs to reconsider just what a "public" means. The "public" today is less an existing community than a rhetorical gesture expressing discontent with the way the human moral center of gravity has shifted from near at hand to far. Or it is a way to mark dissatisfaction with the institutions we have so far devised to ensure a watchfulness over political leadership—elections and representatives, a free press, and voluntary associations.

But if there is a missing public, a phantom public as Walter Lippmann spoke of it seventy years ago, we will not find it in eighteenth-century coffeehouses or nineteenth-century torchlight parades. We will have to invent it for ourselves, in a world with cars and malls and subways and suburbs and televisions—but also a world with talk radio, electronic mail, mass higher education at colleges and universities with stronger traditions of free speech and inquiry than the eighteenth or nineteenth centuries could have imagined. This is a world where once-vital institutions—of public oratory and political parties—have a diminished hold on popular sentiment, but where judicial attention to the Bill of Rights is stronger than ever. I do not know that the gains and losses can be neatly totted up. But I think it is nonsense to believe, out of abhorrence of capitalist rapaciousness or a diffuse intellectual Weltschmerz or wistfulness about time passing and the virtues of the good old days, that there can be no "public" today. The public has ever been fictional. It is the democratic fiction par excellence, carried by the imaginations of people in authority who want to get things done or by people without authority who believe a better world can yet be made, and sustained in good times and bad by republican institutions—elections, a free press, parties, the rule of law, and the arts of association. It is the fiction that brings self-government to life.

Our moral destiny turns, Williams James said, on "the power of voluntarily attending." But he recognized, a century ago, that these acts of voluntary attention are "brief and fitful." Even so, he argued, they are all-important to our individual and collective destinies.[72] In a way, James was only echoing Tocqueville, who observed that "even when one has won the confidence of a democratic nation, it is a hard matter to attract its attention."[73]

It is a hard matter indeed, and one that, to be honest, affects all of us. Each time I visit friends in Washington I find myself shamed by how much better informed they are than I about the news of the day—shamed, that is, until I remember that the "news of the day" is made by people they know or work with or chance upon and that the "news of the day" to which we attribute so much moral import is for them local gossip. They are not necessarily better human beings than I. They are human beings differently situated.

Can the media help people pay more attention? As I suggest in Chapter 10, this is one of two questions that the media should be asking themselves. The other question is: in the *absence* of wide readership or mass viewership, how can the media improve democracy? If the media cannot by themselves entice an audience to attend to public issues, if most of the time most people will have better things to do than watch the news or read the front page, can the media still serve a democratic function? Congress itself faces the problem of attention: how can congressional representatives make reasonably informed votes on issues where they have not been able to inform themselves? What happens in practice is that legislators do not gather information so much as they "take cues" as they vote on complex issues about which they are largely ignorant. They follow the lead of better informed, trusted colleagues whom they would probably agree with if they had time to make independent evaluations themselves.[74]

It will not do to blame the victim, the underinformed citizen, for the failures of American democracy. Nor will it suffice to blame the messenger, the media burdened with greater expectations than they could ever meet. The structure of our polity and our parties is implicated. The fabric of our everyday lives at home, work, church, and school, on the freeway and in the supermarket, at the Little League game or on the street, is involved.

The news serves a vital democratic function whether in a given instance anyone out there is listening or not. The news constructs a symbolic world that has a kind of priority, a certification of legitimate importance. And that symbolic world, putatively and practically, in its easy availability, in its cheap, quotidien, throw-away material form, becomes the property of all of us. That is a lesson in democracy in itself. It makes the news a resource when people are ready to take political action, whether those people are ordinary citizens or lobbyists, leaders of social movements or federal judges. This is the necessity and the promise of the public knowledge we call news and the political culture of which it is an essential part.

I The News in Historical Perspective

1 Three Hundred Years of the American Newspaper

The American newspaper is a remarkable institution, an intriguing and important historical achievement, today the most representative carrier and construer and creator of modern public consciousness. But its very familiarity may make this difficult to keep in mind. It is both remarkable and ordinary at once, and it has been so at least since Ralph Waldo Emerson wrote about it in his journal 140 years ago: "The immense amount of valuable knowledge now afloat in society enriches the newspapers, so that one cannot snatch an old newspaper to wrap his shoes in, without his eye being caught by some paragraph of precious science out of London or Paris which he hesitates to lose forever. My wife grows nervous when I give her waste paper lest she is burning holy writ, and wishes to read it before she puts it under her pies."[1]

But, then, of course, she does put it under her pies, a practice that says something important about the everydayness of the newspaper as opposed, say, to books—or as opposed to newspapers a few generations earlier. In the eighteenth century Samuel Sewall of Boston collected and bound his newspapers, and Martha Moore Ballard, a Maine midwife, did so as late as 1799, when she recorded in her diary that she spent the day "putting the newspapers in regular order and sewing them."[2] Notice, in Emerson's remark, the dubious attitude toward those paragraphs of precious science and toward any inclination to see them as holy writ. And notice also that Emerson takes the newspaper to be relaying information about the world, paragraphs of precious science, rather than picturing some aspect of the world from a given point of view for an appointed purpose. He takes what we call the newspaper to be a purveyor of news rather than a promoter of views.

This was not always so in journalism. Indeed, it is probably not going too far to say that the penny press invented news in the 1830s, and that the nineteenth century invented reporting.[3] It is true that Shakespeare's Richard III inquired of Ratcliff, "How now! What news?" and of Lord Stanley, "Stanley, what news with you?" But Richard sought military intelligence, not what we know as news. That is, he did not seek to satisfy a general curiosity about the world. He did not seek to keep abreast of current affairs as part of a general surveillance of the world or as currency in social relations. He certainly did not seek a journalist's evaluation of what is of general interest and importance in the world happening that day. He did not, in a word, seek what we think of as news.

In this chapter I want to pursue the notion that news is a historically situated category rather than a universal and timeless feature of human societies. I want also to suggest that if the very category of news is a historical precipitate, so is any particular news story a social construction. That is, a news story is an account of the "real world," just as a rumor is another kind of account of the real world, and a historical novel another sort of account of the real world. It is not reality itself (as if any sequence of words and sentences could be) but a transcription, and any transcription is a transformation, a simplification, and a reduction. The newspaper, as the carrier of news stories, participates in the construction of the mental worlds in which we live rather than in the reproduction of the "real world" we live in relation to. This does not suggest that when we read about a military battle in the newspaper we should necessarily doubt that a battle took place. It does mean that when French citizens read in their newspapers about the battle of Waterloo they read a very different story and incorporated it into a very different scenario than did the English reading their newspapers. As Walter Lippmann insisted in *Public Opinion,* people respond not to the world but to the "pictures in their heads," something very different.[4] The pictures people have, or fail to have, in their heads have very real consequences: the battle of New Orleans was fought in 1815, and people died in it, because their picture was that they were engaged in a war when, in London and in Washington, the war was already over. But military officers in New Orleans had fatefully and fatally different pictures in their heads.

It should come as no surprise that there is confusion about the social and, particularly, the historical construction of news because standard treatments of general history omit journalism altogether. I say this with some caution about European history, since I am less familiar with those materials, but I will say it with assurance about American historiography. Take, for instance, a leading college textbook in American history, John Blum's *The National Experience*.[5] What do we learn there of Zenger and Franklin and Greeley, Hearst and Lippmann and Paley, not to mention the likes of James Franklin or William Lloyd Garrison or Edward R. Murrow or Woodward and Bernstein? Well, James Franklin, the first journalist in the world to report the vote count on a bill in a legislature, is not mentioned. John Peter Zenger, the printer found not guilty in 1735 when his lawyer argued that the press could not libel the government by printing the truth, is not mentioned. Garrison is mentioned as a peace movement activist and then as an antislavery activist and editor of *The Liberator*. His brief treatment takes in more of his journalistic role than any other figure I looked up, although this is backhandedly used to diminish his historical importance: "But he was more an editor and publicist than an effective leader and tactician, and the movement soon grew too large for him to control." Greeley is mentioned as a presidential candidate in 1872. He is described as editor of "the influential" *New York Tribune*, but there is not a word about what that influence was. Paley is cited as head of the Materials Policy Commission in 1952. CBS is not mentioned. Hearst is mentioned briefly in connection with the Spanish-American War and in a sentence that declares that the assault on privacy and taste in the 1890s begun by Pulitzer was "continued and intensified by his imitator, William Randolph Hearst." Pulitzer is also mentioned as the father of a new school of journalists who reached the masses by making the news "more sensational and vulgar." Lippmann gets eight mentions, but who Lippmann is is not made clear. Early on, he is described as an intellectual; later, in the 1960s, a commentator; later, as a critic of the Vietnam war, a foreign-policy expert. In every case, he is quoted as an articulate observer of the political or economic scene around him, but nowhere is he cited as a journalist, an influence on journalism, or a theorist of public communication. Murrow's one mention is similar. He is quoted as a critic of television's homogenizing influence on American life, but nothing is said of his journalism. Of the fifteen references to Benjamin Franklin, only the first mentions his role as a journalist, almost parenthetically, noting that he gained success in everything he tried, "whether it was running a Philadelphia newspaper in his youth or wooing the ladies of Paris in his old age." As a printer, the text says, Franklin "defended his right to publish what he pleased" but says nothing of what that might have meant to Franklin or how that distinguished him, if it did, from others, nor how much his view was an expression of a belief in commercial liberty rather than political freedom. And Woodward and Bernstein? This is one of the most interesting citations. In the text, the Watergate break-in happens in June 1972; a grand jury indicts the burglars in September; the trial begins in February, and only then are Woodward and Bernstein described as "meanwhile beginning to uncover sources in the executive branch, especially a mysterious and knowledgeable figure whom they identified only as Deep Throat." By that time, Woodward and Bernstein's main Watergate work was behind them, and the *Washington Post*'s courage in pursuing the Watergate story was already past. But it's hard to criticize a general textbook when you read Stanley Kutler's valuable new study of Watergate, *The Wars of Watergate*, which, however, in some 600 pages of text devotes but a few paragraphs to the news media. It mentions Woodward and Bernstein, but you won't find the names Katherine Graham or Benjamin Bradlee anywhere. The *Washington Post*'s pursuit of the Watergate story is a small sidenote in Kutler's account.[6]

Why should journalism be so invisible in American historiography? When we are writing about the rise of a peculiarly democratic society, a nation that organized its politics through parties and its parties through newspapers for a century or more, when we are writing about a nation that at least rhetorically takes the First Amendment as its most distinctive constitutional feature and the Constitution as its most distinctive political legacy, why, after three hundred years of the American newspaper and after two hundred years of the Bill of Rights, can we still write American history without American journalism?

The answer to this has to do, no doubt, with the way history writing is institutionalized in American universities, but it has also to do with the great gap between the character of communication as a social function and the conventions of historiography. To borrow James Carey's useful distinction, we operate with two models of what communication is and how it works. The first is the transmission model, which takes communication to be the transportation of ideas or information from a sender to a receiver. This is the dominant popular and academic concept. Alternatively, there is a ritual model that takes communication to be a social function of building solidarity and reaffirming common values within a community. Communication constitutes a community rather than transports a message.[7] When the paper says what the mayor did yesterday, it transmits information. But in reporting what the mayor did yesterday, the newspaper also reaffirms the reader's connection to the city he or she lives in or lives near. In the transmission model, a medium of communication tells us what happened; in the ritual model, a medium of communication tells us who we are. I want to suggest that the transmission model of communication fits the presuppositions of history writing but in a way that guarantees the invisibility of the press. The ritual model of communication does not fit the epistemological or narrative conventions of historiography, but it is better suited for understanding the role that communication has played in our national past.

In the transmission model of communication, the press would have a place when it could be identified as the originator or exclusive or predominant disseminator of an idea or program or piece of information that affects what people think. The transmission model draws our attention to the press, if the press acts intentionally with clear consequences. The media may try to advocate, to mobilize, to organize. Even when they do, however, it is rarely possible to identify clearly the consequences of their actions. Even in Watergate, an argument can be made that Woodward and Bernstein and Graham and Bradlee were much less important to the discovery of wrongdoing than security guard Frank Wills, the district police, Judge Sirica, the Federal Bureau of Investigation, the Department of Justice, and the United States Senate. Most researchers today have pretty well given up the idea that the media are responsible for directly and intentionally indoctrinating the public. Communication scholars write less of direct influence than of agenda-setting, how the media help to shape not what people think but what they think about.[8] Or they talk of priming, not what to think about but how to think about what we're thinking about. For example, during presidential elections we know without media coaxing that we're supposed to think about evaluating the candidates, but the priming hypothesis suggests that the media "prime" us to think more about economics than foreign policy, or more about foreign policy than economics, as a measure for evaluation of the rival figures.[9] Or, more subtle still, the media tell us not what to think, not what to think about, not how to think about what we think about, but when to think about the things that we have on our minds anyway.[10] The media are then cue-givers, telling us which of our lines that we already know comes next. It may even be that the media often do little more than re-present to us ideas and opinions we already have. This would seem to be insignificant—a kind of redundancy, but we should know that redundancy is functional, that the stories we tell ourselves and circulate among ourselves serve as reminders of who we are and what we're about, and that these stories, this culture, as a system of reminders, make a very big difference in what we do with and in our lives.

But at that point we have stepped from a transmission to a ritual model of communication. The "representational" function of the press bridges these models. The media, in transmitting ideas authored by others, are voicing, if not authoring. They are, in the language of Mikhail Bakhtin, "ventriloquating." Even editorials seem normally to speak *for* as well as *to* some community of opinion; only rarely do they present a distinctive human voice. They express as much as direct a community. The newspapers transmit information when they tell us that a certain person died of AIDS. They express something about who we are when they adopt a new practice of saying "He is survived by his companion."

If we operate with the transmission model of communication, we have almost full assurance that the newspaper will be absent from general accounts of American history, because causal links in the study of communication are so hard to pin down. If we recognize the ritual rather than causal power of the media and put aside the cause-and-effect narrative of conventional history writing, we may come closer to the central role of the media in American life.

This is something I think Benjamin Franklin may have appreciated even when he was seeking to use the newspaper, transmission-style, to urge specific social change. He did not seek to make print do the work of politics. It would not mobilize. It would not convince. It would simply and importantly, as he put it, "prepare the minds of the people." So he wrote in his newspaper about the benefits of establishing a hospital for the poor in Philadelphia before undertaking solicitation for its support and before bargaining and politicking with members of the assembly for public subsidy to match private giving. He did not trust the newspaper to do everything but only to sow the seeds of support in the public.[11]

The media are a central institution—one might even claim *the* central institution—in the cultural construction of American nationhood and cityhoods and communityhoods across the land. The eighteenth-century newspapers were key instruments of commercial and, later, political integration. The nineteenth-century newspapers were key instruments of urbanization, providing not only the advertising forum that made new institutions like department stores possible but also providing a community identity that held a city together when it was no longer a face-to-face community or even a "walking city." The newspaper industry in the mid to late nineteenth century, as Gunther Barth has put it, "represented the response of one instrument of communication to a new market created by the longing of urban masses for identity."[12] The newspaper helped provide that identity but, I would add, not only in metropolitan areas.

William Gilmore's wonderful study, *Reading Becomes a Necessity of Life,* is instructive about the role of the press in rural communities. Gilmore looks at reading habits in the Upper Connecticut River Valley from 1780 to 1835. There rural weekly newspapers promoted commercialization. Nearly all news of manufacturing that they provided was favorable, and a majority of the poems and letters and essays they printed about economic life exuded faith in manufacturing and commerce.[13] Newspapers, along with other print media, helped to develop "vastly increased involvement in public life" in the district Gilmore examines. In his view, the thickening network of print communication helped to promote and increase the value of "the highly prized ideal of citizen awareness—defined by the speed, accuracy, regularity, and currency of one's knowledge about the world."[14]

Gilmore argues that the spread of reading modernized and secularized citizens' knowledge. Modernization meant, among other things, "greater acceptance of change as a normal part of daily life." The weekly newspapers were instrumental in accommodating and naturalizing change and, no doubt, also in promoting "a newfound ideal of intellectual currency" that "imputed great value to 'timeliness' and accuracy in information diffusion."[15]

At the same time, the newspaper press, among other print media, promoted regional, national, and international perspectives rather than localism or parochialism. Now this is a matter that, as Richard Kielbowicz tells us, was anything but simple or straightforward. European visitors were, as always, shocked at the spread of newspapers and believed that the newspapers "divested" American rural dwellers of "that air of ignorance and rusticity which characterize the greater part of the peasantry in Europe."[16] This no doubt ascribes too much to the media, but certainly it is impressive that a Lexington, Kentucky, coffeehouse in the first decade of the nineteenth century had files of forty-two newspapers that it maintained from around the country.[17]

In the 1830s, Jacksonians insisted on maintaining newspaper postage, while opponents sought to reduce or even abolish it. (Their efforts failed to pass the Senate in 1832 by a single vote.) The Jacksonians' aim was to prevent the widespread circulation of city papers beyond their city borders. The city papers sought rural subscribers and created special country editions; Greeley's *New York Tribune* had as many as a million readers spread across the country, and many rural editors blamed their own business problems on competition from the city press. ("All I used to know," Will Rogers said on a lecture tour in 1925, playing off his famous aphorism, "was just what I read in the papers. But that was when I was 'Shanghaied' in New York, because all anybody knows in New York is just what they read in the papers. But now all I know is just what I see myself." Of course, it's not so easy, then or now, to escape New York.)[18]

This very competition helped spur the rural papers to cover local affairs rather than to emphasize, as had been their wont, international, national, and state capital reports.[19] But the desire for paragraphs of "precious science" from the cities could not be stifled. By mid-century, some papers began Pacific Coast editions, transported by steamship.[20] In a few cases, West Coast papers established steamer editions for Easterners, such as the *Alta California for the Steamer* in 1849.[21]

In some cases, as David Paul Nord has observed, the newspaper was a kind of association in itself. Hundreds of religious, political, and other directly associational papers spoke intimately to the specific needs and interests of their constituent audiences. Even newspapers that sought a more general readership and proudly claimed, like James Gordon Bennett's *New York Herald*, that they did not know and did not care to know their readers, established what Daniel Boorstin calls a "consumption community," a nonlocal and sometimes even nonregional association of people, a new cross-cutting loyalty in a society just learning to use the new powers of communication and transportation that the rotary press, the railroad, entrepreneurial capitalism, and the telegraph made possible.[22]

These are the kinds of subtle community-building functions for which the press is truly effective, but they are very hard to see or to ascribe agency to. They shift our attention from what the newspaper does—what its effects on opinion or action are—to what the newspaper is—what kind of social function and literary or cultural outlook it portends.

What the newspaper is is not preordained by human nature or the nature of "news" as a human cognitive or social category. Indeed, I tiptoe around the term "news" to describe what appeared in colonial and early national papers for the good reason that this category was not the sum and substance, not even the primary purpose, of those journals. *Publick Occurrences,* the first American newspaper, claimed that it would furnish readers monthly—oftener, only if "any Glut of

Occurrences happen"—with a faithful account of "such considerable things as have arrived unto our Notice." Editor Benjamin Harris did not plan to report anything himself. He intended no affirmative action for news-gathering. That was not part of his plan, or anyone else's project, for about a century to come. He promised to provide notice of "Memorable Occurrents of Divine Providence" and "Circumstances of Publique Affairs, both abroad and at home." But Mr. Harris neglected to get government approval for his sheet, and it was dead after one issue. The first paper to last any length of time was the *Boston News-Letter* published by John Campbell. Campbell, too, had a sense of his project quite different from our own sense of news. He saw his task as the recording of recent history. He wanted to keep his reports in chronological order, but because of little space and occasional suspension of publication, he could not print all the news he received from London. He got further and further behind. By 1718 he was printing news that was a year old, and he began to print more frequently to make up for this.[23] The idea of skipping to the most recent events did not occur to him. Nor, certainly, did he think to focus on local, rather than London, news. He got official sanction for each weekly issue before publication, but it is unlikely, given the paucity of local news in the paper, that there was anything that the local authorities could conceivably object to.[24]

As for James Franklin's *New-England Courant* begun in 1721, it was as much a satirical send-up of its newspaper rivals as a newspaper as such, full of sham advertisements and "mock-serious attention to trivial subjects." Throughout its five-year run, it generally began with a literary essay, and Charles Clark has classified it, and several other Boston papers that followed, as a "literary newspaper," whose primary feature was not news but a "locally-produced piece of creative writing that served as the voice of the paper."[25]

The newspaper that Benjamin Franklin came to in Philadelphia in 1729, Samuel Keimer's *Pennsylvania Gazette,* took yet another view of newspaper production. The full title of Keimer's sheet was *The Universal Instructor in All Arts and Sciences and Pennsylvania Gazette.* This revealed Keimer's plan to print serially Ephraim Chambers's *Cyclopaedia,* A through Z. Keimer's paper began in 1728, and when Franklin bought it in 1729 it was still on the A's, the entry for "air" taking up almost the entire paper for two months running.

This hodgepodge of purposes and formats may seem an unlikely beginning for American newspaper history, but it did not stop there. Stephen Botein's analysis of colonial newspapers left him bewildered as to what these papers were up to. Their contents seemed a miscellany, and their assortment of news appeared to be far from anything that could possibly have been of interest to the colonists. Botein arrives at two possible explanations. One is that this was not secular news at all, but, much as Benjamin Harris had suggested, news of Divine Providence. If you take world history in the eighteenth century to be a war of evil popery against good Christians, then what the American newspapers provided was "an archaic geopolitical view of Protestants united in the face of their ancient enemy."[26] But Botein offers this hypothesis rather diffidently, holding equally that "exactly what view of the world colonial printers communicated to their neighbors by reprinting foreign news is difficult to specify."[27] He is more confident in suggesting that printers operated by an economic rather than political logic in determining news content. In these terms, he argues, the object of news selection was incoherence. Printers sought to use particularly those news items to which no one would respond at all. The less interesting, the better—at least it caused no controversy. Avoiding controversy, not relaying what the news was, was the task of the colonial printer up to about 1765. But on the edge of breaking with England after the Stamp Act controversy, printers were compelled to choose sides. They did so, in most cases reluctantly, but they did so. From that point on, journalism became intensely political.

The newspaper, then, was at first a kind of periodical advertisement for the printer's trade, an entertainment, and certainly an updating of sorts, but it is hard to picture colonials in the first seventy-five years of the American newspaper rushing to the news office for knowledge of "news." Samuel Sewall, a regular newspaper reader early in the eighteenth century, almost never, as far as we can tell, got "news" from his copy of the *Boston News-Letter*—he read the London papers directly, after all—but he used the *Boston News-Letter* as "a reference source that recorded political texts such as royal and gubernatorial speeches and proclamations," and he cites the paper as a reference in his diary and letters.[28] In the next seventy-five years, if we imagine people rushing to the printer's office, it would be for controversial views, not reliable news. Remember that colonial assemblies normally met in secret. When a newspaper in South Carolina printed an accurate report of the proceedings of the colony's assembly sent to it by an assembly member in 1773, the printer was thanked for his efforts with jailing. The Continental Congress and the Congress under the Articles of Confederation barred the press. "Through the 1780s," the historian Thomas Leonard writes, "when Americans found a speech in their newspapers it was more likely to have been made in the Parliament of the kingdom they had rejected than in the assemblies of the new nation they had joined."[29] Congress, in its early days, was hostile to the press; the Senate met entirely in secret for its first six years. Congress did little to record its own debates before the 1820s, and no newspaper outside Washington itself kept a correspondent in the capital until the new nation was a full generation old.

As for what the earliest Washington reporting was like, Leonard gives us a sardonic portrait of a world in which reporters took it as their duty to turn rough oratory into acceptable English. This was not pure invention, Leonard suggests, but "rather a complex process of composition in which the leader and the reporter might share responsibility for the citizen's record of political discourse." Politicians sat down with reporters to go over the reporter's notes and to improve upon their own views for the purposes of the printed record. It was also common practice for them to delay publication until the memory of what they actually had said would not jar too sharply or freshly with the printed record (which they would then make sure reached their constituents).[30]

Journalism in the early nineteenth century, especially when given a push by the penny press, shifted from a miscellany of facts and fancy about strangers far from home, practical information for doing business, occasional political essays and bits of folklore, to a miscellany about one's own community, both its local manifestation and its wider connections. At that point, news became a kind of knowledge with a new standing and currency, an intimate part of citizenship and politics. News in newspapers became not the extension of gossip but an institutionalized, competitive marketplace commodity. It also became a public good, a collective and visible good, important in part precisely because it did not pass, like rumor, from person to person but, like divine instruction, from a printed text to hundreds of people at once.

William Gilmore writes of a new ideal of "citizen awareness" that the newspapers helped spawn in rural New England in the early nineteenth century and of the newly fashionable habit of "keeping up with the world." Did people before this time never care about what else was happening around the globe or beyond the reach of their own eyes and ears? Did they have no thirst for news? Contrary to common-sense assumptions, I think the answer to this is largely yes. This is not to say curiosity was a new feature of the human landscape. But it is to suggest that the availability of a product, in this case news in a newspaper, is as often the spur to a desire for it as a desire is the incentive for the marketing of a product. A British newsbook as early as 1548 announced that it would satisfy "the thursty desyer that all our kynde hath to know."[31] But I suspect the author expressed higher hopes for the widespread prevalence of that desire than he in fact discovered. The newspapers of the nineteenth century, in contrast, far from being vessels for a perennially desirable wine, were vintners of something new, a fermenting, modern, democratic popular culture.

In the nineteenth century, as reading the newspaper became a part of what it meant to be civilized in America, newspaper editors came to understand their social function as the provision of news. In 1869, when John Bigelow assumed the editorship of the *New York Times* (for a brief few months), about the same time that the British journalist Edward Dicey defined the American as a "newspaper-reading animal,"[32] he could still assert as something that needed saying that news had become the mainstay of the press. As he wrote in his maiden editorial, "News as an element of interest in the Press has so far transcended all others since the construction of the telegraph that the force of a newspaper is now largely concentrated in that department."[33]

The "consultative" process of speechifying in the antebellum period declined as printed records of proceedings became more available, but a new consultative process emerged that, in one form or another, is with us yet: interviewing. It was not a common practice until the late nineteenth century. Indeed, it was not a known practice before the 1850s for a reporter to speak to a politician or other public figure to gather spontaneous comments on the record. When Horace Greeley interviewed Brigham Young in 1859, it was an odd enough situation that Greeley had to explain to his readers what he was doing.[34] But by the 1880s, the essentially American invention of the newspaper interview was spreading to Europe. A French writer criticized his countrymen who "submit to the presence and indiscretion of certain foreign correpondents."[35] American journalists were, in the early decades of this century, the first to interview the Pope, the first to interview British cabinet officers, the first to interview German ministers.[36] In the United States, in contrast, the interview was by the 1890s so well established that in New York a political figure's refusal to be interviewed could become a news item itself.[37] By the 1930s, interviewing was a well-developed part of journalism, with reporters willing to offer advice on gamesmanship in getting interviews. A famous European journalist cautioned against note-taking, but a British journalism handbook advised that in the United States, "the native heath of the interview," taking notes was good practice because American public men "are more willing victims to the interviewer than those over here, who generally are reserved and not very partial to publicity."[38]

The interview suggests several things about the American newspaper. First, it suggests a change in the standing of the journalist and the newspaper. An interview is a media event and calls attention to the interviewer as well as to the person interviewed. The reporter at the end of the nineteenth century was taking on new authority as interpreter of public life. This new stature was marked not only by the rise of the interview but by the development in the straight news story of a summary lead rather than a chronological lead. The summary lead, much as we may take it for granted today, was a literary invention that asserted the journalist's authority to define for readers the most important elements of a news event.[39] The interview, of course, did this and more. It asserted the journalist's authority to *construct* a news event, to orchestrate an encounter and then to write it up as news. The institutionalization of interviewing also shows that, insofar as the newspaper is an agent of community morals and a form of cultural control, it was presenting a new model of human relations. It promoted a novel form of communication between interviewer and interviewee, in which the most important auditor, the public, was present only in the imagination. That imaginative construction of a public for whom the words of the interview were designed helped to construct and define the concept of the public itself.

Newspaper reporting, along with credit reporting and private detective work, was a new information-gathering profession that arose in the mid-nineteenth century as a specialized, systematic, one-sided, and oddly amoral form of surveillance. That is, the relation of the interviewer to the interviewee is amoral. The interviewee, for the interviewer, is a means to an end and no more. Where newspaper reporting differs from private detective work is that the object of surveillance is a public person or a person in his or her public light, and the client of the surveillance is not an individual but a readership, an entity with a plausible moral and political claim on us. Interviewers accommodate readers to a certain set of expectations of privacy and publicity, of journalist as account-giver and accountant, of professionals as proxies, of irony as a mode of assertion. In this they also flatter the public, give it an overinflated sense of its importance, encourage in leaders not only sensitivity to public opinion but sycophantic submission to popular prejudice. I do not propose that the new journalistic forms of the late nineteenth century were altogether progressive; I suggest simply that they were a vital, characteristic cultural invention and cultural force.

At least from the outside, it seems that the "media" as we call it today, or "the press" as it is still sometimes known, is a source of danger, of foreign influence, of large and unaccountable risk. Today the complaint is that television leads our children to violence or our fellow citizens to submit to 30-second demagoguery or makes us incapable of separating fact from fiction.[40] A century ago, Charles Beard saw the newspaper press as a major cause of neurasthenic disease,[41] and the Women's Christian Temperance Union of Iowa worried that "the influences that today push young people down are intensified beyond those that our fathers and mothers confronted in a proportion corresponding to the increased speed of locomotion and communication, and to the vastly greater use of the press." They worried that, "in these rushing days of telephone and typewriter," the barbarisms of the cities easily reached the secluded villages of Iowa. "Indeed," their report continued, "we have no secluded places. Everywhere through these nerves of steel we feel the feverish pulse of the age."[42] Three-quarters of a century earlier, Thomas Jefferson complained that truth itself became suspicious when printed in the newspaper. He believed that news accounts are not faithful records of world affairs. In fact, he pitied his fellow citizens who imagined that they learned something about their world by reading the papers, when "the accounts they have read in newspapers are just as true a history of any other period of the world as of the present, except that the real names of the day are affixed to their fables." He urged a new organization of newspapers that would divide the paper into four chapters—Truths, Probabilities, Possibilities, and Lies, and he feared only that the first of these chapters would be very short indeed.[43]

But the newspaper is not only an outside force with its paragraphs of precious science as dangerous news. It is also very familiar to us. We throw it away easily. Like Mrs. Emerson, we, at least metaphorically, still put it under our pies. The eighteenth-century newspaper reader was, often enough, also a newspaper writer, and this was not uncommon for the associational press of the nineteenth century. Even in the metropolitan press, letters to the editor continued to occupy large chunks of newsprint. The country edition of the *New York Tribune* in the 1870s regularly devoted a page or more of its sixteen pages to agricultural correspondence, a kind of mass-mediated communal self-help column, with letters titled "My Way with Manure" or "Balky

Horses" (January 30, 1878). There was no Ann Landers interme-diary—these were correspondents writing directly for publication for the benefit of other readers and correspondents. But the metropolitan press, as it became a more insistent, self-conscious, and lucrative big business, increased its distance from its readers. As the link between press and party weakened, the newspaper voice no longer presumed even a broad political agreement with its readers. More and more, the voice of the professional newspaper was separated out from the voice of the readers; where once the two were undifferentiated, they became sharply divided.

Even so, reading the newspaper, if not writing for it, remained, as David Paul Nord has put it, "a form of active citizenship, a way to participate—in solitude perhaps, but a very communitarian solitude—in the on-going conversation of their community."[44] But I don't want to let the romance of this phrase—the conversation of the commu-nity—prevent our recognizing how much the newspaper as it has come down to us is only vestigially conversational. There are still letters to the editor. It is still relatively easy for an ordinary citizen to write a letter, or even an article, for a local or community newspaper and see it in print. There are still columns, like "Confidential Chat" in the *Boston Globe,* that have the same person-to-person character as the agricultural column of last century's *New York Tribune.* But the news-paper is today, and was to a large extent much earlier, distinctly not conversational, even anti-conversational. The shift from interpersonal communication to mass-mediated communication is not something to mourn but to understand. David Fischer has shown that the movement to popularly contested elections after 1800 was a development that Jeffersonians spearheaded and Federalists accepted only reluctantly. Older Federalists conceived the electoral process as a relatively pri-vate exercise and felt that the best electioneering was through private letters rather than newspaper essays. Younger Federalists objected: "They write private letters. To whom? To each other. But they do nothing to give a proper direction to the public mind. They observe, even in their conversation, a discreet circumspection generally, ill calculated to diffuse information, or prepare the mass of the people for the result."[45]

There's that useful verb again—preparing the people, here spoken with a less optimistic ring to it, preparing "the mass of the people" in contrast to Franklin's preparing "the minds of the people." Our atti-tudes to the newspaper today probably represent about the same range of views—from the newspaper as propaganda to the newspaper as education and self-education; from the newspaper as directing to the newspaper as enabling; from the newspaper as business to the newspaper as watchdog and guardian; from the newspaper as disturbing outside influence and vested interest to the newspaper as essential, if imperfect, instrument of democratic self-government; and from the people as mass to be shaped to the people as minds to be informed.

"Few things that can happen to a nation are more important than the invention of a new form of verse," wrote T. S. Eliot. And Jacob Bronowski, defending the sciences in a discussion of seventeenth-century science, added that "few things that can happen to the world are more important than the invention of a new form of prose."[46] I would add to these propositions that few things are more characteristic and revealing of modern culture than the invention of and changes in the ways it declares itself anew each day in its presentation of news. The world may be "out there," as so many of us commonsensically believe. But no person and no instrument apprehends it directly. We turn nature to culture as we talk and write and narrate it. We humanize it, as Hannah Arendt said, but only in part do we humanize it in a general way. We grow up not only human but American, situated in a particular historical moment, and the ways we humanize speak to and speak of our time, our place, 1690 or 1790, 1890 or 1990. Nowhere is that speaking more evidently a preparation of the minds of the people than in the newspaper.

2 The Politics of Narrative Form

Television, a central locus of activity in American culture and politics, is often cited as a dominant force in changing our political structure—and for the worse. But television has not changed our conception of politics; rather, it crystallizes and expresses a transformation of political narrative that was well established in the print media decades before television appeared.

Speaker Sam Rayburn's decision in the 1950s to keep television cameras out of the House of Representatives was an act of great significance—or so David Halberstam believes:

> ... making the House less able to compete with the executive branch, and diminishing its importance in the eyes of the public ... Characteristically, the only time the Congress of the United States appeared on television in this era was when the President of the United States came to the House to deliver his State of the Union speech. Then the congressmen could be seen dutifully applauding, their roles in effect written in by the President's speech writers.[1]

But this credits television with having far more influence on the political system than it actually had. Press treatment of the State of the Union message *did* change dramatically, to emphasize the President at the expense of Congress, but this happened over eighty years ago, in the days of Teddy Roosevelt, William Howard Taft, and Woodrow Wilson. Conventions of covering the presidency established then continue to shape not only the way print journalism covers the President, but how television does it as well.

The evidence I will present in this chapter cannot resolve the debate surrounding the influence of television—the debate between those awed by its power and those inclined to discount it. Instead, it changes the question at issue. While it is true that a new technology can condition politics and society, such a technology appears and comes into use only in certain political and social circumstances. The way the technology is used has a relation to, but is not fully determined by, the technology itself. In light of this, it is somewhat off the mark to ask about the impact of television on the presidency, since there is no way that question can conceivably be answered. We must ask, rather, What is the impact of *this* television, *our* television? To answer that requires more than understanding the new hardware, more even than understanding the social role of the TV set in America's living rooms, dens, and bedrooms. It requires an examination of the national networks as business enterprises; the uneasy relationship of a visible, regulated industry to government agencies; the traditions of American journalism that have shaped the preconceptions and intentions of network news departments; and the decades-long traditions of relations between the President and the press. Our television has a life of its own that plays a role in presidential politics; it is part of the environment that any new development in American politics will be related to. But the form television takes in covering the presidency has been foreshadowed, if not foreordained, by earlier changes in the relationship between print journalism and the presidency.

In this chapter I will show the changes that have taken place in the way print journalism has treated the presidency since the early days of the Republic, changes that reflect new developments in both politics and journalism. I will suggest that the power of the media lies not only (and not even primarily) in its power to declare things to be true, but in its power to provide the forms in which the declarations appear. News in a newspaper or on television has a relationship to the "real world," not only in content but in form; that is, in the way the world is incorporated into unquestioned and unnoticed conventions of narration, and then transfigured, no longer a subject for discussion but a premise of any conversation at all.

Generally speaking, people do not see news as it happens; rather, they hear or read about it. Parents do not experience their child's day at school directly, but learn of it as it is narrated, turned into a story by the child. Children learn that the accounts of their experiences, like the stories and legends they are told, must have certain formal qualities. A child I know told his older sister the following story: "Once upon a time there was a small boy who went out into the forest. He heard a sound. A lion jumped at him and ate him but he tore out the lion's stomach, killed the lion, and dragged it home. The end." Then he told the story again: "Once upon a time, a small boy went into the forest and a lion tried to eat him, but he killed the lion. The end." Then once more: "Once upon a time, a boy killed a lion in the forest. The end." And at last he said: "Once upon a time. The end."

The child had learned something important about form.[2] Journalists know something similar. They do not offer boys, forests, and lions raw, but cook them into story forms. News is not fictional, but it is conventional. Conventions help make messages readable. They do so in ways that "fit" the social world of readers and writers, for the conventions of one society or time are not those of another. Some of the most familiar news conventions of our day, so obvious they seem timeless, are recent innovations. Like others, these conventions help make culturally consonant messages readable and culturally dissonant messages unsayable. Their function is less to increase or decrease the truth value of the messages they convey than to shape and narrow the range of what kinds of truths can be told. They reinforce certain assumptions about the political world.

I want to examine in detail the emergence of a few of these conventions:

1. That a summary lead and inverted pyramid structure are preferred to a chronological account of an event.

2. That a president is the most important actor in any event in which he takes part.

3. That a news story should focus on a single event rather than a continuous or repeated happening, or that, if the action is repeated, attention should center on novelty, not on pattern.

4. That a news story covering an important speech or document should quote or state its highlights.

5. That a news story covering a political event should convey the meaning of the political acts in a time frame larger than that of the acts themselves.

All of these are unquestioned and generally unstated conventions of twentieth-century American journalism; none were elements in journalism of the mid-nineteenth century, nor would any have been familiar to Horace Greeley, James Gordon Bennett, or Henry Raymond.

Unlike reporters today, the nineteenth-century reporter was not obliged to summarize highlights in a lead, to recognize the President as chief actor on the American political stage, to seek novelty, to quote speeches he reported, or to identify the political significance of events he covered. How, then, did the conventions emerge, and why?

A study of reports of the State of the Union message[3] demonstrates that these conventions, among others, incorporate into the structure of the news story vital assumptions about the nature of politics and the role of the press. They make it plain that American journalists regard themselves not as partisans of political causes, but as expert analysts of the political world. They make it equally clear that, although as journalists they hold to principles of objective reporting, they nevertheless view their role as involving some fundamental translation and interpretation of political acts to a public ill-equipped to sort out for itself the meaning of events. Further, these conventions institutionalize the journalists' view that meaning is to be found not in the character of established political institutions, but in the political aims of actors within them. The journalist's responsibility, as they see it, is to discover in the conscious plans of political actors the intentions that create political meaning.

The Constitution of the United States provides that the President shall report to Congress "from time to time" regarding the "state of the Union," and every American president, following the custom inaugurated by Washington, has delivered a message on this subject at the beginning of each winter's congressional session. Although the event itself—the way in which the annual message is presented—has changed several times in the past two centuries, these changes have no connection to the transformations in the way the message is reported. The latter must be linked to changing precepts in journalism about the nature of politics and what a news story should be.

Reports of the State of the Union message have taken three basic forms: the stenographic record of congressional business, from 1790 to about 1850; a chronology and commentary on congressional ritual, from 1850 to 1900; and the report of the message, with an increasing emphasis on its content and its long-range political implications, from 1900 on. Despite journalism's vaunted objectivity, the reporting of the presidential message in each successive period became more interpretive, more divorced from what an ordinary observer could safely assert the message said or what Congress itself heard. This has not made reporting less truthful, but has widened the scope for the journalist's discretion—indicating that, over time, the journalistic function has served rather different intentions.

Early newspaper reports of the message printed it in its entirety, framed as part of congressional proceedings. The report of Washington's 1791 message by the weekly *Boston Gazette*, for instance, appeared on page two under the heading, "Columbia. Congress of the United States. (First Session—Second Congress). House of Representatives. Monday, October 24." The item notes that a joint committee of the Congress waited on the President, who agreed to meet with the Congress the next day in the Senate. Then, in the same column, under the heading, "Tuesday, October 25," there is a one-sentence account of the President's arrival in the Senate Chamber. The reader is then referred to the paper's last page for the full message, and the account moves on to proceedings in the House of Wednesday, October 26. The *Gazette* followed this pattern for all of Washington's messages, although in most years the speech followed under the first heading. But in no case was there any commentary on the speech.

The most significant change in the message as an actual event was initiated by Thomas Jefferson, who felt that for the President to address Congress in person was too imperial a gesture, and so chose to give his State of the Union message in written form. It remained so until Woodrow Wilson reverted to the Federalist precedent of a personal appearance. Despite Jefferson's change, the message continued to be printed in full, either without any reported context or as part of a briefly sketched list of the day's proceedings in Congress. Any commentary on the message was confined entirely to the editorial column, where from the early 1800s on the message was discussed at length, and the President's statements praised or castigated from an engaged and partisan stance.

By mid-century, and especially after the Civil War, the news report of the President's message was set in a much fuller discussion of Congress. The frame for the message continued to be provided by the congressional ritual of appointing a committee to wait on the President, announcing its readiness to hear a written communication from him read by a clerk. But two additional elements became standard. The first was the coverage devoted to the "spectacle" of the opening of Congress, which typically provided the beginning of the news story. As early as 1852 we read in the *New York Times:* "It is a bright and beautiful day, and the galleries of the House are crowded with ladies and gentlemen; all is gaiety." In 1870 the *Times* story began, "A beautiful Indian summer sun, a balmy atmosphere, and crowded galleries, resplendent and brilliant hues of gay toilettes, greeted the return of Congress to its chambers." The press noted, sometimes in great detail, the cordial greetings across party lines as congressmen reassembled. Reports described the lavish bouquets of flowers on the desks of senators and representatives, gifts from loyal supporters.

The second change, which became standard from 1870 on, and which was more notable in the long run, was the attention given to congressional reaction to the President's message—several decades before reporters took it upon themselves actually to *report* what the message said. Where at first only the general response to the message was noted on the House and Senate floors, in 1870 the *Times* reported that two or three Democratic senators "appeared to go to sleep" when the portion dealing with foreign relations was read. In the 1870s, reporters typically confined themselves to observations of congressmen's behavior on the floor, though they sometimes attempted a general characterization of the congressional response, as in the *Times* in 1874: "It may be said there is little fault found with the President's message as a whole, though some of its views find strong and special opposition." Occasionally, notable congressmen were singled out. A *Times* reporter observed in 1870 that when the message discussed revenue reform, many people looked at Carl Schurz, "whose consciousness of the fact caused a faint smile to play over his face." In 1878 the *Times* reported that the message's mention of investigating people who disfranchise Southern voters "gave encouragement to the Republicans while the Democrats exhibited unmistakable signs of disapprobation" and caused a "scowl . . . to overspread the faces on the Democratic side."

In the late 1870s and the 1880s, journalists interviewed individual congressmen. Reporters on the *Chicago Tribune* and *Washington Post,* for example, did interviews at the reading of the message in 1878, as these papers and others began to publish separate news stories on congressional responses to the message. The *Post*'s story in 1886 began: " 'Didn't hear a word of it. Must wait until I see it in print.' That was the general response made by congressmen to any question asked about the President's message, after it had been read in both houses." This was typical. Rarely did the congressmen in these accounts regard the interview as an opportunity for publicity; rather, they seemed irritated that they had been asked questions.

Stories of congressional response to the message grew more elaborate in the 1880s and 1890s. Occasionally there were stories of the response of other bodies, particularly editorial comments in foreign newspapers. But by the end of the century the attention given to the splendor of the opening of Congress, so prominent in the 1860s and 1870s, seemed to wear on the press. The *Washington Post* dryly observed in its December 3, 1878, report that the public showed curiosity at the opening of Congress, "as if it were a new thing." The *Chicago Tribune* teased in its headline of December 4, 1894, "Toil of the Solons / Makers of Laws Resume Business at Washington." Evidently bored, the Washington *Evening Star* announced in its 1890 story, "Here We Go Again."

Thus, at the same time that the press took Congress as its beat, and regarded the opinions of individual congressmen more and more seriously, its respect for the ritual and spectacle of office declined, and it began to delight in the lampooning of congressional affairs. The change taking place in the relation of journalists to officials was part of the new view that journalists took of their own purpose. They began to strain at the tradition of reporting normal occurrences and everyday proceedings. No longer the uncritical reporters of congressional ritual surrounding the reading of the State of the Union message, they became increasingly uneasy over writing about something that happens again and again, year after year. The uneasiness came out in humor or in self-conscious commentary about how everything is the same as ever but people get involved nonetheless. The notion that the journalist should report original events and not record ongoing institutions grew stronger as the journalists of the 1880s and 1890s found themselves torn between two modes of activity, one might even say two forms of consciousness.

By 1900 the news story had been partially transformed, as the strictly chronological account of the reopening of congressional proceedings gave way to a descriptive account of the reopening of Congress, with a summary lead focusing on the spectacle of Congress, and some affectionate, jocular remarks about the reassembly of the group. The President's message remained buried within the story on Congress, though always printed in full on another page. The account, beyond the descriptive overview in the lead, tended to be chronological, but it was not as dry and formal as it had been in the early part of the century.

It is clear that with the establishment of the summary lead as newspaper convention, journalists began to move from being stenographers, or recorders, to interpreters. Still, in 1900 there was no mention of the content of the President's message in the news story, nor was the President mentioned by name, but referred to simply as "the President." Although he was the author of the message, attention in newspaper reports continued to focus on Congress. Journalists stayed in the here-and-now, reporting on congressional reactions on the floor, and turning to interviews only to supplement the central work of observing the event itself.

After 1900 all of this changed: the President's message, not congressional response to it, became the subject of the lead paragraph, and the President became the chief actor. The highlights of the address were summarized before noting congressional response to the address, as reporters increasingly took it as their prerogative to assert something about the larger political meaning of the message. Although these changes did not happen in all newspapers simultaneously, or with utter consistency, the trend is unmistakable.

Take, for example, the 1910 account of William Howard Taft's message. The main *New York Times* news story begins: "In the longest message that has been sent to Congress in many a day President Taft today announced the practical abandonment of the unenacted portion of the great legislative programme with which he began his administration." The message, not Congress, is the subject. The content of the message is cited, and the content, not congressional response to it, emphasized. Indeed, rather than taking the message as a litmus test of congressional opinion, congressional response now becomes a way to characterize the content further. The *Times* reporter includes his own observation that the message was "obviously aimed at giving reassurance to business," and supports this comment by reporting that congressmen regarded the message as "eminently conservative." Moreover, the President is treated as a person, and is mentioned by name in both the lead paragraph and the headline, something that happened rarely in the body of the story before 1900, and never in the lead.

This form of the news story is still familiar to us today: it incorporates what have become the givens of modern politics into the very form of the story. First, it emphasizes the preeminence of the President; he and his views, not Congress and its reactions or its rituals, are the main theme of the news story. Second, it incorporates the assumption that the President is in some sense a representative of the nation, a national trustee, rather than merely the leader of a political party. He speaks for himself to the Congress and the nation, not as the leader of a party to that party in the Congress. After 1910 stories about congressional response to the message continued to emphasize partisan differences, yet the message itself was read not as a party program, but as an indicator of the President's personal program and political career.

If this form of the news story incorporates, in its very structure, assumptions about our political system, it incorporates as well assumptions about the role and intention of our news media. It takes for granted the journalist's right and obligation to mediate and simplify, to crystallize and identify the key political elements in the news event. It takes for granted that the journalist should place the event in a time frame broader than that immediately apparent to the uninitiated. And it is here that the simplest notion of objectivity—that one should write only what another naive observer on the scene would also have been able to write—is abandoned.

News stories of the 1910s and 1920s illustrate these points admirably. That the preeminence of the President is assumed in these stories requires no illustration: the President and his views, as expressed in the message, are the key elements in nearly every news story lead from 1910 on. That the President is viewed in a time frame characterized by personal career, not by party, needs more illustration. There begins to be more attention paid to comparing the message to other messages of the same president and other presidents, a subject that long had a place in editorial comment, but that only now becomes a regular part of news coverage. The *Times* reports of Taft's message in 1912, "This message ranks with the best in the literature of Executive utterances."[4] The 1918 *Tribune* story begins, "Appearing before congress this afternoon on the eve of his departure for France, President Wilson explained his reason for attending the peace conference and submitted recommendations for legislation on domestic questions which he desires initiated during his absence." Here, the turnaround from nineteenth-century reporting is dramatic: congressional activity is presented within the context of the presidential schedule, rather than the presidential message being viewed within the time frame of congressional activity.

The 1928 *Evening Star* lead is also instructive: "President Coolidge, in his annual message submitted to congress today, gave a report of his stewardship and recommendations for the future. No more remarkable picture of American development and no more virile and optimistic view of the future have been drawn by a President of the United States." Note here not only the editorializing, but the sense of the historic role of the President, connected not to party but to "stewardship" of the nation, compared not to other contemporaries with whom he may or may not agree, but to other presidents. In a less intrusive lead, the *Chicago Tribune* that year held to this wider focus: "The valedictory message of Calvin Coolidge as the thirtieth president of the United States was read in both houses of Congress today."

By the 1930s, the additional factor of broadcasting made it clear that the President speaks not only to Congress, but to the American people and the world as well—something the press promptly noted. In 1934 the tradition of appointing a congressional committee to wait on the President was done away with and replaced by a telephone call to the President. Radio and sound-picture recording were present and noted in the press. (Attention to the spectacle of the opening of Congress continued, but more of it focused on the President, with the *Evening Star* noting the presidential motorcycle escort down Pennsylvania Avenue, the *Washington Post* observing Mrs. Roosevelt's presence in the gallery.) On January 4, 1936, Turner Catledge mentioned broadcasting in his lead:

> In his opening message to the second session of the 74th Congress, delivered personally at an unprecedented joint session in the House chamber tonight, and broadcast by radio to millions of listeners throughout the world, President Roosevelt threw down a challenge to critics of the New Deal to come out into the open at once and fight in Congress, the people's forum, for repeal of the administration's measures.

The 1938 *Evening Star* story observes that the address was broadcast, and notes in the lead that "in an address of absorbing interest President Roosevelt today told Congress *and the world* this Nation must prepare to defend itself."[5]

If these stories reflect a new political reality, they reflect also a new journalistic reality. The journalist, no longer merely the relayer of documents and messages, has become the interpreter of the news. This new role allows the reporter to write about what he hears and sees, and what is unheard, unseen, or intentionally omitted as well. For instance, the *Chicago Tribune* in 1909, in a story dated December 8 by John Cullan O'Laughlin, begins: "President Taft's first annual message, which was read to the two houses of congress today, is more notable for what it omits than for what it says." In a less provocative manner, the *Times* on December 4, 1924, wrote of Coolidge's message: "President Coolidge's annual message, sent to Congress today by messenger and read in each house by a clerk, was notable for its lack of specific recommendations." In the 1920s, attention to what the President omitted was a regular feature of news reporting. On December 8, 1926, the *Times* story noted that "the message was marked by only two omissions, the world court and Muscle Shoals, and these perversely enough were among the first to be placed before the Senate." The *Evening Star* on December 7 noted that the message omitted mention of Mexico and the World Court. In 1928 Richard Oulahan's story in the *New York Times* told of what was omitted and what was said implicitly: "Perfunctory and colorless as it may have seemed to most of those who heard it read in the Senate and the House this afternoon, President Coolidge's last annual message to Congress contained certain suggestions between the lines calculated to disarrange legislative plans for the session which was begun yesterday."

In 1930 G. Gould Lincoln in the *Evening Star* observed that President Hoover did not say, but "clearly implied," that the one percent reduction in the income tax would not be continued. Reporters even felt free to put words in the President's mouth. On December 3, 1930, Arthur Sears Henning in the *Chicago Tribune* wrote: "In his second annual message on the state of the Union, President Hoover told Congress today, in effect, that good times are just around the corner." Richard Oulahan did something similar in his 1926 story: " 'Let well enough alone' might be a description of the attitude the President implies in the document which the Constitution requires him to submit to Congress annually."

As more of the stories in the 1920s became interpretive, so too were more by-lined, a phenomenon typical of changes in journalism in that era. A content analysis of the front page of the *New York Times* by Christine Ogan and her associates[6] found no by-lines in the five-year periods from 1900 to 1905 or from 1910 to 1915. Six percent of stories were by-lined in 1920–1925; 16 percent in 1930–1935; 47 percent in 1940–1945; and 85 percent in 1970. This study also found a difference in the "time orientation" of front-page stories. Ogan distinguishes between "immediate" and "long-range" time orientation, between stories that focus on events where knowing about them is useful in the short run (a baseball game, a fire, stock quotations) and stories that focus on events where knowing about them has more long-range value (a ball player's profile, a story on arson patterns in the city, or a report on economic indicators). In the period from 1900 to 1905, 87 percent of stories were of immediate interest. By 1920–1925 this figure had dropped to 72 percent, and it was 67 percent in 1930–1935, 61 percent in 1940–1945, and 57 percent in 1970.

Changes in the reporting of the annual message, where the same event, once treated as something of immediate significance, came to be treated in a long-range time frame, buttress this suggestive finding. The reports do not rest with noting on-the-spot congressional response, but focus on the significance of the address in the political career of the President. The reporter does not leave the long-range significance of the event to the reader, but interprets it for him.

Why have these dramatic changes in reporting presidential addresses occurred, and what might they signify? The changes I have found may not, of course, be representative of news reporting as a whole. Yet I believe that similar kinds of transformations have occurred in other types of news stories, and I offer this account as both a hypothesis and a model against which other researchers might compare changing conventions in other types of news reporting.

The simplest explanation is that news reflects reality, and the political reality itself must therefore have changed. The new conventions of journalism can be viewed as predictable responses to the growing power of the presidency. The form, not just the content, of the news story mirrors the fact that the President and his addresses had, by about 1910, become more important than the Congress and its reactions to presidential policy.

Without question, the power of the presidency grew, and as it did, a shift from a "congressional" to a "presidential" system of government evolved. Theodore Roosevelt, especially, forged a symbolically more central presidency by the force of his personality and by his assiduous efforts at cultivating journalists. Yet, as important as Roosevelt was in bringing new authority to the White House, his actions do not sufficiently explain the changing conventions of journalism. First, some of the most significant changes in the presidency, changes that could be assumed to be causes of new modes of reporting, *followed* the change in news conventions. Woodrow Wilson, for example, revived the precedent, abandoned by Jefferson, of appearing before Congress to deliver the State of the Union address and other messages. In his first such message, he said, "I am very glad indeed to have this opportunity to address the two Houses directly and to verify for myself the impression that the President of the United States is a person, not a mere department of the Government . . . a human being trying to co-operate with other human beings in a common service." Wilson's action reinforced the centrality of the President and the habit of seeing the President as "a person," but the habit was already being encouraged by journalistic practice.[7]

Another significant change was the establishment of the Bureau of the Budget in 1921 and the beginning of a presidential role in budgetary policy and government-wide policymaking. Until then government agencies submitted budget requests to the Secretary of the Treasury, who passed them on, with little change, to Congress. The President played, at best, "only a limited role."[8] Despite Teddy Roosevelt's importance, then, in enlarging the prestige of the presidency, his real contribution lay not in establishing a powerful presidency, but in paving the way for its institutionalization. In this context, the changing conventions of news reporting may have been less a simple result of a change in the political world than a constituent of that process itself.

There is another way to look at the situation. Remember that the press always treated the State of the Union address with great seriousness. The full address was always printed and, as in the early 1800s, was sometimes the entire editorial material for a given issue. Later on, though the news story focused on congressional proceedings, the full text continued to be printed, and the editorial—much more the heart of the newspaper in the nineteenth century than it is today—focused on the substance of the President's message itself.

The change in conventions of news reporting, then, while giving greater emphasis to the presidency in describing an altered political reality, more importantly provided *a different form* for describing any political reality at all. It is a very different matter to say that the news reflects the social world by describing it, and to say that it reflects the social world by incorporating it into unquestioned and unnoticed conventions of narration. When a changed political reality becomes part of the very structure of news writing, then the story does not "reflect" the new politics but becomes part of the new politics itself.[9] There is not only a narration of politics in the news; the news is part of the politics of narrative form.

In the nineteenth century, reporters had little or no political presence as individuals or as a group. Editors, not Washington correspondents, set the political tone of a paper, and their views were political acts to be reckoned with. In the twentieth century, reporters have taken on a more pronounced political role and acquired political self-consciousness. Although critics bemoan the sensationalism and commercialism of the press and its failure to treat politics with appropriate solemnity, it is still true, as David Riesman observed years ago in *The Lonely Crowd*, that journalists accord politics a prestige that it does not have in the public mind. "They pay more attention to politics than their audience seems to demand . . . Many of the agencies of mass communications give political news a larger play than might be dictated by strict consideration of market research."[10] In a sense, journalists are the patrons of political life.

To the degree that this is so, the journalism of the national newsweeklies, most large metropolitan newspapers, and the network television news does not mirror the world, but constructs one in which the political realm is preeminent. But what is politics, and how are we to understand it? The changing conventions of reporting State of the Union messages suggest and support a major shift in the public understanding of politics. The changes in story form do not indicate that journalism was once stenographic and is now interpretive, but rather that political commentary, once a partisan activity of the newspaper editor, has become increasingly a professional activity of the journalist. This change, far from being a product of the sixties or of the growing affluence and autonomy of national political reporters in the 1970s, began around the turn of the century.

The transformation of the news story is clearly related to the idea of politics promoted by the Progressive movement. Briefly, progressivism emphasized a "good government" view of the polity; it distrusted political parties and their machinery, and sought more direct public participation in government. The secret ballot; initiative, referendum, and recall; primary elections; direct election of senators; and other reforms—all were products of the Progressive movement. If there was an effort to remove power from the parties, it was not all to be returned to the public. The movement supported "expert" management of the political system, ranging from city-manager municipal government to the establishment of federal administrative agencies for the conservation of natural resources. In the Progressive vision, faction could be avoided, conflict overcome, and politics transformed into technique. Politics itself was to be professionalized.[11] Although the Progressive idea of politics did not cause the changes in conventions of news reporting, it was consonant with them and can be seen as part of the same climate of opinion. As Progressives sought to have politics viewed as technique, so journalists strove to have reporting viewed as political commentary by skilled analysts.

Within journalism itself, three factors may have made this an especially likely ambition. First—and I think most important—reporters as a group were becoming more self-conscious and autonomous. At the end of the nineteenth century, as Robert Wiebe has observed, the identification of the middle class with political parties weakened,

while their identification with, and allegiance to, occupations and occupational associations grew.[12] In journalism, press clubs began to
form in the late nineteenth century, the prestige and the pay of reporters began to rise, professional journals appeared in New York, and
at least an elite of reporters like Richard Harding Davis or Sylvester
Scovel became quite famous and thereby relatively independent in
their work. At the same time, as newspapers became successful big
businesses, and publishers increasingly took more interest in making
money than in making policy, journalists, freed from the necessity of
adhering to their publishers' party lines, came to regard themselves
as "professionals." But they did not gain complete autonomy, nor did
they achieve all at once the relative independence they now have.
What is clear is that editors were losing power relative to reporters as
early as the 1890s, when newspapers shifted from reprinting documents to relying on reporters' contacts for news. As Anthony Smith
puts it, "The power of brokerage . . . thus passed from news editor to
correspondent and specialist reporter, and as a result the editor . . .
[could not] wield the same kind of authority he did in previous generations."[13]

Second, newspaper readership grew enormously from the 1880s on,
especially among the working class. If this had influenced the conventions of news reporting directly, the expectation would be for the
more popular, mass-oriented papers to be the first to adopt the modern
interpretive conventions; papers catering to a smaller and better-ed-
ucated middle-class audience would lag behind. Yet very different
papers adopted the new conventions, all at about the same time. Nevertheless, it is plausible to hold that, at some level of consciousness,
journalists changed their practice to accommodate the real or presumed demands of a different kind of audience.

Third, the telegraphic transmission of news may have provided a
model of how news reporting might be more brief and interpretive. The
earliest news reports focusing on the substance of the President's message were stories telegraphed to midwestern newspapers, such as the
Chicago Tribune, as early as 1858. These reports did not substitute
for a full transcript and a largely chronological account of congressional proceedings; these were printed a day later and were clearly
regarded as superior. The telegraphed summary of the address was, in
fact, offered apologetically, and readers were urged to wait for the full
account. So the new format that the telegraph helped to invent did not
become the working norm for half a century. When the new conventions finally emerged, there was apparently no overt connection be-

The Politics of Narrative Form   67

tween them and early telegraphic communication. Still, the terse form of news by wire may have lodged somewhere in the literary unconscious of journalists and their readers.[14]

The vital point remains that the modern conventions of news reporting emerged at a time when politics was coming to be thought of as administration. Politicians, then, could legitimately be evaluated according to their efficiency as political leaders rather than on the basis of their political positions. The new conventions of reporting helped take partisanship out of politics. This does not "reflect" a politics grown more independent of party; it incorporates and so helps construct a nearly preconscious set of assumptions about what politics is. The news story today, as in the past, not only describes a world "out there" but translates a political culture into assumptions of representation built into the structure of the story itself.

By the 1920s, a more self-conscious, autonomous journalistic corps covered the President. Reporters felt free to analyze the significance of presidential messages, even if they did not believe it appropriate to comment on the rightness or wrongness of presidential views. They took responsibility for highlighting salient points of the message and for stating how the message related not only to congressional business at hand, but to the President's career and his place in history as well.

It should not be surprising, then, that when television came along, network news departments devoted disproportionate time to covering the presidency. The technology and economics of television make this a likely choice, of course. Since television equipment is expensive and awkward, and can be moved around less easily than the lone reporter with pencil and notepad, film crews tend to be centered in just a few locations, with the result that those locations—especially Washington—gain great emphasis in the TV news. And with the still-current understandings of politics that began decades ago to shift attention from Capitol Hill to the White House, the TV watch on the president was an obvious choice.

Other choices, of course, could have been made. In Britain, for years after the introduction of television, the BBC refused to cover general elections and took great pride in this decision. Elections were deemed too important for television.[15] Even in America, television began its fascination with news, and with presidential news in particular, only when the quiz show scandals prompted the networks to take their public service function more seriously, and when John Kennedy tried to use his considerable personal charm on television to enhance his political standing. There was a real question whether television would become a news medium. But once it began to function as one, what kind of news medium it would be, what kind of political assumptions it would incorporate into the news, and what kind of political and journalistic culture it would draw on were in little doubt.

It is not unusual that a new medium comes to serve purposes that older forms are already trying to address. In *On Photography*, Susan Sontag observes that photography enlarges our view of what is worth looking at, until we have come to believe that *anything* may be worth photographing or looking at.[16] This is a far cry from conventional Western image-making. For centuries, only religious subjects were thought worthy of painting; even in the seventeenth and eighteenth centuries, the repertoire of subjects was quite restricted. But in the eighteenth and early nineteenth centuries, the subject matter for painting expanded. In this more democratic era, artists began to paint common people, street life, and a variety of landscapes. For a time, in fact, in the middle of the last century, the range of subject matter for painting was far wider than that of the budding art of photography, which was restricted primarily to portraiture. Within a few decades, however, photography became the more democratic art, as all aspects of life became its subjects. But this could not have been imagined if a profound cultural change were not already under way.

Photography, of course, is not mechanized painting, nor is the news on television only newspaper news with pictures. Television news has its own possibilities. In covering the State of the Union address, television ironically brings back an abandoned print form: a chronological account of the day's event, the full text of the speech, and the pomp and circumstance, the spectacle and ritual, surrounding the event. Guided by the camera's eye, we see a revival of attention to on-the-scene congressional response to the address, much as the reporters of the late nineteenth century provided. Still, too much has changed in both journalism and politics for this to satisfy the journalists, and presumably the public. The broadcasters provide a "follow-up" that summarizes the high points of the address and suggests the political significance of the message. When the story is retold on the late evening news, the President speaks for himself, *and* the broadcast journalist points out the highlights of the address and uses film of the speech to illustrate them. Television thus inherits the trend toward analytical reporting and nonpartisan political commentary that the print media had already established by the 1920s.[17]

News, as we imagine it in its ideal state, is all information, no form. Or, to use Kenneth Burke's distinction, it is supposed to be all semantic meaning, no poetic meaning. But as Burke observes, these categories are not easy to separate. In the ideal of semantic meaning, we aim to "evolve a vocabulary that gives the name and address of every event in the universe." Thus Burke takes as a good example of the semantic ideal the address on an envelope: name, street and number, city or town, state, nation. This is a very efficient system for locating one individual out of several billions. In a sense, it is purely informational, purely semantic, without affective color or significance. But it is nonetheless neither neutral nor objective. Its content is tainted because its form *assumes* certain values and structures. Burke writes of the envelope address: "It depends for its significance upon the establishment of a postal structure, as a going concern . . . It *assumes* an organization. Its *meaning*, then, involves the established procedures of the mails, and is in the instructions it gives for the performance of desired operations within this going concern."[18]

A news story is also in the business of giving instructions for desired operations within a going concern. The news story informs its readers about politics, but in a specific way. Its meaning lies in the instructions it tacitly gives about what to attend to, and how to attend, within the going concern of American political life. It asks readers to be interested in politics, but politics as the community of journalists conceives it.

The community of journalists (at least, national political reporters) is "progressive," as Herbert Gans has observed, but this is so even more fundamentally than he implies.[19] Reporters are progressive in their implicit, conscious, but not often worked-out political views. They are progressive even more in their sense of what their job is, their view of what reporting politics always (as they see it) has been and should be. Without knowing it, and sometimes while actually fighting against it (thoughtful journalists frequently complain that, in writing primarily about agility in winning and losing, they and their colleagues treat politics too much like a sport), journalists are persuaded that politics is a matter of running campaigns, handling pressure groups, and disarming oppositions, and that this is an engineering task appropriately analyzed by experts, not by partisans. For more than half a century now, this is the story our news stories tell us, even when their authors intend them to say something else.

Theodore White wrote of the press corps, on the presidential campaign trail in 1960, that the talk of correspondents with one another is more than gossip; it is a critical process of consensus-formation. The group becomes a "brotherhood" that "influences and colors, beyond any individual resistance to prejudice or individual devotion to fact, all of what they write. For by now they have come to trust only each other."[20] This is not entirely true. They trust *also* the very forms of discourse around which their work is oriented and their gossip centered. These forms—which they must control if they are to be respected professionals—have an extraordinary power to control the journalists themselves and, through them, their readers. Like reporters, American citizens expect to find power exercised in the conscious intentions of actors. But we, like the journalists themselves, will better understand our politics as well as our news media when we recognize the substantive message and substantial authority of narrative form.

3 Question Authority: A History of the News Interview

The interview is the fundamental act of contemporary journalism. Reporters rely overwhelmingly on interviews; according to a study of Washington reporters in the 1980s, journalists depend so heavily on interviews that they use no documents at all in nearly three-quarters of the stories they write.[1]

This has not always been the case. Although newspapers in America date to the early 1700s, the interview as accepted journalistic practice cannot be traced back before the 1860s. The early colonial press devoted most of its editorial space to news items found in London papers, with a sprinkling of essays of moral instruction, humor, and letters. After about 1765, as the press grew overtly partisan, essays and letters on topics of political controversy became central, but there was little that a modern reader would recognize as "reporting." In the 1820s, as both political combat and commercial competition increased, leading urban dailies began to hire reporters to gather news; with the coming of the commercially-minded "penny papers" of the 1830s, reporters covered local news as never before, especially news from the police and the courts. The *Boston Herald* observed in 1847 that "reporting is now one of the specialties of the press."[2]

Despite the advent of "reporting," interviewing was not practiced. Much reporting remained nothing more than the publication of official documents and public speeches, verbatim. Reporters talked with public officials, but they did not refer to these conversations in their news stories. Politicians and diplomats who dropped by the newspaper offices—as many of them did regularly—could feel secure that their confidences "were regarded as inviolate," as *Baltimore Sun* reporter Francis A. Richardson later recalled.[3] President Lincoln often spoke with reporters in informal conversations, but no reporter quoted him directly.[4] Charles Nordhoff, managing editor of the New York *Evening Post,* spoke with President Andrew Johnson in 1867 and relayed the conversations to his editor at the paper, but he never mentioned them in print. "Typically, Nordhoff used his access to politicians to lobby for causes he believed in, to cajole, and sometimes to act as a mediator between opposing political camps."[5]

Asking questions, like other human social practices, is an activity distributed unequally across cultures, eras, domains, and social stations. It may be that asking questions turns up in some form in all societies in all periods, but it is not a practice that appears with the same frequency, the same moral tone, or the same cultural significance.[6] In American journalism, asking questions was not regularly practiced at all until the 1820s and it was not an activity acknowledged in print until after the Civil War. How did a practice, unknown to journalists of the early nineteenth century, become the centerpiece of the reporter's trade? How did an "unnatural act," this "relatively new kind of encounter in the history of human relations," come to be accepted?[7] My aim here is to sketch the institutionalization of interviewing in journalism, as both a social practice and a literary form.

Historians of journalism have tried to date the first newspaper interview. Some authorities have traced it to James Gordon Bennett's coverage of the Helen Jewett murder in 1836, others to Horace Greeley's account of a conversation with Brigham Young in 1859, and still others to the period just after the Civil War and the work of the Cincinnati journalist Joseph McCullagh, among the first reporters to interview a president (Andrew Johnson).[8] This search for an individual inventor naively assumes a "great man" theory of history and neglects to ask why the interview should have emerged when and where it did. The institutional and cultural acceptance of the interview, as opposed to its birth, has not been the subject of any published research at all. On this fundamental transformation of how news is written, historians of journalism have been silent.

Whenever the first interview appeared, it was a form generally unfamiliar in American journalism and even unnamed as late as 1859 when Horace Greeley wrote in his *New York Tribune* about Mormon leader Brigham Young. This was indeed what we would recognize today as an interview, but Greeley had no straightforward way to identify it for his readers. He had to explain, in concluding his "question and answer" format article, just what he was doing: "Such is, as nearly as I can recall, the substance of nearly two hours of conversation, wherein much was said incidentally that would not be worth reporting, even if I could remember and reproduce it."[9]

"Interview" refers both to a social interaction between a person of public interest and a professional writer and to the literary form that is the product of that interaction. The term was widely used in the nineteenth century in a much broader sense, to refer to any kind of meeting and conversation between two people. But within a decade of Horace Greeley's awkward use of the interview form in its narrower, journalistic meaning, the "interview" was the recognized name for the new practice. By the turn of the century, there was no question that the interview was the central act of the journalist. "In one sense a Washington correspondent's work is a steady round of interviews," wrote one observer in 1900. "In interviewing in all its phases is best brought out the mutual confidence which exists between a Washington correspondent and public men."[10] "Practically the whole of the newspaper is based on the interview," Hutchins Hapgood wrote in 1905. "What makes a good newspaper man is his ability to obtain facts from public men and his skill in inferring from what he has secured to what he has been unable to extort."[11]

The Nature of the Interview

The news interview is much more than an interaction in which a reporter seeks to elicit information. That is what a person does, very often, when asking a question of another person in ordinary conversation. But that does not adequately describe what happens in a news interview. While I do not presume that in the 125-year history of the news interview its features have remained constant, a few general norms and expectations define for it a relatively invariant structure:

1. The reporter may ask either a question to gather information or what is called a "known information" question. If the questioner is actually seeking information, the normal sequence in the interaction is (1) question (2) reply and (3) acknowledgment. Alternatively, the questioner may already know the information and may be testing the interviewee. The "known information question" is the standard format in elementary school classrooms where teachers ask students to provide information that they themselves already have. The standard sequence is (1) question (2) reply (3) evaluation.[12] In a news interview, the interviewee may not know whether the question on the table is a

"known" or "unknown" information question, and this creates a special tension. The reporter is *both* inquiring *and* testing. The interview tests not only the source's veracity but his or her consistency with the views of others in the same party, agency, or administration, as well as self-consistency with his or her own previously expressed beliefs. The normal sequence of turns in the news interview is (1) question (2) reply and (3) next question. The "next question" serves as a brisk acknowledgment at the same time as it represses any evaluative response. If the reporter does not follow the reply with another question but acknowledges the reply, he or she tries to do so in as neutral and nonevaluative a form as possible.[13]

2. The news interview has at least three parties, not two; it is a triadic relationship in which an unseen public is an "overhearing audience." Its literary outcome is a written or broadcast presentation of the source (and to a lesser extent the journalist) through the medium of the journalist to an anonymous public. Although the reporter in the news interview refrains from making evaluations, there is an inferred—and deferred—evaluation *by a third party*, the always present "public" or audience. It follows from this that the news interview is normally "on the record." Any talk that is privileged and not spoken for publication must be specially marked. Normal interview talk is consequential, talk for which the speaker will be held publicly responsible. (It would not be too much to say that in many interviews there are as many as five parties involved: the source, the reporter, the absent audience, and also the reporter's employing institution and the institution or organization the source is taken to represent. A reporter from a prestigious news institution is treated very differently from a reporter for a student newspaper.)

3. In the news interview, the relative power of the reporter and the source is an ever-present consideration. In any conversation, there is potentially a tension between talk as a form of solidarity that establishes or reinforces an egalitarian relationship between two people and talk as an assertion of power, establishing or restating hierarchy. Questioning, as Esther Goody says, is both a "device for seeking the truth" and a "vehicle for demonstrating authority."[14] In news reporting, the power relationship is the central frame for interaction. The reporter's dependence on the words and views of the interviewee for his or her reputation, or even livelihood, is balanced against the interviewee's vulnerability to public exposure or need for public recognition controlled by the journalist. Each party exercises leverage potentially damaging to the other.

In spite of this, egalitarian trust, affection, and loyalty may emerge.

"Questioning," Esther Goody writes, "binds two people in *immediate* reciprocity."[15] There is a norm of reciprocity in interviewing, a direct human bond that affects both what the interviewee tells the reporter and what the reporter is willing to write publicly. Even so, reciprocity does not imply equality or communion; the centripetal binding of the face-to-face interview is in tension with forces tugging the reporter and the source to different corners and conflicting purposes.

The Early Reputation of the Interview:
The American Barbarism

The history of the interview is an account not only of the form's modernity but its American-ness. The *New York World*'s correspondent Thompson Cooper referred to the interview in 1871 as "this modern and American Inquisition."[16] "The interview," wrote the famed British journalist William Stead in 1902, "was a distinctively American invention."[17] The *London Daily News* as early as 1869 worried about a new practice of some of the daily newspapers in New York who "are bringing the profession of journalism into contempt, so far as they can, by a kind of toadyism or flunkeyism which they call 'interviewing.' "[18] In America, the Irish-born, European-style journalist E. L. Godkin, editor of *The Nation,* attacked the practice of interviewing, calling it "the joint production of some humbug of a hack politician and another humbug of a newspaper reporter."[19] Godkin's main concern was that the interview tended to increase the independence of the reporter from editorial control. A French writer, Paschal Grousset, compared the French press unfavorably to the British, noting that the former had borrowed too freely "that spirit of inquiry and 'espionage' " from the Americans. "The mania for interviewing, which is so rampant in America, and which has a tendency to acclimatise itself here, will never take root in England," he wrote. English public men, he said admiringly, laugh at the "naive resignation" of their French counterparts who submit to "the presence and indiscretion of certain foreign correspondents."[20]

European journalists associated reporting in general, not just interviewing, with the American press. "The English press belongs to the leader writers, and the American press to the reporters," wrote a visiting Scottish editor in 1887. A French journalist, after his 1886 visit to America, held that "reporting is in the process of killing journalism," and he feared that "reporting is creeping into the French newspapers" too.[21] Reporting as a journalistic practice was far more advanced in the United States than in Europe, although the "new journalism"—with an emphasis on reportage—was by the 1880s becoming more popular in England as well.[22] But even in the United States, a nation accustomed to reporting since at least the 1830s, interviewing appeared as a novel practice and was sometimes treated derisively by old-time journalists. Take Mark Twain, for example, in 1868:

> I came across one of the lions of the country today at the Senate—General Sherman. The conversation I had with this gentleman therefore ought to be reported, I suppose. I said the weather was very fine, and he said he had seen finer. Not liking to commit myself further, in the present unsettled conditions of politics, I said good morning. Understanding my little game, he said good morning also. This was all that passed, but it was very significant. It reveals clearly what he thinks of impeachment. I regard this manner of getting a great man's opinions a little underhanded, but then everybody does it.[23]

Still, once initiated, the practice of interviewing seemed to take hold quickly. The *Baltimore Sun* correspondent Francis Richardson suggested that McCullagh's interview with President Andrew Johnson in 1867 "excited sensation" and helped publicize and popularize the new form.[24] The Atlanta journalist Henry Grady wrote that "the idea took like wild-fire." He himself claimed to have interviewed "nearly every prominent man in the South and many of the greatest men in the North and West."[25] Direct quotations from "public men," apart from transcripts of their speeches, were still not integrated into everyday journalistic practice, but Grady has a point. A perusal of the *Atlanta Constitution* suggests that in the early 1870s any sort of interview was highly unusual; by the mid-1870s, direct quotation in news stories or other indications that interviewing was at the root of a news item could be found frequently.

After 1900 the English began to accept the interview, too, but often through American tutelage. American journalists taught Europeans that their own elites would submit to interviews. In 1906 Frederic William Wile was working for the *Chicago Daily News* in Berlin when R. B. Haldane, Secretary of State for War in the British Cabinet, came to the city. Wile was also representing the (London) *Daily Mail,* substituting for its vacationing correspondent. "To an American-trained reporter it was the obvious thing for even a pro-tem correspondent of a London newspaper to interview Mr. Haldane." He headed to Haldane's hotel for an interview, despite being informed by the reporter for the (London) *Morning Post* that British ministers "were never molested" by reporters, especially when visiting a foreign capital on government assignment. "That sort of thing isn't done," the reporter told him, "in accents that mingled pity and contempt."[26] Wile got his interview. Wile interviewed King Oscar II of Sweden in 1906 at a time when, he later wrote, "a direct-quote interview with a reigning monarch for American newspaper publication was unheard of. It was at least rare."[27]

Wile's *Chicago Daily News* colleague Edward Price Bell also succeeded in interviewing Haldane in 1915 when, under the pressure of war and with the British seeking to influence American public opinion, he agreed to an interview. The enterprise of American journalists combined with a growing British sensitivity to American public opinion was breaking down British officials' resistance to the interview.[28] Bell did not hesitate to point out to the British leaders he sought to interview after the war that their policies were widely misunderstood: "I have been pestering Curzon steadily since he took over the Foreign Office to give me an interview covering the whole question of British foreign policy, pointing out to him how persistently, mercilessly, and often mendaciously this policy is attacked almost everywhere."[29]

The war transformed the standing of the interviewer and gave it, as the American magazine journalist Isaac Marcosson wrote, "a whole rebirth of distinction. You saw the immemorial aloofness of the King of England wiped out at a tea party for American journalists at Sandringham; you beheld the holy of holies of the British War Office as the setting of a weekly conference with reporters."[30] After the war American journalists accompanying President Wilson in Europe paid their respects to Lloyd George. Instead of withdrawing gracefully after their brief audience, they asked the Prime Minister questions directly, "to the utter astonishment and great embarrassment of our British escorts," as the *Baltimore Sun*'s Washington correspondent recalled. Lloyd George responded and seemed to enjoy the exchange; he gave the reporters permission to quote from the interview.[31] Journalist Willis Abbot recalled that his assignment to interview European heads of state in 1909 seemed "ridiculous and impossible" (and he failed at it), but twenty years later it was easily managed, the interview no longer "a shocking innovation to the rulers of Europe."[32]

British journalists had begun to conduct interviews in England in the late nineteenth century. What seems to have been much more rare than in America were impertinent interviews. Interviews were conducted with public figures who sought publicity, and generally the interviewee spoke only to the representative of a newspaper favorably disposed toward him. The primary contribution of William T. Stead, sometimes considered the inventor of interviewing in England, was finding ways to question people not eager to be interviewed. What made Stead original was "his stalking of an unwilling subject."[33]

But frequently an American stalked first. An American correspondent for the *New York World,* Thompson Cooper, is supposed to have been the first to interview the Pope (Pius IX in 1871). The *World,* of course, took great pride in this coup, and crowed over its triumph: "The Roman Catholic Church is the oldest, as the interview is almost the youngest, of the institutions of mankind. And they are this morning presented faced to face in the persons of their respective representatives—his Holiness Pius IX and Mr. Thompson Cooper upon the part of *The World* of New York. The spirit of the Church and the spirit of the age, in concrete and accurate types, have met together. The Church and the Press have kissed each other."[34] James Creelman was reportedly the first to be granted an interview by the president of France (Félix Faure, in 1897).[35] The *World* scored with the Pope (Benedict XV) again in 1915. Karl von Wiegand, the interviewer, reported that this was the first interview with a pope since Leo XIII (1878–1903) and only the second audience of its kind "in the modern history of the church."[36]

Late nineteenth century European contempt for the American interview was not universal. The liberal Danish journalist Henrik Cavling visited America several times in the 1880s and 1890s and admired the American style. "The reporter and the interview are the focus of these papers . . . this is ideal journalism," he wrote, thinking especially of the *New York World* and other "new journalism" papers. "These papers are produced by journalists, not aesthetes and politicians, and they are written for the lower class to help them, inform them and fight corruption for them." Cavling sought to introduce the American style to Denmark.[37]

The interview was not accepted without tension. As late as 1897 reporter Lincoln Steffens was rebuffed by New York Governor-Elect Frank S. Black in an exchange Steffens preserved for his readers:

> "Is this for an interview?"
> "It is to ask you—"

"I never am interviewed."

"The subject is important," said the reporter. "It is—"

"I make it a rule to say nothing whatever in this way."[38]

The naturalization of the interview, then, was by no means complete at the turn of the century. It is not complete yet; its cultural awkwardness survives.

Standard Interview Practices

Interviewing had to develop its own practices, its own etiquette, and its own lore. Should a reporter take notes? No, Frederic Wile learned while interviewing the famous Chauncey Depew, head of the New York Central Railroad and senator-to-be. A beginner at reporting, he took notes, in shorthand, on everything Depew said during an interview he shared with veteran reporters from other Chicago papers. What he came up with, however, was no better than the articles of his rivals who took no notes at all. He learned that "a trained reporter has no need of notes. What he requires is a memory for essentials, and the capacity accurately and interestingly to reproduce them." On momentous occasions, "when a precise account of words or ideas is essential," some note-taking is acceptable, but for background issues, "seasoned Washington newspapermen and women trust to their memory, just as my elders did at the Depew interview."[39]

Joseph McCullagh reported that in his historic interview with President Andrew Johnson, he took no notes at all and wrote nothing until the next morning, when he took two hours to commit his story to paper.[40] The general practice of taking few or no notes in an interview adds to the impression that "interviewing" and "reporting" were regarded as separate activities. Skill in stenography had long been an asset to a reporter; the archetypal act of reporting earlier in the century was sitting in a legislative session writing down speeches. Interviewing changed that. Now memory, not stenography, was the reporter's prized tool.

The reliance on memory was codified in textbook pronouncements. A handbook on reporting (1901) urged reporters to write "as few notes as possible" and never to use shorthand. "Notebooks are used only by reporters in stories and plays."[41] Another textbook agrees that "the stage has hardened us to seeing a reporter slinking around the outskirts of every bit of excitement writing excitedly and hurriedly in a large leather notebook . . . But real reporters on real newspapers do not use notebooks. A few sheets of folded copy paper hidden carefully in an inside pocket ready for names and addresses and perhaps figures are all that most of them carry."[42] This text urged journalists not to take notes—except for interviews with prominent men "who are used to being interviewed and prefer to have their remarks taken down verbatim. Such an interview, however, is little more than a call to secure a statement for publication."[43] Yet another book claims that "a notebook or pencil wrongly displayed" can instantly suppress news; reporters must learn to cultivate their memories. Politicians especially clam up when pencils appear, and so "political reporters aware of the fact never take notes if they can help it while getting interviews."[44] A 1911 handbook advised journalists to take notes only on names and important facts.[45]

Leading journalists counseled against taking notes. Julian Ralph observed, "Note-books and pencils frequently alarm and put upon his guard a man who would talk freely in an ordinary conversation."[46] Edward Price Bell agreed, although he recommended that the reporter write out notes as soon after the interview as possible.[47] Isaac Marcosson advised against note-taking, too. "Some men are note-shy. This is especially true of the great American financiers. To write down what they say while they are saying it shuts them up like a clam."[48]

But sometime between 1900 and 1930, there was probably a change in journalistic practice; at least there was a change in the nature of advice offered young journalists. A text coauthored by Walter Williams, one of the pioneers of journalism education, agreed that "there is danger in putting too much stress in the taking of notes." Still, he recommended note-taking as a useful "guard against inaccuracy" even though he also advised that "the reporter who, producing a note-book and pencil, assumes the attitude of one making a formal stenographic report, instills a feeling of hesitancy and restraint, or tends to frighten his informant so that he will refuse to be interviewed."[49] In the 1922 edition, Williams and his coauthor Frank Martin recommended "the discriminate and intelligent use of notes." Misquoting, they observe, is often the result of reporters' relying too much on memory, so "many public men who have given interviews that were incorrectly written, now ask that as a safeguard, notes be taken by the reporter."[50] By 1934 another textbook could report that shorthand is rarely used by American reporters because "it deflects attention from highlights to minute details." In reporting speeches, beginners take down too many quotes, although better too much than too little.[51]

In the 1930s, European reporters were still urged not to take notes.

But in America by that time, according to a British source, taking notes was acceptable practice because public men in the United States "are more willing victims to the interviewer than those over here, who generally are reserved and not very partial to publicity."[52] A *Chicago Tribune* reporter advised that taking notes flatters an interviewee, who "immediately thinks the occasion momentous and inwardly feels he must give his best to the reporter."[53] Although advice varied, the apparently growing acceptance in journalism of note-taking suggests a degree of naturalization of the interview.

Standard practices in writing up, as well as conducting, interviews have changed over time. At first, as I have suggested, the interview seems to have been regarded as an independent genre of journalism separate from reporting and regarded as a news event in itself, a journalistic coup. Its printed format might be a straightforward "Q and A" style, as was the case with Greeley's 1859 interview of Brigham Young. In interviews with President Andrew Johnson in the *New York World,* conducted by "J.B.S." (Jerome B. Stillson), the format was more or less novelistic, the reporter giving as much attention to his own comments and questions as to the President's. Again, as with Greeley, the novelty of the form occasioned some prefatory discussion—and puffery:

> The following is a synopsis of a desultory conversation had by the writer with President Johnson last evening. As no man's utterances are so important or so eagerly sought for at this momentous time as those of the Chief Executive, I am convinced that the dignified tone of these unofficial remarks will be hailed with satisfaction by every true friend of the Republic and of constitutional government.

The interview then follows with long paragraphs of Johnson interrupted by occasional interjections from J.B.S., as in the following:

> "Yes," I observed, "the Radicals in Congress appear to take precious little warning from the Northern reaction. One would think, from what they are now doing, that their pressure was increasing."
>
> The President smiled grimly. "The Radicals in Congress are desperate."[54]

An interview might be printed with little or no direct quotation at all. John Swinton's interview with Karl Marx in 1880 describes Marx's look, characterizes his conversational style, and paraphrases his answers to questions. Only in the closing paragraph is Marx quoted directly. Reporter Swinton, "going down to the depths of language and rising to the height of emphasis, during an interspace of silence," inquires of Marx, "What is?" And "in deep and solemn tone, he replied, 'Struggle!' "[55] The *Chicago Tribune* ran several stories in 1896 based on interviews with William McKinley's presidential campaign manager, Mark Hanna. In one story, there was no direct quotation at all.[56] In another, the lead was a direct quotation from Hanna with all quotations thereafter indirect.[57]

The integration of direct quotation into straight news stories took some time to become standard journalistic practice. As late as 1914 a leading metropolitan paper like the *Baltimore Sun* could go for days at a time with no quotation marks appearing anywhere on the front page.[58] Ten years later, a more modern form of direct quotation was well established. For instance, in a story on a speech in Pittsburgh by Robert LaFollette, the lead ran:

> Andrew W. Mellon was portrayed by Senator Robert M. LaFollette, Independent Presidential candidate, in an address here tonight as "the real President of the United States." Calvin Coolidge, he added, "is merely the man who occupies the White House."[59]

Before the 1920s, it would have been very rare for a speech to be reported in this "sound bite" fashion. During the 1920s long news stories without direct quotation still remained in instances where today direct quotation would dominate, but an approximation of the contemporary format had made its appearance.

The Authenticity of the Interview

Standard practices are not, of course, neutral inventions. They have biases of their own. The very existence of standard practices connotes a corruption of authentic or spontaneous interaction. One early critic of interviewing held indignantly that many interviews are "arranged":

> I mean that the interviewed party, in the awfulness of his dignity, does not wish to appear in the light of seeking to "put himself right" before the public; and so one of his "friends," for example—sometimes his modest self—arranges with the editor or proprietor of a newspaper to send a reporter "around" at a certain time and "interview" him; and it

is a remarkable fact that the reporter always finds the "great man" in his private office, "on time."[60]

In a period dominated by the partisan press, politicians ordinarily spoke to reporters whose papers supported them. Interviewing was often no more than puffery for the politician interviewed. General Ben Butler went so far as to write up his own "interviews" and pass them on to reporters. "Self-interviewing," often for handsome financial reward from the newspaper, became common practice.[61]

Still, reporters came to hold to an ideal of authenticity, even if it was rarely achieved in practice. President Theodore Roosevelt manipulated reporters with extraordinary skill. A *New York Times* correspondent who covered him, Charles W. Thompson, wrote: "He gave out many statements, some of them in the form of interviews, and sometimes, too, he was actually interviewed, but in such cases he always directed the form the interview should take." A real interview, Thompson went on, is "an unpremeditated thing." The reporter asks as he pleases and, he holds, "There is no escape even in saying, 'I refuse to answer that question,' for that sentence may have a world of significance if the question is rightly framed." So Thompson advised that the best site for interviewing was "in a railroad station as the public man gets off the train. It may be short, but it is spontaneous and revealing." That never happened with Roosevelt.[62]

Can an interviewee revise or take back what he has said? Of course; Frederic Wile remembered an interview with William Jennings Bryan, in the presence of Mrs. Bryan, who sat knitting and listening. "I don't think I'd say that, Will," she interjected at one point. "And 'Will' immediately 'unsaid' it."[63] William C. Hudson, a reporter for the *Brooklyn Daily Eagle*, interviewed President Grant at his summer cottage in 1874 or 1875. He wrote up the interview without attributing the views to the President, as at that time "etiquette demanded." He referred instead to "the highest authority" for his knowledge of the President's views, "the customary euphemism." But he had qualms about using some of Grant's phrases in print and so sent the draft article to Grant, calling attention to the doubtful sentences. Grant thanked him, changed some things, and added a new piece of information on a different subject that was a coup for Hudson.[64]

What Hudson reports as an act of his own initiative Charles Dana made a general precept—"Never print an interview without the knowledge and consent of the party interviewed."[65] Standard practice in the early 1900s was to send the interview to the source for corrections before submitting it for publication. Isaac Marcosson, writing for *Munsey's* Magazine, interviewed Governor Woodrow Wilson in 1911 and returned from New York to Trenton to go over proof with Wilson.[66] For Edward Price Bell, getting the source's authorization of finished copy was a seal of approval for the interview: "The formally authenticated interview bears a definite seal upon the accuracy of the interviewer's work, and so safeguards, not only the interviewee, but the journalist who reduced his exposition to black and white."[67] Bell, though the most celebrated interviewer of his day in foreign news, was vulnerable to the manipulation of his sources. In an article on the art of interviewing, Bell wrote about his interviews with the leaders of Germany, Italy (Mussolini), France, and Great Britain, and said of them: "To these statesmen I said we were looking for truth, for light, for candor, for that which would be of lasting educational value to the world, and I am convinced they did their utmost to give us what we sought." Bell was indiscriminately optimistic on this point. He felt that he met the real Hitler in a 1935 interview where Hitler portrayed himself as an apostle of peace. He read events of the next years as evidence of pressures placed upon the well-meaning Hitler by other nefarious forces.[68]

The interview can be a conspiracy of the reporter and the source against the audience. One part of the conspiracy is whether information gathered in an interview will be attributed or not. Chauncey Depew would sometimes be quoted by name and at other times under the general phrase, "It has been learned from a reliable source."[69] There was already at the turn of the century concern over what was called, as today, the "leak."[70] There was collaboration also in the discretion of reporters who knew much more than they wrote and kept confidences of the public officials with whom they had ongoing relations. Reporters could protect a favored, or simply a naive, public person from himself. Reporters interviewing William Howard Taft when he served as Secretary of War under Roosevelt were astonished one day when he spoke frankly to them of his disagreement with the President on an important issue. "Taft sat beaming, waiting for the next question, wholly unconscious of the bomb he had touched off," wrote *New York Times* correspondent Charles Thompson. "He was safe enough in the hands of most of us; but the Hearst representative would assuredly print it under streamer head-lines in bold face type on the front page." So the Associated Press representative, Arthur Dunn, told

Taft that the comment he had just made was not under an injunction of secrecy and assured the Secretary they would print it unless he enjoined secrecy upon them. "We strongly advise you to place the injunction of secrecy upon us. Do I speak for all of you, gentlemen?" And everyone agreed. As the reporters left, the Hearst man said to the AP reporter, "Dunn, why do you hate a good story so intensely?"[71]

There is a tidiness to this anecdote that makes one suspect it has been told and retold and polished before finding its way into print. Still, Thompson's easy assurance that Taft was "safe enough in the hands of most of us" is a notable acknowledgment that reporters routinely protected sources from their own indiscretions. A decade later, Karl von Wiegand arranged an interview with Germany's Crown Prince Friedrich Wilhelm, just a few months into World War I. The Crown Prince told von Wiegand to tell his father, the Kaiser, something he dared not tell him himself: that he was convinced the war was already lost. Von Wiegand, abiding by normal understandings of the day, kept this sensational opinion confidential. As von Wiegand was leaving, Wilhelm said: "I have trusted you. All I ask is, don't write anything that will add to my troubles."[72]

Eleanor Roosevelt had a devout following of women reporters who tried to protect her. In 1933 Mrs. Roosevelt leaked to four women reporters the news that President Roosevelt had refused to sign a joint proclamation with Herbert Hoover to close the banks the day before the inauguration. The reporters told Mrs. Roosevelt that such a story could start a worldwide panic, and they refused to print it. One of the reporters, Dorothy Ducas, recalled in an interview many years later that "the women always covered up for Mrs. Roosevelt. All kinds of things were said (by her) that shouldn't be said in print."[73]

The artificiality of the interview, its association with "new journalism" where journalists create or make the news rather than report it, at first kept its status within journalism precarious. Although Isaac Marcosson, an advocate of the interview, could declare in 1919 that interviewing was "merely a phase of reporting," the Associated Press prohibited its reporters from writing interviews as such until 1926.[74] Kent Cooper, who had become AP general manager a year earlier, introduced interviewing as part of his plan for the AP to cover not only "important" news but news of human interest. Indeed, the first interview the Associated Press ran was with the golf champion Bobby Jones.[75] But the sense that an interview was a way of "making" rather than reporting news, marking it as inauthentic, has remained.

The Interview as Invasion

Cooperative as the interview might be, even conspiratorial, this is only one side of the ambivalent relationship that modern journalism establishes between reporter and official. Early commentators on the interview regularly refer to the aggressiveness and deviousness of the interviewer. Grousset refers to the interview as a form of "espionage."[76] Grant Milnor Hyde in his 1912 textbook writes of the interviewee as "the victim."[77]

If the interview can be criticized as an act of aggression, it can also be admired as manly performance, exploit, or coup. The interview was seen early on as an enterprise attesting to the bravado of a reporter. In the 1870s a New York reporter, Joseph I. C. Clarke, interviewed Cardinal John McCloskey in his home, recalling in his memoirs, "No one, they said at the office, could do it." So he asked the Cardinal about the progress of building St. Patrick's Cathedral, took a good many notes on this, and then closed his notebook. At that point he casually asked about events in Europe, from which the Cardinal had just returned. When he published his story in the *New York Herald*, he featured the Cardinal's views on Europe and all but ignored the cathedral.[78]

Karl von Wiegand took his 1915 interview with the Pope to be a great triumph, and his paper rewarded him with a $1000 bonus.[79] In the reported interview, he wrote:

> Only those newspaper men who have made attempts to get an audience and interview with the Pope can appreciate the difficulties and obstacles to be overcome. In my case the difficulty was considered greater because, as it happens, I am not a Catholic.
> "Impossible," I am told in Berlin.
> "Impossible," was the answer that met my first efforts in Rome.[80]

Interviewing the Pope seems to have been the next best thing to interviewing God for American journalists, and they kept on citing papal interviews as earth-shattering achievements, from Cooper in 1871 to von Wiegand in 1915 to Thomas Morgan for United Press in 1929. Although Morgan was not the first to interview Pope Pius XI, he was the first to do so, the United Press claimed, "in the private library of the Pontiff."[81]

Exploit might require a bit of deception. A journalist for the *New*

York Evening Sun advised reporters who succeeded in getting someone to say something he might "later wish to have left unsaid" to "retire before a change of mind comes" by changing the subject, playing the admirer, and gracefully making an exit.[82] The journalist could do much more than this to manipulate the interview form. The reporter could determine what he wanted the news to say and then choose an interviewee he believed would be willing to say it.[83] It appears that in the late nineteenth century, "interviews were routinely faked. If reporters sent to hotels in search of newsworthy visitors found the pickings slim, they sometimes simply conjured up quotable characters."[84]

Although the rudeness of the American interviewer was widely acknowledged, even by journalists themselves, this may be a case where people wanted to claim more vices than their behavior demonstrated. G. K. Chesterton found American interviewing "generally very reasonable" and "always very rapid"—it had, he remarked, "many of the qualities of American dentistry." Reporters portrayed themselves in print as "far more rowdy and insolent" than the interviews had actually been. The American reporter, he concluded, was "a harmless clubman in private" but "a sort of highway-robber in print."[85]

Not surprisingly, the interview form raised questions about privacy. A German observer, Emil Dovifat, writing a comprehensive book on American journalism in 1927, refers to the interview as "an American invention" and notes that in seeking out interviews the American reporter "has become almost a public figure. In middle and small sized towns, even private travellers are being attacked by reporters and are asked the most incredible questions."[86] Waylaying prominent people at hotels and train stations was standard practice, raised to a high art by the *Chicago Journal*'s Martha Dalrymple in the 1920s, who habitually interviewed movie stars as they changed trains in Chicago in traveling from Hollywood to New York.[87] The distinguished American editor Henry Watterson complained of importunate interviewers, describing them as capable of producing "the hold-up in the station" and "the ambuscade in the lobby of the hotel," thereby giving "an added terror to modern travel."[88] G. K. Chesterton reports that even before his ship touched land in New York, interviewers had "boarded the ship like pirates."[89]

Though Americans as well as Europeans could be taken aback by the effrontery of the American interviewer, the main source of concern about the press and privacy in the late nineteenth century centered on newspaper illustrations and straight reporting, not on interviews. The interview depended, as the sketch or photograph did not, on the victim's cooperation; so it was taken to be less an invasion of privacy than a social indiscretion for someone of a reporter's station. Thus Ben: Perley Poore (1820–1887), an old hand in Washington journalism, speaks disparagingly of the new journalism by recalling that in the old days Washington correspondents "were neither eavesdroppers nor interviewers, but gentlemen, who had a recognized position in society, which they never abused." Interviewing he took to be a "pernicious habit" and "a dangerous method of communication betwen our public men and the people."[90] Charles Nordhoff took to quoting sources directly in his columns but disdained the practice of "ignorant" reporters who, "active and brassy," run after public men to ask them pointed questions; he preferred the informal socializing of public officials with respected journalists that he had experienced earlier in his career.[91]

Conclusion

A history of the news interview contributes to the history of cultural and social modernity, but it is no easy matter to specify just what the interview's emergence signifies. Perhaps it should be seen as part of the history of "intrusive perception," as Edward Shils has called it, a form of surveillance characterized by "the scale, the existence of specialized occupational cultures, the elaborate, scientifically based technology, and the goodwill which accompanies much of it."[92] People have always gathered information about other people, to orient themselves in a social encounter and to manage social relations strategically, to control the behavior of others. But ordinarily people gather information about other people in ways that tend to be (a) unspecialized, (b) relatively unsystematic and often unconscious, and (c) mutual. The people-watching and information-gathering that arose in the nineteenth century were specialized, relatively systematic, and one-sided.

The nineteenth century gave rise to occupations that practice what I would call *impersonal* surveillance: the relationship of the observers or reporters to the person they are gathering information about is formally impersonal. They are not engaged in *personal* social control, a relationship of trusteeship, as is the parent who watches and gathers information about the toddler crawling about the room or the children playing in a wading pool. Neither are they engaged in *interpersonal* social control, a relationship of contract, as is the supervisor observing workers or the police officer walking a beat on behalf of civic order. The new professions of intrusive perception engage in a form of impersonal social control. In personal and interpersonal surveillance, the physical movements of the person watched may be grounds for intervention; in impersonal surveillance, physical movement is just one more bit of information to be gathered. Indeed, the locus of control is information about the person, not the bodily person as such. The information gatherer has no authority and little motive for intervening in the activity of the person observed. The personal watcher reports to no one but interacts directly with the person observed; the interpersonal watcher reports to a constituted authority to which the person watched also has a direct relationship as employee or citizen; the impersonal watcher reports to an audience with which the person watched may have little or no connection. The reporter may write about people who lost their homes to a devastating fire in Tucson for an audience in New York, just as the anthropologist may write for graduate students in Chicago about South Sea islanders.

Personal surveillance is characteristic of the family, the neighborhood, and the traditional society. In these settings social contacts are few in number and face-to-face in character. Interpersonal surveillance grows and becomes specialized with the rise of industry, city life, and large-scale, dense human groups. Social contacts become numerous and are increasingly mediated by formal organizations or by the etiquette of relations among strangers. Impersonal surveillance increases when the technologies of communication, transportation, and information storage enable dense human interaction among people who are neither face-to-face acquaintances nor united by membership in common organizations nor connected by the propinquity of shared public space. People may be connected, instead, in the more abstract relationships made possible by markets, "consumption communities," and mass media. There are specialized roles and even specialized occupations of interpersonal surveillance (the police officer), as there are specialized roles of impersonal surveillance (the news reporter, the news photographer, the credit reporter, the social scientist, the public opinion pollster, and others). But it is primarily in the occupations of impersonal surveillance that there is a literature of self-doubt and anxiety about the authenticity of the occupational task. For the police officer, relations with the public are the core activity, and the officer's responsibility is to the people with whom he or she interacts in public. The news reporter or the social scientist is in a different position altogether. The anthropologist in the field, for example, is engaged in the defining feature of the job. But field research is an initiation rite, not a regular assignment, and the test of the anthropologist is in presentation before professional audiences, not before natives.

When people in everyday life gather information, they use it or consume it on the spot. The reporter, in contrast, saves or stores information and reinvests it in an institutional setting in which the reporter and his or her source both have relatively little power. People in everyday life also store information when they bear grudges, make plans, or anticipate the social moves of others. But people in impersonal information-gathering jobs adopt a relatively disinterested relationship to the information they gather. They do not internalize information for personal use; they externalize it. They manufacture cultural objects—reports, photographs, or news stories. Their vested interest is not in the information they have but in the fact that they have information. They thereby respond both to the specific institutional needs of their organizations for data about individuals and to general popular desires for such information.

The interview is one form in which the news reporter exercises autonomy and demonstrates to the public and the news institution alike an intimacy with powerful people. Reporters are judged professionally by the sources they keep. This was already beginning to be true at the turn of the century when Julian Ralph reported that getting "beats," still the "chief aim and glory" of every news reporter, "is growing to be more and more a product of intimate acquaintance with public men, and less and less a result of agility of mind and body."[93] Reporters publicly demonstrate through interviews their proximity to news sources and thereby increase the authority of their writing for the audience.

The rise of the interview coincides with the rise of newspaper reporters as relatively autonomous workers who self-consciously achieve an occupational identity. Reporters in the late nineteenth century came to identify with one another across newspapers (in addition to identifying with their own employers).[94] Other professionalizing changes in news writing occurred in the same era. There was a shift from 1880 to 1920 from a fairly informal address from reporter to editor ("The sky was blue and air was clear when I set off to the Capitol this morning . . .") to a formal and professional address to the reader ("Rep. Jones today introduced a path-breaking spending measure . . ."). Chronologically presented news gave way to a summary lead and inverted pyramid structure that required the reporter to make a judgment about what aspect of the event covered mattered most. News stories increasingly conveyed the meaning of the act reported in a time frame larger than that of the act itself. In these ways, journalists proved themselves not relayers of documents and messages but legitimate interpreters of news, able to write not just about what they, like any observer, can see and hear but also about what is unheard, unseen, or intentionally omitted.[95] The summary lead and the interview enlarged the reporter's field of action and sphere of discretion. They helped make of the reporter a visible public type, even occasionally a celebrity, throughout this century.

Even though interviewing is a well-established journalistic practice, it continues to raise uncomfortable issues of whether an interviewer makes news or reports it; of whether the journalist is responsible to the interviewee or to some other force—"truth" or the "public" or the news institution; whether the reporter or the interviewee has or should have the upper hand. In recent years, particular styles of questioning (was Dan Rather of CBS News too aggressive in asking Vice President and presidential candidate George Bush about Iran-Contra in 1988?) and even particular questions (should Paul Taylor of the *Washington Post* have asked Gary Hart "Have you ever committed adultery?") have become public controversies.

Whether an interview represents an act of solidarity between reporter and source or an act of domination with each trying to wrestle the other to the floor is as ambiguous as ever. The journalist still is taken to be predatory. Janet Malcolm has put this baldly: "Every journalist who is not too stupid or too full of himself to notice what is going on knows that what he does is morally indefensible. He is a kind of confidence man, preying on people's vanity, ignorance, or loneliness, gaining their trust and betraying them without remorse."[96] Interviewing, for all of our familiarity with it, for all of our reliance on it, remains deeply disturbing.

This may be true even for reporters themselves. But for them, conducting interviews shows that the reporter is "on the job."[97] It is a way to demonstrate—to the audience, to the editor, to other journalists, to other sources—not that the reporter speaks truth to power but that he or she speaks close to power. Quoting practices, Barbie Zelizer writes, are "the credit cards of contemporary public discourse: They lend credit to speakers who use them in their messages."[98] Contemporary quoting practices lend authority to journalists as a group. But this was not the point of interviewing in its earliest days. The interview was at first the invention of a new journalistic form. Marked by the absence of note-taking and by a premium placed upon the spontaneous and the authentic, it was a new locus of journalistic artistry. It became a point of competition among journalists, a coup that glamorized an individual reporter more than it lent credit to the profession of reporting.

Over time, interviewing became less the occasion for a separate feature article and more a routine technique of news-gathering incorporated into a large majority of news stories. The interview served as a means of cultural control over people in the public eye, especially government officials or candidates for office. Appearing first in the unusually democratic culture of the mid-nineteenth-century United States, the interview offered a novel mechanism for public watchfulness over the powerful. This intimate surveillance, especially suited to a democratic society, became well institutionalized by the 1930s, without shedding its contradictions—including the vulnerability of the reporter to the source, and of the public to both.

4 What Is a Reporter?

What first strikes a reader of Harrison Salisbury's auto-biography, *A Journey for Our Times*, is that it begins with two pages of "Acknowledgments." An autobiography is always an acknowledgment. One written at the end of a long public career cannot help being a series of acknowledgments, some certainly heartfelt, some painful, some politic. It is nonetheless a surprise to find Salisbury thanking his parents and aunt "for creating the family archive and writing the letters that enabled me to reconstruct so much of my early life," and thanking his sister for preserving this archive. He then makes explicit what the reader already senses: "I have approached my memoirs like a reporter and have drawn on many sources to refresh, correct and extend my recollections."[1] He is a reporter first and last and he knows it.

But what is a reporter? That is not so obvious a question as it appears. Is a reporter a kind of historian? A political activist or reformer? A skilled stenographer? A writer? Reporting as an occupation is an invention of the nineteenth century, a result of and a contributor to a democratic market society and an urban commercial consciousness. But it has evolved a life of its own and a unique self-consciousness. It is through that self-consciousness, reflected in the autobiographies of Lincoln Steffens (1866–1936) and Harrison Salisbury (1908–1993) that I seek some insight into the meaning of news reporting as a vocation with a distinctive outlook and a distinctive meaning.

Autobiographies, of course, provide direct evidence not of the life of the writer but of how the writer conceives his or her life. An autobiography is necessarily an apology, and the autobiographical project shows us primarily "the effort of a creator to give the meaning of his own mythic tale," as George Gusdorf puts it.[2] What is revealing, in examining the autobiographies of Steffens and Salisbury, is that journalists of different eras repair to different myths. This is a difference between the two individuals, to be sure, but it is also one that reflects the changing career of journalism itself.

In 1908, the year Salisbury was born, reporting in anything like the modern sense was just three generations old. Although newspapers date back to the early 1700s in this country, reporting as a specialized journalistic activity did not begin until the 1830s. Even after the Civil War, the activity that is today the archetypal act of the journalist—the interview—was a novelty, as we saw in the previous chapter. As late as World War I, American journalists were teaching their European colleagues that it was not uncivil but professionally responsible to interview powerful government officials. The reporter, and reporting, were inventions of the nineteenth-century middle-class public and its institutions. Reporting is not an ancient art. It is a historically specific, historically created activity. It does not necessarily transfer well or easily to other cultures. It does not maintain itself untouched as the world around it changes. What reporters report on, how they report, what they aim for, and how they go about their work vary from one era to another. But some features of reporting, bequeathed to contemporary journalists by the nineteenth century, mark the authority and character of news-gathering in ways that still shape the world of reporters and the world of the rest of us who read and listen to the news. We may get some insight into this by inquiring about what a reporter is, about the ontology of this novel occupational type.

For a general reader of Salisbury's memoirs who sails right by the acknowledgments, there is still no doubt, from the first sentence of the first paragraph of the first chapter, that Salisbury is a reporter and sees, or at least portrays, even his own life through the reporter's eyes: "To a workingman, head tucked into collar against the wind, hurrying home in the dark Minnesota November, the figure of a small boy slowly stomping across the snowy lawn beyond the yellow arc of gaslight was almost invisible, a blur against the crepuscular shadows of the gabled house" (p. 1). We are not surprised to learn in the next paragraph that this small boy, marching back and forth as if he were standing guard in the snow, is Salisbury, age nine. We are shown him at first as someone else might see him. Who that someone else is is a matter of some surprise: a workingman hurrying home after work. This workingman could be just a figure to give the whole scene a Victorian, nineteenth-century flavor (the gaslight certainly does that), but there is more to it than this. Salisbury's father was a doctor's son who found himself trapped in an office job in an industrial plant that meant little to him besides his paycheck. He was a workingman. Salisbury's father-in-law had been a miner in the coalfields of Illinois. Salisbury finds a natural identification with the worker, not a Marxist romance but a plain-spoken, simple respect. And so he first pictures himself to his readers watched, nonjudgingly, and watched over, by a worker. What a reporter is depends in large part on whom a reporter reports to. Who is the audience? Who is the public for the reporter's words?

Salisbury, age nine, called "Bunny" by his parents, seen or not seen by a workingman passing by, is outside in the snow near his home on Royalston Avenue in Minneapolis. It is November 1917, shortly after the Russian Revolution. What he is doing there is problematic. Salisbury the memoirist reconstructs a conversation after Bunny goes inside. His father asks him what he was doing in the yard. "Just playing," he replies. But what he was playing at was imagining himself a member of the Children's Regiment, standing guard at the Winter Palace, wearing a helmet with a red star. Was this "just playing"? The memoirist writes, "I've looked back a hundred times at that nine-year-old youngster, particularly during my long years in Russia, wondering whether, in fact, I was 'just playing' " (p. 2).

I will worry the same question here. The question is about imagination, about play, about how children or the reporters they grow into construct a career for themselves and a world for their readers. It is a question, again, of what a reporter is, because no reporter just "gets the facts." Reporters make stories. Making is not faking, not lying, but neither is it a passive mechanical recording. It cannot be done without play and imagination.[3]

Lincoln Steffens was also concerned with "play" in his autobiography. Born forty-two years before Salisbury and half a continent away in San Francisco, Steffens in the first pages of his autobiography is attempting not to pose a question but to assert an answer, to propose a theory—that his is the story of a happy life and one that has come full circle from his own golden infancy to his pleasure at being, for the first time, in his sixties, the father of an infant son who laughs when he tumbles out of bed.

Certainly this is how Steffens deals with the serious topic of child's play. For Steffens, the magic and beauty of childhood are in play, fantasy, and imagination. Books were a great source of fancy for the young Steffens. Riding around Sacramento on his pony, he would be Napoleon or Richard the Lion-Hearted or Byron and lose himself in his daydreams. One day, as he tells it, his father brought home an artist, W. M. Marple. Marple wanted to be taken to the dry basin of the American River, which, as it happens, was Lincoln's favorite stomping ground, a playground filled in his imagination with Indians, Saracens, and elephants. Marple set up his easel and painted while young Joseph Lincoln watched. Not impressed with the realism of the painter's work, he criticized it. Marple replied that he was not interested in the details of the sun-baked mud. "I see the colors and the light, the beautiful chord of the colors and the light." Steffens then admitted to his Indians and Saracens and felt embarrassed: "Your golden light is really there and my Indians aren't." The painter replied:

Your Indians are where my gold is, where all beauty is, in our heads. We all paint what we see, as we should. The artist's gift is to see the beauty in everything, and his job is to make others see it. I show you the gold, you show me the romance in the brush. We are both artists, each in his line.[4]

For Steffens, play creates reality, imagination finds and makes worlds. At the same time, imagination is the consolation for disappointed hopes. The young boy keeps discovering that each adult he gets to know is "playing he is really something else besides what his job is" (p. 66). They are all, in their minds, enacting life scripts they would like to be different or reenacting life stories that might have taken a more favorable turn.

Salisbury and Steffens—two different reporters, two different people, two different eras of journalism, even two different kinds of journalism: Steffens a magazine writer in his heyday as a muckraker; Salisbury a foreign correspondent for United Press and later the *New York Times*. It would make no sense to try to extract from these different lives some qualities we could describe as "essence of journalist." But by examining how they present themselves in their autobiographies, how and what they remember of their lives as reporters, we can learn something about the contours of twentieth-century journalism. What does a reporter report—and how? To whom does a reporter report? What is the reporter's objective? What does this imply for the inner life of the person who is a journalist? What does the prominence of reporting in contemporary life imply for all of us?

What Is a Reporter? 97

What a Reporter Feels

Let us go back some distance to a prehistoric journalist for contrast. Benjamin Franklin was a printer, not a reporter, and his journalism was of a very different order from that to which we are accustomed. Indeed, "reporting" was not a part of his task as conductor (the term *editor* was not in use) of a journal (the term *newspaper* was not widely in use either), nor was the journal necessarily the place for the promotion of political opinions. Not that Franklin entirely refrained from political jousting in the *Pennsylvania Gazette*. But he was as likely to launch his plans for civic improvement by publishing a pamphlet as by placing the article in his journal.

For Franklin, journalism—printing—was a trade. It was a trade that suited him, but was not in any central respect an expression of or a mold for his soul. In his autobiography he is, as Robert Sayre has shrewdly observed, a kind of trickster figure who takes on different masks, different trades, different persona, and passes on—in some measure untouched by them.[5]

There is nothing of the sort in Lincoln Steffens, an artist in his own line. For Steffens, becoming a reporter meant becoming a distinct human subspecies. Writing to a friend in 1897 as a young, ambitious, and rather successful reporter for the *New York Evening Post,* he took a characteristic stance:

> I have no longer any inclination to answer you the moment I receive your letters. It seems so hopeless. You are living your own life out, while I am living that of others, hundreds of others. My thoughts and my feelings, my purposes and desires and doings are of no moment; they hardly engage my own attention, never any protracted reflection. My observations are worth while. Others are the objects of them, so they interest me,—I can work them over and there is a market for what I say. So I am the spectator. I am not grumbling, mind. But my concern is with anybody but myself, and my life is the life of the millions, the Greater New York.[6]

This last is a bit strong. Despite some reporting on crime and on the Jewish ghetto on the Lower East Side, Steffens had devoted most of his career to reporting on Wall Street. So his life was scarcely the "life of the millions." The whole letter seems a concealed put-down: "I am not concerned with myself, you are preoccupied with navel gazing while there is a whole world out there to know." And yet the letter expresses a genuine, one could even say breathless, sense of enthusiasm for the work of the journalist, the spectator, the watcher. And for Steffens, this *is* ontology. Journalism is not one trade among many. It is a distinct way of experiencing the world. It is a separate consciousness.

But what is it to be an onlooker? For Steffens, it is an activity that reaches far beyond itself. The events he witnesses are to be understood not as important in themselves but as revelatory of deeper significances, underlying laws of human behavior. He is not merely an observer—observing is an active, constructive, reforming activity. He wrote Ray Stannard Baker what he hoped for his magazine work: "I have great ideas of what can be done by telling the facts and telling the stories of life about us. I would have the *American* report and report and report, till men had to see in what a state of servitude they are in, and fight for very shame."[7] For Steffens, the people he witnesses are instances and he is in search of the general law, and the truth of the general will set people free.

For Salisbury, in contrast, general laws do not exist except in the instances. He takes pride in his Minnesota, commonsense, down-to-earth turn of mind. He is skeptical about grand theories of human behavior. "I am wary of precise rules. Precision puts human conduct into a straitjacket. We are a disorderly species. Clean-cut cases are rare, and unless we recognize that there must be exceptions, we bind ourselves to rigidity and nonsense." Salisbury wrote to me, responding to an earlier draft of this chapter, "Stef was a crusader and quite a public figure. I am, as you note, basically a reporter, not an exhorter. I try to dig out what is what and present it and let the facts (as I see them) move people's minds."[8]

For Steffens, his life is a life of his own exploits. He is his own hero. Rarely does any outside event impinge on his recollections. He tells, in the book's opening paragraph, how the San Francisco earthquake of 1868 pitched him, two years old, out of bed—unhurt and, as usual, smiling—and tells how his mother repeated this story over and over as evidence that Joseph Lincoln, Jr., was a remarkable boy. Nowhere else in the book does an event of general magnitude affect him—and even here, of course, he suggests that the effect was on his mother more than on himself. The world's events are, for him, a textbook. They instruct him. They influence his theories. But they do not touch him.

Salisbury, in contrast, regularly marks his own passage through life in terms of the world's passage through history. He recalls the cries of the newsboys, the "bushwhackers," the night the news came of the

What Is a Reporter? 99

Titanic, the family awakened after everyone had gone to bed—at least he thinks he recalls it, acknowledging some doubt on the subject. The sinking of the Lusitania he remembers clearly. Much more important, he remembers the news that "Minnesota's Slim Lindbergh" had touched down in Paris. "It was an extraordinary moment, the biggest moment for me since the armistice of November 7, 1918, the 'false' armistice which I and everyone in Minneapolis thought had ended World War I" (p. 14).

"Slim" Lindbergh was a kind of alter ego for young Salisbury. "I could never have flown across Lake Minnetonka, let alone the Atlantic, but my emotion was there never quite to vanish" (p. 15). It is, of course, the one thing the reporter of Salisbury's temperament can never do— fly, be the center of the world's attention, soar beyond what others have done rather than following close behind them. Reporters may be close to the history-makers, but they are not the history-makers. Salisbury knew this from the beginning of his career, writing to a friend in 1933 that he found working for United Press "a grand seat for viewing things over the world from the grandstand" and that "I think that after all the grandstand is the place I would rather view them from" (p. 62). This sharp distinction between reporter and participant, so vital to the con- temporary journalist, is not something Steffens was clear about. Stef- fens lived, as he saw it, on the frontier of knowledge. Salisbury lived in the folds and furrows of history. Steffens seeks a future; Salisbury, a location. What makes them exemplary journalists is that they both seek—both expand out over their jobs—though Salisbury did not manage this, truly, until Russia. He had, retrospectively, a destiny; Steffens had, prospectively, a mission.

It would not be fair to say that Steffens represents an active and Salisbury a passive view of reporting. Salisbury was a man of great energy, his 75-word-per-minute leads his trademark, stubbornness a key virtue he admired in himself and others, enterprise—and not a little imagination—something he exhibited in his reporting. But he certainly found that the job of reporting created a unity for his life, provided him a whole world, in ways it did not and could not for Steffens. In part, this reflects a general development in which profes- sional lives have become more and more absorbing and defining. In part, it indicates a modesty of ambition in a world where specialized roles are more carefully constructed than in Steffens's heyday. In part, I suppose, it indicates a growing tradition in journalism itself. Steffens could imagine himself a pioneer. Salisbury's exploits were ones he could always see as part of a continuity in journalism. While Salisbury was editor at his college newspaper, his heroes were the likes of Upton Sinclair, Ida Tarbell, Frank Norris, and—of course—Lincoln Steffens. He thought of himself as a muckraker at first; later he thought of himself simply and proudly as a reporter. It may be generally true that muckraking more often recruits people to journalism than keeps them there.

What a Reporter Knows

Both autobiographers describe, in cinematic detail, a street scene of the reporter as a young man. This follows something of a tradition in American autobiography. Benjamin Franklin, of course, in one of the most famous scenes in American literature, describes himself as the newly arrived Boston printer walking through the streets of Philadelphia, poor but prosperous in outlook, two loaves of bread under his arms. Philadelphia is for this young man not a city to describe nor a city to understand but a city in which to work. Franklin includes the scene of the young man as a comic interlude and as a moral lesson— behold how far I have come since then! Steffens offers a scene of Pittsburgh that we can compare to Franklin's description. He goes there in the heyday of his muckraking articles for *McClure's* Magazine. Pittsburgh, he recalls,

> looked like hell, literally. Arriving of an evening, I walked out aimlessly into the smoky gloom of its deep-dug streets and somehow got across a bridge up on a hill that overlooked the city, with its fiery furnaces and the two rivers which pinched it in. The blast ovens opened periodically and threw their volcanic light upon the cloud of mist and smoke above the town and gilded the silver rivers, rolling out steel and millionaires. (p. 401)

He was afraid because it was the first city he "muckraked" without knowing ahead of time a reformer or friend who could guide him through it.

> As I wandered, a stranger, through that vast mystery of a city, looking for a place or a person to begin my inquiries, I wanted to run away. I could not. I had to stay. "We" had announced that I was to investigate and expose the corruption of that invisible government which looked so big and strong, so menacing and—so invisible. (p. 402)

What Is a Reporter? 101

This is a very different kind of entry into a city—not to be a part of it but to take it apart. Steffens assumes, from the outset, that the only truth worth getting to would take digging and the wits to deceive the dissemblers. And all this in a place that looked like hell.

Salisbury has a street scene of his own. He leaves the Twin Cities for the first time to take up a job with United Press in Chicago. He comes to that city with a whole set of associations ahead of him. "I kept thinking in capital letters. The Big Test. Sandburg's Chicago, Frank Norris's Chicago, Colonel McCormick's Chicago, Al Capone's Chicago. The Big Time." The train pulls in at 7:00 in the morning, a chill January day in 1931.

> I put on my camel's hair coat, my throat sore from the hot air, the feverish naps, the cigarettes. I picked up my bags and walked through the great waiting room and out over the bridge, dirty ice floating on the green puke of the Chicago River, men and women, mostly men, hurrying head down against the wind, I hurrying too, under the "L" and up Monroe Street to the Great Northern Hotel. I got a room, paid in advance, three dollars. I gave the bellhop a dime tip, my first tip. I remember coming down to the street and out into the cold, the wind blowing off Lake Michigan. Not eight o'clock yet and on my way to the office, my throat ached, my eyes ached, my head ached. I breathed in the cold air, big breaths, threw back my shoulders, put my head up, held it high and walked east toward the lake. I leaned into the wind and walked through the crowds pouring down from the "L," starting their day's work. They did not know me. They did not know who I was. They did not know what I was going to do. (p. 96)

Salisbury walks through the Loop, down Michigan Avenue,

> tall and skinny, six feet tall, 142 pounds, a long cantering gait, my ankle-length coat swirling around me, a comic figure, likely to be splintered by the wind, but not splintering, not aware of the comedy, deathly serious, stalking Chicago like a camel-coated panther. I was going to take this city. I was going to take Chicago. Words out of some book I had read. Well, that was my fantasy. (p. 96)

There is what we might call a reflexivity in Salisbury's self-portrait that is missing in Steffens, an ironic edge, an irony created not only by the bemused view of an old man looking at himself as a young man (after all, Steffens shows no such bemusement) but by the sense that the young Salisbury was reenacting rather than acting, that he was living out a dream he had evidently already read about. The dream is serious, but the fact that the young Salisbury was a dreamer keeps it at one remove.

In classical tragedy, there is a vital "scene of recognition" where all becomes clear and Oedipus or Lear stands face-to-face with the truth about himself. He knows, in a moment of tragic insight, who he is. It is a culmination and a turning point. Reporters, as they tell their stories to us, have no such turning points. Their scene of recognition is a scene of challenge, of a new assignment, another task, another world to conquer, yet one more Philadelphia or Pittsburgh or Chicago before them.[9]

Steffens's and Salisbury's street scenes share the reporters' conviction that life is a confrontation with the world outside. It is not that the reporter has no inner life but that he is relatively uninterested in it. Indeed, both reporters suggest that such interest would be self-indulgent. Reporting, for Steffens and for Salisbury, is a challenge to manhood. The job is to penetrate, to get beyond appearances, to find the facts that make the meanings. But Steffens is confronting politics; Salisbury is confronting a career in journalism and a name for himself. Steffens still has an aim outside reporting; Salisbury is the more consummate professional—his only aim is defined within reporting itself, a passion to master the trade.

Salisbury, in this regard, is the more modern reporter. He has no great use for ideas and a "fierce antagonism to ideologues" (p. 249). As a young man, he liked to think of himself as "a hard-hitting, two-fisted, call-them-as-they-come reporter." For him, the detail, the fact is all. His "Minnesota turn of mind" (p. 348), his "commonsense approach" dominate. He learned, he reports, to understand Russia by relying less on codes and doctrines and textbooks "and more and more on reality" (p. 348). He is not anti-intellectual. He makes apparent his respect for scholars who taught him about Russia and his respect, indeed, his love, for the Russian poets he came to know. But "ideas" are sentimentalized for him; they are romantic, they are poetic, they do not seem critical to his understanding of what goes on in the world. They are, in a sense, similar to his experience with great works of literature as a preteen, reading volume after volume: "I read them all, serially in continuous wonder shelf by shelf, between the ages of nine and thirteen. I grew up knowing what culture was—it was the books on the walls of my grandfather's study" (p. 7). Ideas, for him, though beloved, remain on the walls of the study.

Steffens seems different. He had a sense that a "science of ethics" lay just beyond him, and his muckraking days were spent in search of a "theory of corruption." In short, Steffens saw himself as an intellectual; intellectuals were not for him, as for most journalists today, a different species. But his was a simple, simpleminded in retrospect, theory; not so much a theory as a simple thesis that processes of corruption are the same in different cities and different countries and have to do not with the moral qualities of individuals but with the social organization of business and politics. (In retrospect, it would have been easier for Steffens had he studied sociology and not psychology, but sociology was not yet born when he was in school and he did not become better acquainted with it later.)

Despite Steffens's passion for facts and for science, he held some information as a reporter that he did not put into the public domain. If a reporter's job is to get the news out to the public, we may be able to define reporting better by seeing what news the journalist fails to carry through to print.

Steffens, first of all, would not print information given to him "confidentially" by a source for fear of losing the source (p. 184). The reporter, in pursuit of an ongoing or long-term commitment to provide information to the public, made short-term compromises that kept information from the public.

Second, Steffens as a young reporter withheld information about criminal activity on Wall Street because he simply could not believe it. "I was too imbued with the Wall Street spirit . . . I was a Wall Street man myself, unconsciously, but literally." Information does not fall upon a blank slate. No reporter is a blank slate but rather an uneven terrain in which some information will settle and some will not be absorbed at all. For Steffens, the information on Wall Street criminality was such that "I would not, could not, take it in" (p. 194). Steffens also reports how his rival police reporter, Jacob Riis, responded to news at police quarters of a raid on a homosexual resort. When the situation was explained to him, he could not believe it; he denied the existence of homosexuality. "Not so. There are no such creatures in this world." He would not report the raid (p. 223).

Third, Steffens learned that some information would never be printed by any paper. News of police brutality against strikers never made the papers. From his own account, Steffens never tried to buck this system. He accepted the reality, if not the necessity, of it (p. 207). When writing on political reform in New York, Steffens realized that no one he talked to had any good idea how to get to the bottom of corruption, how to make a real difference. It was his job to find such people—"it was my job as a reporter to seek them out and report them," but, he wrote, "within the limit of my search I found not one." And then he adds a curiously acquiescent clause: "I could not interview radicals, of course, there were not many of them anyhow, they were only faddists: cooperators, socialists (a few), anarchists, whom nobody would listen to" (p. 249). Here he reports his failure as a reporter, followed by a set of excuses—there weren't very many radicals (and presumably they didn't represent many others), those who existed were not very serious anyway, and even if they were serious, "nobody" would listen to them. Well, not "nobody" of course. Steffens suggests here that he, for one, recognized that they might have something important to say. But of course "nobody" is a metaphor standing for a smaller body of people: Steffens's editors, first of all; and then his readers, the wealthy and established readers of the *Evening Post;* and perhaps also the wider elite circles of power in the city. That is the "nobody" who would not listen.

Finally, Steffens refers more philosophically to a large category of information: "What reporters know and don't report is news—not from the newspapers' point of view, but from the sociologists' and the novelists' " (p. 223). It is a sober recognition all too often denied or ignored by reporters—that "news" is a peculiar form of information, a peculiar genre, by no means the totality of what might be interesting but only what might be interesting from a certain point of view.

We might define a reporter in these terms: a reporter is someone faithful to sources, attuned to the conventional wisdom, serving the political culture of media institutions, and committed to a narrow range of public, literary expression. This is scarcely a flattering definition, but there may be more honesty in it than more celebratory definitions of journalism would care to admit. It also leads naturally to a set of questions that would be good starting points for a systematic study of journalism. Who are the reporter's sources? Where does the reporter pick up conventional wisdom? What is the economic, political, and social structure of media institutions? What is "news" as a genre of literature and public expression?

Salisbury would add a fifth limitation to the four Steffens acknowledges: the reporter is constrained by the competition and camaraderie of other reporters. (And this would lead to a fifth question in our sociology of journalism: Who are journalists and what are their background and training?) Steffens identified with science and with reform, not with "journalism." Salisbury, in contrast, is part of a profession of journalism with which he identifies and in which he wants to succeed. He is part of a circle of journalists. Conversations with other reporters recur throughout his book—in Steffens's, most reported conversations are with politicians. For Salisbury, the search for truth is a collective search as it never was for Steffens. It is a story of friends and comrades in arms. And it is a story of competition. Salisbury is passionately competitive—and this is what led to one of his compromises with truth: he kept to himself a tip that there was a plot to assassinate the mayor of Chicago, in hopes of getting a jump on the competition in reporting the assassination when it happened. It is also the occasion of a comical, but perhaps not so comical, admission: that when he heard the news, via Associated Press, that the war in Europe was over, he found that "to a competitive UP man like myself, the disaster of an AP exclusive on the war's end overshadowed the event itself. All day I called one diplomat after another, looking for confirmation—or better yet, denial" (p. 291).

This suggests a sixth question for a sociology of journalists and journalism, but the hardest one of all to answer: What does it all mean? What does this fact-gathering, competitive, implicated news bureaucracy mean for how people, journalists or their readers, come to experience the world?

What the Reporter Wants

What, finally, does the reporter seek or strive for? What does the reporter want?

For Steffens, the task is to find the truth and thereby change the world. For Salisbury, it is to keep the faith. To find the truth, for Steffens, is both a scientific task and a political task. For Salisbury, to keep the faith is an act of homage to the past and an act of defiance toward those who will not honor it.

Salisbury feels a deep connection to his parents and their heritage, to Minnesota, to a Progressive political tradition (although he was a lifelong Republican), to a patriotism in which no holiday in the calendar, sacred or secular, could match the fourth of July. His great-great-uncle Hiram, a farmer in the early 1800s, celebrated no holiday except the fourth of July (pp. 20–21). It was the same for Salisbury as a boy, celebrating the Glorious Fourth. And he misses the special qualities the day once had.

But even as a boy Salisbury sensed a world he cared about slipping away. He mourned the demise of the passenger pigeon in 1914, and "for years I kept hoping I might discover a survivor" (p. 20). Salisbury's effort for much of his life was devoted to discovering survivors. In Russia, he hoped to discover survivors of the revolutionary hope and humanist commitment that he learned of from a neighbor across the street in St. Paul, a Russian émigré committed to the revolution. (He did not really find what he sought but "came to realize that nowhere in that gray wasteland would I ever taste the wine of Revolution as pungent and pure as that of my childhood in the Oak Lake Addition" [p. 6].) In his travels in the 1960s and 1970s across America he kept looking for survivors or survivals of dreams and hopes and desires. It is no accident that he was a Civil War hobbyist, enthralled with that terrible era and remembering, perhaps, that his father, as he grew older, "looked like Lincoln, not so tall, but with Lincoln's deep-set eyes and melancholy" (p. 42).

With Steffens, whose journalistic career was focused on American cities and American national politics rather than international affairs, connections to the wider world are less personally crucial. Salisbury was something of the traveler and anthropologist, intent on understanding the peculiarities of different peoples. Steffens, who studied in German universities and spent some time at the laboratory of Wilhelm Wundt, the first psychological laboratory in the world, was more the social scientist seeking laws of invariance to explain the variations of human behavior. Steffens, indeed, ultimately became bored with muckraking; at the end of his muckraking days, in Boston, in the year Salisbury was born, he turned over much of the legwork to a young assistant, Walter Lippmann, because of this boredom: "I had reported the like so often that my mind or my stomach revolted at the repetition" (p. 606). Oddly enough, it is Salisbury, with the more scholarly sense of his subject—the Soviet Union—who never got bored. Disappointed, pessimistic, and angry, but not bored. Steffens, with more scientific ambition and a more formal, organized mind, was more lost as a journalist, groping for a stance between the scientist, the reformer, and the scold.

Steffens is intent on explanation. Salisbury is content with "getting the facts." Steffens sometimes delights in the role of observer and outsider but at other times chafes at it; Salisbury slides into it comfortably. Steffens is restless, Salisbury—for all his evident energy—comes across as "old shoe" in his memoirs. Steffens is a public figure, and he tells us in chapter after chapter how the political and business bosses of the great American cities confided in him and used him as a father confessor. Salisbury's friends are journalists or poets or his

What Is a Reporter?   107

own family, outsiders to the political struggles Salisbury chronicles. The image Steffens gives us is heart-to-heart talks with Teddy Roosevelt; the image Salisbury leaves us with is his waiting, alone or with other reporters, outside the Kremlin for news of Stalin.

The 1890s was the age of the reporter. Not now, not even in Salisbury's account of traveling to Hanoi as the first American reporter there during the Vietnam war. Here he soft-pedals his own efforts; where Steffens is his own hero, Salisbury, in his own writing, is, if not an antihero, then at least someone more on the sidelines than in the center of history—Rosencrantz or Guildenstern, not the prince. And yet his trip to Hanoi was an act of imagination of a sort very rare in journalism (or in any field). It was the sort of nonpartisanship that makes journalistic objectivity inevitably an impertinence and a challenge to authority. He showed forcefully the unending capacity of the objective stance to be seditious. In doing so, he raised a question in action about what audience a journalist should imagine and what loyalties he should hold dear. (This is a question, by the way, that Ronnie Dugger raised again in his criticism of the American press coverage of the Reagan-Gorbachev summit in Geneva, arguing that the press behaved like sportswriters, writing everything from the point of view of the home team. "As professional journalists, what are our international responsibilities? . . . perhaps, if we ask the question, and answer that reporters do have responsibilities to the human race no less than national leaders do, we will make our way to the second summit as more than sportswriters for the home team.")[10]

In going to Hanoi, to what was Salisbury loyal? To journalism? To his family and regional tradition? To the working man? To his own career? To his alter ego, Lindbergh the flier and the pioneer?

To all of them, I think. What may be important for thinking about the ethics of journalism is that loyalty to journalism and to "career" would not have been enough. Salisbury's objective in this instance was anathema to many journalists, including even the *Washington Post*, which editorialized in criticism of Salisbury's decision to go to Hanoi.[11] Description is always an act of imagination. Salisbury was willing to play in this case as well as to work, to locate a personal destiny consistent with one reading of journalistic ethics but unrecognized by the conventionality in which all professions and all ethical codes come slothfully to lounge until challenged. The journalist with a destiny is willing to go beyond the ethics of the profession, an ethics always limited and limiting, even in the best of circumstances. Salisbury, I suspect, was a leading journalist not just because he committed himself to his profession—though he did—but because he never let that commitment obscure the fact that his father looked like Lincoln, his great-great-uncle celebrated the fourth of July, and his fellow Minnesotan flew solo across the Atlantic.

Salisbury had a refined sense of the past and of continuity. Steffens, one of Salisbury's heroes, had no such thing. This is a difference between scientific optimism and realistic pessimism; between a man who thought journalism could serve up truth and another who saw journalism as a modest chipping away at falsehood; between someone whose sense of the line between advocacy and observation was incidental and someone for whom it was cardinal. But even Salisbury's stance is not one of scientific detachment but of personal integrity. The reporter faces more constraints on fact-gathering and more limits on publication than any scientist would tolerate. The reporter, in the face of this, seeks an ethical ideal, and Salisbury finds his in a dedication to observing.

The difference is not just between two individuals but between two eras in journalism. The shift from Steffens to Salisbury is a shift from an individual with a mission to an individual with a role (the detached reporter), a role within a profession that has a collective mission or, at least, a collective responsibility.

Salisbury ends his memoirs by describing himself as a "pilgrim" in "an unending quest for knowledge—knowledge of Russia, whose shadow falls across the planet which in my lifetime has grown so small, so dangerous, so enigmatic; knowledge of America, so filled with promise, so shackled by frustration, yet still pregnant with hope for her people and for the world" (p. 534). The world, however small it seemed to Salisbury, is larger than it was for Steffens. Steffens believed in a unity of humankind, in simple solutions, in the capacity of truth to settle matters. Salisbury is much more aware of human differences, the peculiarities of both Russians and Americans. He is more intent on describing differences and hoping this will help than on finding underlying truths and knowing this will be decisive. Steffens's optimism is naive; Salisbury's hopefulness plaintive. But between them, I think, they define the range of possibilities to which a journalism of dedication and vision can aspire.

The old debates of the 1960s—objective journalism versus advocacy journalism—have abated enough for us to see that the terms were never quite right. No one has ever observed these abstractions in practice. No journalism worthy of the name fails to seek trustworthy facts collected according to the best standards of objective reporting. But

What Is a Reporter?   109

neither is there a journalism worth more than a radio headline service that is not also an act of play and imagination.

Nor are these old debates adequate to the question Salisbury's memoirs raise—without approaching an answer—about the audience. This is a question that never came clear in the 1960s. Who is the reader? What is the public sphere in which the journalist works, which he serves, and which he helps to establish? Neither Steffens nor Salisbury gives us guidance about this. They are exemplary reporters who held to the presuppositions of their craft in their age. When they escape those presuppositions, as both of them had the will and the instinct to do, they are, with so many of the rest of us, adrift without a language adequate to describe or celebrate their best actions.

II Myths of Media Power

5 Trout or Hamburger: Politics and Telemythology

Has television taken over the practice of American politics? Have cynically manipulated images and sound bites mesmerized the American public? Have politicians bypassed the citizen's rational decision-making process with a shortcut to some image center in the brain that values appearance over substance, flash over philosophy? In American politics today, do the eyes have it?

Anyone listening to political commentary in any recent election would surely answer yes. The airwaves teem with political commercials. The newspapers overflow with commentary about the broadcast spots. And then new TV spots incorporate the print commentary about the old spots. At times, candidates and voters seem to be on the sidelines, passively observing the media consultants and ad agencies on the playing field.

As soon as the election is over, however, talk about the brilliance or mendacity of 30-second demagoguery fades. On the day before the election, every politician is a candidate, and takes a candidate's obsessive interest in every little bit of good or harm that might come from advertising. On the day after there are only winning candidates, glad to be in office, and losers, seeking some kind of solace in a bad time. The losers seem to change quickly from activists to philosophers, from political strategists to political scientists. Thus in 1990 Dianne Feinstein's campaign manager, Duane Garrett, was suddenly reminding people that for twenty-five years (with the exception of 1974, the Watergate year) California voted Republican for president and governor—so what else could one expect in 1990? In his post-election assessment, the story was not that Feinstein lost but that she came as close as she did.

Did Feinstein's TV spots make a difference? Did Paul Wellstone's in Minnesota? Or Jesse Helms's in North Carolina? The question is still important, but it is notoriously elusive. Despite all the attention that the press has lavished on political commercials, it is no simple task to evaluate their potency, as opposed to observing their ubiquity and decrying their negativity. Even newspaper "truth box" commentaries, which began in 1990 to monitor the accuracy of political ads on television, have been criticized for focusing on the commercials' explicit claims rather than their visual imagery—for reading television as if it were radio and failing to understand the overwhelming power of the image.

But is the image overpowering? Does the image conquer all in political television? Even that apparently safe assumption can be questioned.

Take, for instance, the story told by the media critic Michael Arlen in *Thirty Seconds* about the making of an AT&T "Reach Out and Touch Someone" commercial.[1] In one version of the commercial, a group of men have gone off to a rural retreat for a weekend of fishing. The weekend is a disaster; it is pouring rain the whole time. We see the men huddled in their cabin in the woods, cooking hamburgers, while one of them talks to friends back home, singing the praises of their manly adventure. The man on the phone is staring into a frying pan full of hamburgers while he says into the receiver, "Boy, you should see the great trout we've got cooking here." When test audiences were asked what the men were cooking for dinner, they replied overwhelmingly—trout. One of the advertising executives in charge of the project comments:

> I have to tell you we were very discouraged. Some of our guys were even talking of junking the commercial, which was a good one, with a nice humorous flow to it. Well, we ended up making it, but what we had to do was, when we came to that segment, we put the camera almost inside the frying pan, and in the frying pan we put huge, crude chunks of hamburger that were almost red. I mean, just about all you could see was raw meat. This time, when we took it to the audience, it tested OK. That is, most of the test audience—though, in fact, still not everybody—finally said "hamburger."

The trout/hamburger story has not made its way into the common culture of media consulting, political journalism, or academic criticism. The ability of verbal cues to trump the visual is forgotten, while the contrary lesson, that a picture overrides ten thousand words, is regularly retold.

A current favorite is the story of the Lesley Stahl four-and-a-half-minute piece that CBS ran during the 1984 presidential campaign. Its subject was how the White House staged events for Ronald Reagan and manipulated the press, especially television. Stahl later said that a White House official called her soon after the piece aired and said he'd loved it. "How could you?" she responded. He said, "Haven't you figured it out yet? The public doesn't pay any attention to what you say. They just look at the pictures." Stahl, on reflection—but not, I think, on very much reflection—came to believe that the White House was probably right: all she had done was to assemble, free of charge, a Republican campaign film, a wonderful montage of Reagan appearing in upbeat scenes.

In the world of media criticism and political consulting, the Stahl story is presented as powerful evidence of the triumph of pictures over words and emotion over rationality in American politics. It is a major piece of evidence for *New York Times* reporter Hedrick Smith's conclusion that the eye is more powerful than the ear in American politics; it opens journalist Martin Schram's account of television in the 1984 election; it is cited to similar account by *Washington Post* columnist David Broder and communications scholar Kathleen Jamieson.[2] But the story's punch depends on our believing that the White House official knew what he was talking about. Did he?

In this case, no one really knows. But in another case we have information that indicates that the Reagan White House did *not* understand the power of pictures on television. In 1982 the country was in the midst of a recession and the Reagan administration was faring badly in the polls. The networks were making efforts to dramatize the country's economic plight not only by reporting the national unemployment figures, but also by focusing on a particular person or family hurt by hard times. The White House was outraged and criticized the networks for presenting the sad tale of the man in South Succotash and missing the general economic trends that, according to the White House, were more positive. Obviously, the White House assumed that the emotionally compelling, visually powerful vignette had much more impact on the American public than dry statistics. But when Donald Kinder and Shanto Iyengar conducted a series of careful experiments on television viewing, they found that the captivating vignette on economic affairs did no more than the bare statistics to lead viewers to believe that economic affairs were a major problem facing the nation.

In fact, the evidence in Kinder and Iyengar's *News That Matters* ran modestly in the other direction—viewers were more impressed by statistics than by down-home stories about the gravity of the economic crisis.[3] This result runs counter to common sense. Isn't it true that a picture is worth more than all those words? Are the social scientists in this case (and not for the first time) just plain wrong?

I don't think so. There is a way to understand their results that is consistent with other well-established research. People do not automatically extrapolate from individual experience, even their own, to the nation as a whole. When American citizens go to the polls, for instance, they distinguish between their own personal economic situation and their sense of how the nation as a whole is doing—and typically they vote according to their sense of how the nation as a whole is doing. They do not cast reflex-like "pocketbook" votes.[4] When people see a television story on the plight of an individual family, they do not automatically generalize to the state of the nation. Indeed, the form of the vignette encourages them to discount the story as unrepresentative. If, say, the vignette pictures a black family, a significant number of whites may routinely discount the story as a special case, not a representative one, because they do not identify with blacks. If the news pictures a farm family, an urban family may not identify with them. In a sense, these viewers are not "visually literate"; they do not follow the visual logic by which one instance of poverty or unemployment is meant to represent the general phenomenon. Viewers find more general significance, then, in Department of Labor statistics than in artfully composed and emotionally compelling photographic essays on the economy.

The Lesley Stahl episode has become part of our telemythology, a set of widely circulated stories about the dangerous powers of television. With respect to politics, three key episodes contribute to the general mythology:

- Kennedy defeated Nixon in 1960 because he presented a more attractive image in the first television debate.
- Television's graphic portrayal of the war in Vietnam sickened and horrified American viewers, who were led by harsh photographic reality to oppose the war.
- The unprecedented popularity of President Reagan has no rational explanation but can be accounted for only by the power of an actor skilled at manipulating a visual medium.

But look again at each of the episodes. Kennedy just barely defeated Nixon in November 1960, and perhaps did not actually defeat him at all—we will never know just how many ballot boxes were stuffed in Cook County on election day. Many observers of the election, including Kennedy himself, attributed his success to his fine showing in the television debates. The most discussed part of the debates concerns the failure of Nixon's makeup artists to prepare him properly for the hot lights of the television studio. Where Kennedy seemed cool, Nixon appeared to be sweating; where Kennedy was self-assured, Nixon seemed to strain. Kennedy's appearance on national television galvanized his campaign; crowds instantly seemed larger and more enthusiastic in his campaign appearances. For Nixon, who added to Kennedy's stature simply by accepting the challenge to debate in the first place, the first debate was deeply unsettling.

Social scientists cite the finding that citizens who listened to the Kennedy-Nixon debate on the radio judged Nixon the winner; those who watched television found Kennedy the winner. As with the Stahl story, this is presented as conclusive evidence of the distorting lens of television. On radio, it is assumed, one listens to pure argument; on television, one is distracted by the appearance of things, the superficial look of people rather than the cogency of their arguments.

The basis for all this is a study undertaken by a Philadelphia market research firm that found that radio listeners judged Nixon the winner by 43 percent to 20 percent, while a majority (53 percent) of television viewers judged the debate a draw or refused to name a winner. Of those willing to name a winner, 28 percent chose Kennedy and 19 percent Nixon.[5]

Even if we accept this study as valid (and it was never reported in a form to make serious analysis possible), there are two problems with the way it has been used. The first problem concerns the presumption that radio is a distortion-free medium. Is the human voice itself not a medium? Is radio not a medium, too? Are words conveyed through radio a pure rendering of logical relations? Or does the voice—specifically, the radio-transmitted voice—give special weight to sonority and to the verbal tics and tricks of an experienced and skilled debater that have no necessary relation to the validity of the arguments themselves? Might radio have exaggerated Kennedy's Boston accent as part of his nature and therefore put people off? The human voice, from the cry of a baby onward, can stir passions. It can as easily be an enemy of reason as its epitome. A medium like radio that separates the human voice from the body is not necessarily a guardian of rationality.

Second, is television imagery so obviously superficial? Was it not important, and truthful, to see that Kennedy, despite his relative youth, was able to handle the most public moment of his life with assurance? Was it not important, and truthful, to see Nixon, despite his vast experience, looking awkward and insecure? Isn't it possible to argue that the insecurity he showed betrayed his manner and motive in public life?

Let me turn briefly to Vietnam. Here we have been told repeatedly about the power that television had to turn the American public against the war. The general argument has been that the horror of war, graphically shown to the viewing public, sickened Americans. Anything that the narration might have said about the legitimacy of the military effort, the pictures stunningly undermined. What is the evidence for this belief? There is, it turns out, almost no evidence at all. The public did, over time, become more and more disenchanted with the war in Vietnam—but at just about the same rate and to just about the same degree as the public became disaffected with the untelevised Korean war. Moreover, contrary to some popular reconstructions of television coverage, the TV coverage of the Vietnam war provided very little combat footage in the years during which opposition to the war mounted. It is possible, of course, that isolated instances of combat coverage had great impact; but, as Peter Braestrup points out in his book *Battle Lines*, the television archives provide no basis for the view that a day-in, day-out television portrait of bloodshed was ever presented to the American public.[6]

The general understanding behind the "TV-turned-us-against-the-war" argument is that TV photography comes to us unmediated—it forces itself upon the viewer, who then recoils from war. In fact, Daniel Hallin argues in *The Uncensored War* that "television's visual images are extremely ambiguous." We don't know very much about how audiences construct the meaning of TV images, but "it seems a reasonable hypothesis that most of the time the audience sees what it is told it is seeing."[7] Trout, in short, not ground beef.

The final piece of telemythology I want to examine is the view that Ronald Reagan's mastery of television led to his mastery of the American public. This is another curious story. Reagan's extraordinary popularity was heralded by the news media months before he took office. The sense in Washington of his popularity was so powerful that on March 18, 1981, not yet two months into Reagan's first term, James Reston reported that Congress was very reluctant to vote against the budget of so popular a chief executive. Reston's column appeared prominently on the *New York Times* op-ed page on the same day that, in a three-inch story at the bottom of page 22, a report on the latest Gallup poll coolly stated that Reagan's public approval ratings were the lowest in polling history for a newly elected president.

As it turned out, Reagan's average approval rating for his first year in office was, according to the Gallup survey, 57 percent compared with Carter's 62 percent, Nixon's 62 percent, Kennedy's 76 percent. His second-year average was 43 percent compared with Carter's 46 percent, Nixon's 56 percent, Kennedy's 72 percent.[8] Polls that tried to separate Reagan's personal appeal from the appeal of his policies found the President to be notably more popular than his program; however, this has been the case with every president, and the margin of difference was smaller for Reagan than for other presidents.[9] Later in his first term and in much of his second term, Reagan had unusually high public approval ratings. Still, the public impression and the media consensus about his general popularity were firmly established before there was any national polling evidence to corroborate it. How did this happen?

There are a number of explanations (discussed more fully in Chapter 6). The most important, I think, is that the Washington establishment *liked* Reagan. That establishment, Republican and Democrat, politician and journalist, had had enough of Jimmy Carter's puritanical style of socializing and humorless style of leadership. "For the first time in years, Washington has a President that it really likes," *Washington Post* political analyst Haynes Johnson concluded by the fall of 1981.[10] Reagan was very likable, yes. He brought with him the allure and glamour of Hollywood. More than this, he turned out to be a first-rate politician in the most old-fashioned sense: he could count votes, he knew whom to invite to breakfast or dinner and when, and he employed expert staff to deal with the Congress. When his aides asked him to make a phone call here or a public appearance there, he obliged. And if this direct courtship from the White House were not enough, Reagan succeeded in mobilizing a small but highly vocal right-wing constituency that, with just a whisper from the White House staff, would deluge congressional offices with telegrams and letters.

That is probably the heart of it, but I think there is something more—the strong belief of Washington elites that the general public can be mesmerized by television images. Many journalists shared a kind of "gee whiz" awe at the media skills of the White House, according to Laurence Barrett, senior White House correspondent for

Time. Their sense of White House media omnipotence was particularly strong because of the contrast between Reagan's smooth administrative machinery and the ineffective Carter White House.[11] Consider the view of Barrett's colleague at *Time,* Thomas Griffith, who wrote that the "people in Peoria" are more receptive to Reagan's message than people who follow public affairs closely. The Reagan administration, he felt, aimed its message at the television audience, not the close readers of print. Reagan's was a "TV presidency."[12]

What is a TV presidency? Reagan's was scarcely the first to be declared one. There was Kennedy's, of course. Even Nixon gets a vote: "Nixon is a television creation, a sort of gesturing phantom, uncomfortable in the old-fashioned world of printer's type, where assertions can be checked and verified." That unlikely judgment comes from novelist and critic Mary McCarthy.[13] Carter was regularly declared a master of symbolism and images in his first year in office. In 1976, Carter flew into office hailed as a genius at media manipulation. His own media adviser, perhaps not surprisingly, called him "the biggest television star of all time. He is the first television president." The comic strip *Doonesbury* added a new cabinet officer, the secretary of symbolism, early in the Carter administration. The *New York Times* television critic reported in 1977 that Carter is "a master of controlled images." David Halberstam wrote in 1976 that Carter "more than any other candidate this year has sensed and adapted to modern communications and national mood ... Watching him again and again on television I was impressed by his sense of pacing, his sense of control, very low-key, soft, a low decibel count, all this in sharp contrast to the other candidates."[14] Note, however, that as is so often the case with discussions of Reagan, Halberstam attributes Carter's television power to sound, not look. A case could be made that Reagan's presence on television has to do most of all with his voice. People thought of Carter in his first years as a master of images—the President walking, rather than riding, in his inaugural procession; the informal, down-home Jimmy wearing a cardigan sweater. Reagan riding his horse on the ranch never gained the same kind of power. I suspect that we will one day recall Reagan as one of the least visual but most auditory of our presidents. What is memorable is the Reagan with the slight choke in his voice when he told a melodramatic story about a G.I. or read a letter from a little girl, his quick intelligence with a joke or a quip, the comfort, calm, and sincerity in his voice. It was not even his look. It was not his words, as such, but his way with them. Reagan knew, if his critics did not, that it was his voice, his long-lived radio asset, that made his television appearance so effective.

The power of television is perhaps more firmly an article of faith in Washington than anywhere else in the country. There is an odd sense inside the beltway that the rest of the nation is not so much concerned with freeway traffic, paying bills at the end of the month, waiting for the plumber, getting the kids off to school, and finding a nursing home for Grandma as it is with watching Washington, especially in an election year. Otherwise it seems inexplicable that George Will, for instance, should have judged Robert Dole's relatively high poll ratings among Democrats early in the 1988 Republican primary season as "an effect of the televised Senate—he's had a chance to be seen in what is manifestly his home turf, where he is very comfortable."[15] Who is watching the televised Senate? C-SPAN is just not much competition for "Wheel of Fortune," "General Hospital," "Roseanne," or, I'm afraid, even "Sesame Street." How could anyone be so hopelessly out of touch? But so as not to pick on a Republican unfairly, I call to mind Walter Mondale's mournful plaint after his landslide loss to Reagan that television never warmed up to him nor did he warm up to television.[16] Did Hoover lose to Roosevelt because he didn't warm up to radio? Could a Depression have had something to do with it? And might Mondale have lost because 1984 was a time of peace, apparent prosperity, and a likable incumbent Republican?

The phenomenon of people believing that only *others* are influenced by the mass media is what W. Phillips Davison calls the "third-person effect" in communication.[17] The assumption that gullible others, but not one's own canny self, are slaves to the media is so widespread that the actions based on it may be one of the mass media's most powerful creations. The power of the media resides in the perception of experts and decision makers that the general public is influenced by the mass media, not in the direct influence of the mass media on the general public. That is to say, the media's political appeal lies less in its ability to bend minds than in its ability to convince elites that the popular mind can be bent.

If experts overestimate the direct power of the visual, they underrate their own power to reinterpret the visual. In 1976, Gerald Ford said in his debate with Carter that "there is no Soviet domination of Eastern Europe." Although recent events suggest that his misstatement was truer than he knew, that gaffe was reputed to be a major break for Carter and the beginning of the Ford campaign's unraveling. Again, it appears, television demonstrated its enormous power in American politics.

But few television viewers noticed or cared about Ford's remark. A poll conducted by a market research organization employed by the President Ford Committee found that people judged Ford to have done a better job than Carter by 44 percent to 35 percent in the two hours immediately after the debate on the evening of October 6. By noon on October 7, Carter was judged the winner by 44 percent to 31 percent, and by that evening he was judged the winner by 61 percent to 19 percent. On the evening of October 6, not a single person interviewed mentioned the Eastern Europe statement as one of the "main things" the candidate had done "well" or "not well" during the debate. But the next morning 12 percent of the respondents mentioned it, and the next evening 20 percent mentioned it. By that time it was the most frequently mentioned criticism of Ford's performance.[18]

What happened in the interim, of course, is that the news media intervened. Journalists, print and broadcast, told viewers what they had seen and heard. Viewers did not take their hint from the cathode ray tube but from the lessons the journalists taught them after the fact. Trout or hamburger? People did not know until they were told.

In 1984, in Mondale's first debate with Reagan, there was widespread agreement that Mondale was impressive and Reagan surprisingly ill at ease and defensive. Polls conducted during the debate, however, showed that people felt, by a slight margin, that Reagan was winning. An hour after the debate, Mondale had a 1 percent edge in a poll on who won. A day later his advantage was 37 percent, and two days later 49 percent. Again, the evidence compellingly shows that even when people "see for themselves," they take as cues for their own thinking suggestions from experts that come after the fact.[19]

In this respect, Reagan's administration did understand television very well. Reagan's aides did not expect television by itself to implant in Americans a love of Reagan or his policies, and they did not treat a television appearance as simply a matter of finding an appropriate stage set and working on the president's makeup. They did all they could to assure the success of a television appearance by preparing the audience for it in rather old-fashioned ways. Before a presidential TV address, the administration's public liaison office arranged for Reagan to meet personally with groups of allies, several hundred at a time, and brief them on what he would say on television so that they could alert their comrades at home. According to political analyst Stephen Wayne, these briefings helped unleash the flood of responses the White House and Congress received on the budget and tax proposals during Reagan's first year in office.[20] This is not to say that the television appearance was without effect on the public—although recent analysis by political scientists indicates that the influence of staged television appearances was very slight in the Reagan years.[21] It is to suggest that even here Reagan was more successful at manipulating congressional opinion than public opinion—but the manipulation came through encouraging the Congress to believe that the public at large was aroused by television. Since this so readily coincided with a view that Washington elites already held as gospel, it was a relatively easy trick to manage.

If the belief in television power is a large part of what makes television powerful, it may be not television but our beliefs about it that help undo a vital politics. The fascination of critics with television as devil, in any event, takes political discourse off track. We—American citizens, cultural critics, social scientists—seek some kind of reckoning with television, the culture it presents and the culture it represents. But despite the growing abundance of media critics, I don't think we have found the language for that reckoning yet. The object of our attention keeps shifting, for one thing; we've gone from an era of the sponsor to an era of the network to the present (still undefined) era of the proliferation of cable and the declining network-share of the television audience. The kinds of television experience also seem too varied to be easily encapsulated—from the live coverage of the Kennedy funeral, the Olympics, a presidential debate, or a natural disaster to the evening news, daytime soap operas, old movies, or reruns of old sitcoms. The judgment we make of one of these genres is not likely to stick when applied to the next.

Beyond the difficulties in keeping the object of our attention steadily in view, there is the complicated problem of the mixed motives of our own curiosity. There are professional career-making ambitions, an inevitable product of the proliferation of the study of communication in the universities; there is the *ressentiment* of intellectuals who feel unfairly overlooked in an era of celebrity; there is the anger, seeking an object, that arises in the general population from a sense of impotence in dealing with the wider world that both print and television news bring to our homes daily. There is also a sense, one I certainly share, that television executives live in time-and-space capsules closely linked to research reports on market trends but very far from deeper currents of experience in the contemporary world. And since they do not yet know this, may never know this, may not want to know this, they may never tell us the stories about ourselves from which we could genuinely learn.

6 The Illusion of Ronald Reagan's Popularity

with Elliot King

By the time Ronald Reagan was inaugurated as the fortieth president of the United States, he was already widely acknowledged by the news media to have a unique ability to communicate with the American people. Reporting on Reagan's first inaugural address, George Skelton, a staff writer for the *Los Angeles Times,* wrote: "This speech was most striking for its skilled, faultless delivery and straightforward message . . . What Americans saw was a leader with exceptional skills at communicating with the public. Certainly not since John F. Kennedy, and before that Franklin D. Roosevelt, has the country had a President who could match Reagan's skills in front of the microphone or camera."[1]

Skelton's observations were not new. Almost from the moment Reagan entered public life with his campaign for the governorship of California, reporters sensed that he had something special. *Time* reported that Reagan was "the most magnetic crowd puller" California had seen since John Kennedy. "He can hold an audience entranced through 30 to 40 minutes of statistics, gags, and homilies."[2] Reviewing Reagan's first year as governor, Jules Duscha, a professor at Stanford University, reported in the *New York Times Magazine* that "Reagan has enormous plausibility . . . and the glamour of Kennedy."[3] In reflecting on the 1976 primary battle Reagan waged against Gerald Ford, *Time* concluded that Reagan's surprisingly effective challenge came because "Reagan had touched a public nerve."[4]

The assertion that Reagan could touch a public nerve directly became increasingly common in the media, especially after his election in 1980 as president. In the first months of his administration, *U.S. News and World Report* wrote that "many already are acclaiming him as the most adept communicator in the Oval Office since Franklin Roosevelt."[5] On March 14 the *National Journal* wrote of him as a "skilled communicator" and observed that "no President since Lyndon Johnson has had the entire Washington political establishment under the magic of his charm as Reagan, at least at this stage of his Administration."[6] Within six months, Reagan was routinely described as the "Great Communicator."[7] Reagan's mystique as a communicator peaked only in 1986, when *Time* wrote, "The Great Communicator has come to communicate with the American people on a tribal level, a fascinating feat considering the U.S. embraces so many different competing tribes."[8]

When the Iran-Contra scandal broke, the news media suggested that it was the first event in Reagan's six years in office to threaten his general popularity. "For six years, President Reagan floated in a lofty cloud of public trust," stated a *New York Times* editorial.[9] Because of the scandal, political analyst William Schneider wrote in the *Los Angeles Times,* "Reagan has lost the principal source of his political effectiveness, a special relationship with the American people."[10] Indeed, some observers speculated that it was, in part, that perceived special relationship that had allowed the scandal to go undetected. Liberal political activist Mark Green held that Reagan had escaped press criticism for so long because "many journalists were mesmerized by the aura of the presidency in general and Reagan's stratospheric poll ratings in particular."[11]

While many observers speculated about how Reagan established his special rapport with the American people, a more important question is why the news media—and many others—believed that Ronald Reagan in fact had a special rapport with the American people. On what evidence did they base their conclusions?

It wasn't from the available polling data. All the polling data from the first two years of the Reagan administration indicate that far from being the most popular politician in America, as popular memory now has it, Ronald Reagan was, in actuality, the least popular president in the post–World War II period. Far from having "stratospheric" poll ratings, as even his political enemies seemed to believe, his polls were lower for his first two years in office than those for any other newly elected first-term president since such numbers began to be tracked. Just two months into his administration, during what should have been his "honeymoon," Gallup reported that Reagan's job approval rating was lower than that of any other elected president two months into the first term.[12]

This has now been reported widely in popular and professional journals without, I think, having done much to dent the general popular memory.[13] At any rate, the data are so firmly established that we can report them briefly here. Compared to his elected predecessors, Reagan had the lowest average approval rating for the first two years of his administration—precisely the years when his legend as the Great Communicator grew. After a month in office, his rating of 55% compared to Carter's 71%, Nixon's 61%, and Eisenhower's 68%. At the end of a year, his Gallup rating of 47% was lower than Carter's 52%, Nixon's 61%, Kennedy's 77%, and Eisenhower's 68%. At the end of two years, Reagan's 35% job approval rating trailed Carter's at 43%, Nixon's 56%, Kennedy's 76%, and Eisenhower's 69%. In his third year, Reagan still trailed Nixon and Eisenhower, though he had a higher approval rating than that of Jimmy Carter. In January of the fourth year of his administration, Reagan's approval rating once again trailed Carter's as well.[14]

Of course, the first two years of the Reagan administration were marked by a serious recession. So while his policies may have been unpopular, the press regularly reported that his *personal* popularity remained high and that, as *Newsweek* put it, the President's tactical problem was "transferring his glow from his person to his policies."[15]

But was there a personal glow? Although public approval of Reagan's general job performance generally ran higher than that of his specific programs, Reagan did not fare any better than other presidents when the public was asked to rate his personality. In a poll reported by Gallup on May 20, 1982, which compared presidents' personality approval at equivalent moments in their administrations, Gallup observed that "contrary to a widely held belief, Reagan's personal popularity is not disproportionately greater than [that of] his predecessors." At that time Reagan's job approval rating was 44%, while public approval of his personality was 69%. This is a perfectly ordinary disparity. Eisenhower's job approval rating was 52% when his personality approval was 84%; Johnson's job approval was 48% when 80% of the public liked Johnson personally. For Kennedy, comparable figures are 64% and 86%, for Nixon 55% and 78%, for Ford 44% and 69%, and for Jimmy Carter 48% and 72%. Curiously, no leading national publications ran a story on this Gallup report—or on a similar one released the following fall.[16]

It is not these well-established polling facts we seek to explain but the disparity between them and the image of Reagan as an extraordinarily popular president. Why should a sense of Reagan's enormous popularity grow at a time when the best available evidence of popularity—national opinion polls—showed consistently low ratings? How could the press speak so confidently of Reagan's high estimation in "public opinion" while ignoring the conflicting evidence of the polls? In institutions often criticized for following polls all too slavishly, why did the media consistently ignore or misread the polls on Reagan's popularity?

Reagan's Low Poll Ratings, 1981–1983

Reporters should have been well aware of Reagan's performance in the polls. Leading papers dutifully reported the poll results. But these same papers then carried stories that read as if the polls were mistaken or the latest polls an aberration. Our review of coverage in the *New York Times, Washington Post, Los Angeles Times, Time,* and *Newsweek* demonstrates that journalists wrote as if they believed that Reagan's popularity was inviolate and transcendent.

As early as March 1, 1981, the *Washington Post* reported the NBC/AP poll as showing Reagan slightly behind Carter at the same point in his term of office. On March 18, 1981, the *New York Times* ran a report of the latest Gallup poll in three inches at the bottom of page 22. The story was certainly clear enough: "President Reagan's handling of his job after eight weeks in office wins less approval from the public than any newly elected President in 28 years, according to the Gallup poll." It was actually much worse than that for those who read the whole story—not only were Reagan's "approval" ratings the lowest, but his "disapproval" ratings were nearly three times higher than for any other newly elected president. The *Los Angeles Times* placed their Gallup story on page 1 below the fold, the *Washington Post* on page 3.

On the same day's *New York Times* op-ed page, James Reston wrote a column in which he reported that even Democratic leaders in Congress "concede that the President has public opinion on his side." Why did they concede that? What evidence supported this assumption? There seems to have been a great disjunction between what the polls said and what Washington insiders believed.

On April 25 in the *Washington Post,* Barry Sussman's assessment of the first 100 days of the Reagan administration attributed Reagan's high job approval rating (73% according to the ABC/*Washington Post* poll) to his "personal magnetism," and held that "in every personal measure Reagan stands about as high as anyone who espouses such controversial measures could." The story noted the upward turn in the polls after the assassination attempt but did not mention the surprisingly low polls of the first two months in office. There is little doubt that the upward turn in Reagan's April polls was a sympathetic rally-round-the-President response to the assassination attempt on March 30. *Newsweek* made exactly that judgment on May 4, but one week later reported, without any mention of the surprisingly low polls for Reagan's first months in office, that Reagan's presidency was suffused in "a blanket of personal goodwill unmatched since Dwight Eisenhower."[17] In what may have been the low point in press coverage of Reagan's popularity, the magazine reported that Reagan's popularity ratings in some surveys "are the highest in polling history." That was simply false. The evidence *Newsweek* cites was a Robert Teeter poll in which 48% of the public held the country to be on the wrong track, compared to 82% in 1979. This is not a direct measure of Reagan's popularity at all.

On May 18, *Newsweek* reported that Reagan was the most popular and best-liked president since Eisenhower and that "a swell of personal sentiment and political support for Reagan in the outlands" settled the congressional battle over the budget. *Newsweek* cites no source for its intimate knowledge of the outlands.[18]

In August, Hedrick Smith wrote of Reagan in the *New York Times Magazine:* "As a newly elected public figure, he has enjoyed warm popularity and a successful honeymoon."[19] Compared to other presidents, this was not true, if the polls are to be believed. The June Gallup polls, released seven weeks before Smith published his story, showed a 59% approval rating (28% disapproval, 13% undecided or no opinion), compared to Carter's at the same point in his administration of 63% (19% disapproval and 18% with no opinion). Comparable figures for Nixon were 63%, 16%, and 21%; for Kennedy, 71%, 14%, and 15%; for Eisenhower, 74%, 10%, and 16%).[20]

By the fall of 1981, Adam Clymer reported in the *New York Times* that "President Reagan's once solid grip on public support appears to be loosening somewhat because of concern about the economic situation, and his speech Thursday calling for more budget cuts did little or nothing to reverse the slippage, the latest *New York Times*/CBS News Poll shows."[21] All well and good—except for that opening phrase about Reagan's "once solid grip on public support." There is no polling evidence that Reagan ever had such a grip in office. All newly elected presidents get the benefit of the doubt from citizens—but Reagan got considerably less than his predecessors.

The new year began with a new Gallup poll and a report of it in the *New York Times:* "Public approval of President Reagan has slipped below 50 percent for the first time and he now stands lower than President Carter did four years ago, according to the latest Gallup Poll."[22] This is a bit misleading. It suggests (by the word "now") that slipping below Carter in the polls was a new development. In fact, for the first eleven monthly Gallup polls, Carter surpassed Reagan eight times. In Reagan's three winning months, his margin of victory was 4, 4, and 5 points, while Carter's margin averaged 8 points. The Roper polls showed Carter outdoing Reagan every time in the first 30 months in office, with Reagan outpolling Carter for the first time only in the summer of 1983.[23]

On January 21 Lou Cannon, widely regarded as the most astute Reagan watcher in the Washington press corps, commented in the *Washington Post* on Reagan's low poll ratings but then noted that Reagan was personally more popular than his policies (failing to note, of course, that this is typical for presidents). Ellen Goodman wrote two days later in her syndicated column about Reagan's "protective coating of likability." She stressed, as if it were a peculiarity of Reagan and not a normal feature of every presidency, that "it has been as if his personal popularity had a life of its own, beyond his policies."[24]

Reporters did not create their assumptions about Reagan's popularity out of thin air. But since the polls provided no evidence for this popularity, how did the press arrive at their judgment? How did it happen that they were, as Elizabeth Drew said, cowed by Reagan's popularity? Were they, as Lou Cannon said, sharing in a national euphoria of Reagan's popularity after a string of presidents perceived of as failures? How did it happen that, as David Broder said, the press decided "not to make pests of ourselves" even when not bemused by Reagan?[25] Michael Kinsley wrote later that critics of Reagan felt him not bright, nor thoughtful, nor very honest, not really competent for the presidency, "but a large majority of people seemed not to mind." Reagan seemed to have a special magic with the public and, Kinsley recalls, "even Reagan's critics became deeply superstitious about this alleged magic. They became afraid to say, or even forgot that they think, that he's just an old movie actor. They themselves came to believe that to criticize Reagan personally was to cut yourself off from the democratic life force."[26] How did it happen, as Yale professor Edward Tufte put it, that the Reagan team convinced their Democratic opponents, the Washington establishment, and "the 50,000 people that really matter" that Reagan was "really tuned into America"?[27] Why, when available statistical evidence showed President Reagan to have modest public support, did Washington elites and the news media believe in his invincible popularity?

Face-to-Face Communication in the Television Age

Reagan's image as the Great Communicator did not grow because of narrowly defined oratorical skills. Describing the speech outlining his economic program, the start of the "Reagan Revolution," *Time* reported, "The master of the television homily and the after dinner pep talk appeared not only ill at ease, but even a bit defensive." *Time* noted that Reagan rushed his delivery and misjudged his applause lines in a grade B performance.[28] Several other speeches were similarly graded by the press. If the press gave Reagan's platform performances mixed reviews, his ability to handle himself in press conferences was savaged. In his first press conference, held in the "honeymoon period" when the Reagan juggernaut was just beginning to roll, *Time* offered the back-handed compliment that Reagan displayed "charm, aplomb and the indifference to some details in the briefing books that has distinguished his public performances from those of his fact-happy predecessor Jimmy Carter."[29] *Newsweek* described his first press conference after the assassination attempt as "full of faux pas. He may have a foreign policy but he has plenty of trouble explaining it."[30] Commenting on a February 1982 press conference, *Newsweek* wrote of Reagan's ragged sessions "reinforcing the impression that the president is uncomfortable off the cuff." In that particular press conference, *Newsweek* reported, Reagan ducked questions, suffered from slips of the tongue, and made factual errors.[31]

In his first year Reagan held only five press conferences, fewer than any president in fifty years. He held to that pace throughout most of his administration. And the reviews of his performance rarely improved. "The White House press conference," wrote Christopher Hanson (under his William Boot pseudonym) in the *Columbia Journalism Review*, "has been converted by Ronald Reagan into a forum for inaccuracy, distortion, and falsehood."[32] Reagan's embarrassing press conferences became an issue early in his first term; his handlers sought to preserve his image by keeping him secluded from situations of spontaneous communication.

The evidence suggests that at no time in Reagan's first years was the general public as charmed by Ronald Reagan as the news media were. The picture that reporters presented of Reagan as a Great Communicator did not arise from Reagan's ability to communicate to the masses. It can be explained, however, by five other factors: (1) Reagan's skills and the skills of his staff in communicating personally to the press corps and the Congress; (2) a changed political balance of power in Washington after the election of 1980 and a concerted effort to take advantage of this; (3) Reagan's ability to mobilize a key right-wing constituency; (4) the tendency of the press to defer to legislative success and to read it as popularity; and (5) the exaggerated importance that the mass media and Washington insiders attribute to the role of television in shaping public opinion—and to "public opinion" itself.

First, then, it is important to examine the power of face-to-face communication in the television age. What may have been Ronald Reagan's greatest strength as a communicator was not the well-trained radio voice or the professional actor's skills but his frequent roles in Hollywood as the "best friend." He retained that "best friend" persona, the kind of guy you just can't stay mad at, with the press and Congress.

People in Washington genuinely liked Ronald Reagan. *U.S. News* reported as early as March 2, 1981, that a large number of White House reporters liked Reagan even though they did not share his conservative outlook. *Newsweek* reported a year later that "most journalists who cover the White House like him personally." Jody Powell said, a year thereafter, "Most reporters I talk to say they generally like the guy." Steven Weisman's account of Reagan's first 100 days describes him as being able to command the public's attention, court new friends, keep opponents off guard, and maintain a friendly posture. Official Washington, he reported, was captivated by Reagan's affability.[33]

Reagan's likability presented a contrast to outgoing President Jimmy Carter. The press did not like Carter. *Newsweek* reported that Carter hated the Washington establishment, and the establishment reciprocated the feeling. In contrast, Reagan's first post-election visit to Washington showed Reagan sweeping the city's "glitterati" off their feet. Carter, *Newsweek* said, had been too stubbornly the standoffish outsider. He was also too unsocial—even billing congressional leaders for White House breakfasts. Reagan and his aides began meeting with Washington leaders immediately after the election—and, in sharp contrast to the Carter White House, attended Georgetown parties. *Newsweek* happily noted that it had been years since Washington heard a president laugh at himself. Carter's "self-righteousness irritated many reporters," according to John Herbers. So not only did they like Reagan, but they felt a great relief and great contrast to the Carter years. "Ronald Reagan," said his 1980 campaign press secretary Lyn Nofziger, "whether you like him or not, always comes across as a nice man. Carter does not come across as a nice man. And I think that has to have a subconscious effect over reporters."[34]

This likability was not just a matter of Reagan personally but of a public relations staff that received widespread approbation. John Herbers wrote in the *New York Times Magazine* that James Baker had put together a very professional and amiable staff—with Larry Speakes and David Gergen both singled out. Baker assembled "an extraordinarily capable staff," Hedrick Smith later wrote. Morton Kondracke praised Gergen's abilities in *The New Republic*.[35]

Reagan's affability with Congress was as important as his likability with the press. His personal appeal seemed especially important with the Democrats. House Speaker Tip O'Neill was quoted in the press on his personal liking for the President. He said in the *Washington Post*, November 8, 1981: "People like him as an individual, and he handles the media better than anybody since Franklin Roosevelt, even including Jack. There's just something about the guy that people like. They want him to be a success." And in *Time*, February 22, 1982: "Generally, I like the fella. He tells a good Irish story."[36]

Reagan's way with Congress also involved much more than his pleasing personal style. Tip O'Neill recalled later that Reagan's staff work with Congress was extraordinary—"the Reagan team in 1981 was probably the best-run political operating unit I've ever seen."[37] Max Friedersdorf, Reagan's first congressional liaison, was widely praised for the skill with which he guided the Reagan program through Congress in 1981. Friedersdorf arranged sixty-nine meetings for key congressmen in the Oval Office in Reagan's first 100 days. He brought sixty Democrats to the White House the week before the key budget vote in May 1981, and himself accompanied undecided congressmen to concerts and the opera the nights before the final vote. Within hours after the vote, thank-you notes signed by the President were delivered to all who voted with him.[38] James Reston reported early on that the President was solicitous of Congress, calling leaders to private White House dinners and establishing an effective liaison. In his first months, he clearly had better relations with Congress than Carter ever did. Reagan may have delegated much of his work to others, but he did not delegate the job of "Chief Salesperson," as *U.S. News* put it. He spent hours a day selling his policies to legislators. "We had to keep him off the Hill when we first arrived or he'd have been there every day," according to Tom Korologos, the congressional liaison officer during the transition from the Carter administration. Reagan was lavish in his use of social invitations, his distribution of presidential cuff links and signed photographs, and his timely phone calls to key congressmen.[39]

Washington would not long have been impressed if the Reagan administration offered nothing more than bonhomie and good cheer. Washington admires success—and Reagan was quickly able to demonstrate it. Some of this may have been done with mirrors, of course. This is particularly true of the interpretation of Reagan's electoral victory as a great "mandate" for his policies. Before the election, it was reasonably clear that what candidate Reagan had going for him most of all was the public's distaste for an apparently ineffectual Carter administration held hostage by the Iran crisis. Just before the election, for instance, *Newsweek* described President Carter as "the least popular president to run for reelection since Hoover." But within weeks the same magazine, while reporting that four out of five Reagan voters supported him because of Carter's poor performance (according to exit polls), also concluded that the election was a "rousing vote of confidence" in Ronald Reagan and his "politics of nostalgia."[40] The 1980 election came quickly to be remembered as a Reagan landslide and a mandate for his policies. And it was true that Reagan's margin over Carter was substantial—but John Anderson picked up a significant share of votes, giving Reagan under 51% of the popular vote. Most observers now recognize the election as a referendum on Carter, but the Reagan administration worked hard to reshape perceptions of the November test as a validation of Reagan's new conservative agenda. All of this may have been accentuated because the results were a surprise. Days before the election, some pollsters still judged the race too close to call.

In retrospect, most political scientists agree that one need not invoke anything at all about Reagan's personal appeal to explain his 1980 victory (or his 1984 landslide)—a simple model of "economic voting" fits the evidence very nicely.[41] But in what social psychologists refer to as the "fundamental attribution error" in lay judgments about causality, people seek actor-based rather than situation-based explanations of phenomena they want to understand. The media are far from immune to this error, particularly when it comes to understanding elections and presidential popularity. In fact, it may be that making the "attribution error" is a *requirement* of story-telling journalism; identifiable human actors a reader can love or hate, not abstract social forces and social structures, are essential elements in the conventions of news writing.

Reagan followed his electoral victory with an aggressive and uncompromising legislative program. In his first 100 days, he proposed a budget that severely cut social programs and rapidly increased defense spending. With the press drawing battle lines—the President on one side and the Congress on the other—the measure of Reagan's authority and political strength was taken with every legislative skirmish. Reagan did remarkably well at these tests. According to *Congressional Quarterly*'s study of presidential support in Congress, Congress followed Reagan's wishes 82.4% of the time in his first year, the best record for a president since Lyndon Johnson won congressional approval for 95% of his programs in 1965. Perhaps more impressive was the fact that Reagan's bills passed relatively unsullied by compromise with Congress. House Majority Leader Jim Wright complained, "There has never been an administration that has demanded to dictate so completely to the Congress. I don't know what it will take to satisfy them, I guess for Congress to resign and give them our voting proxy cards."[42]

Within his first two months in office, Reagan found the Congress bowing to his legislative wishes. This required much more than a smiling television personality and good congressional liaison. In the 1980 elections Republicans captured control of the Senate, turning a 58 to 41 Democratic edge into a 53 to 47 Republican majority. In the House, Republicans gained 33 seats, giving them 192 to the Democrats' 243. With thirty avowed conservatives numbered among the Democrats, it was clear that the congressional balance of power had swung to the Republicans. There was even a moment in November when twenty-six conservative Democrats thought of joining the Republicans to form a new majority.[43] The Democrats were in disarray.

From the moment the 1980 elections were tallied, then, and the Senate in Republican control for the first time in a generation, it was clear that the House would be the main battleground for Reagan's new programs. This made for a simple story line in the news—a new protagonist in the White House battling an entrenched congressional establishment in the House. When Reagan's spartan budget made its way through the House in May—by a vote of 218 to 214—*Newsweek* wrote, "The citadel fell to an irresistible force named Ronald Reagan and his cut and slash assault on big government."[44]

A leading explanation for Reagan's stunning success—and it was indeed a stunning success—was his ability to take his case to the people to intimidate and overcome the Congress. Recent analysis casts serious doubt on this explanation. In a detailed examination of the politics of Reagan's 1981 tax and budget cuts, Marc Bodnick takes issue with Sam Kernell's influential account of the growing importance to presidential power of "going public" rather than "bargaining" directly with Congress. While Kernell is certainly correct in emphasizing that access both to television and to jet airplanes offers new flexibility to the presidential arsenal, Bodnick argues that for Reagan in 1981, at least, "bargaining" remained the primary weapon of the presidency. It was not public appeals that won the day, according to Bodnick, but real compromises in the tax and budget packages to please a Congress that was already, without pushing or persuasion, notably conservative.[45]

In fact, congressmen were hearing from their constituents that they should support the President. Congressmen take their mail seriously as a measure of public opinion, but there is grave doubt about the wisdom of doing so, especially when the polls are telling a different story. Why did the Congress get so much pro-Reagan mail? We shall assume that, in fact, they did—Tip O'Neill reports that he did. He also recalls that some of the Democrats who supported Reagan's programs "came to me and explained that the people back home really wanted them to support the president—which was undoubtedly true."[46] Certainly the *volume* of mail increased remarkably; congressional mail before 1981 had never reached 30 million letters a year, and suddenly in 1981 it jumped to 40.1 million letters, more than 26% higher than in 1980.[47] But the likeliest explanation for the burgeoning mailbags is that Reagan had successfully mobilized a new constituency, the "New Right," that had never before had one of its own in the White House.

The advent of the New Right led not only to a new slant in the congressional mailbag but to a new orientation in the newspapers as well. A whole set of newly legitimate sources arose and colored the political atmosphere in Washington. Between 1979 and 1981, the number of stories written about the conservative movement soared. In 1979, for example, in magazines indexed in the *Reader's Guide to Periodical Literature*, 22 articles about the conservative movement were listed. In 1980, there were 57; in 1981, 106. Spokespeople for the leading elements of the conservative movement—Terry Dolan and Richard Viguerie for the New Right, Irving Kristol for neoconservatives, and Jerry Falwell for the religious right—became extremely newsworthy. In 1979 Jerry Falwell had been the subject of one magazine story; in 1980, 22 stories; in 1981, 32 stories. Terry Dolan and the National Conservative Political Action Committee were covered once in the *Washington Post* in 1979, three times in 1980, twenty-five times in 1981. By 1982, it was clear that the media had oversold the New Right.[48] But by then, in a sense, the damage was done, Reagan's momentum in Congress well established, and the self-fulfilling legend on a roll.

There was no question but that Reagan effectively mobilized this conservative constituency for political action. "From 15 years of crisscrossing America in the cause of conservatism," Hedrick Smith wrote in 1982, "Ronald Reagan has developed the most potent network of political activists in the nation." Smith's essay in the *New York Times Magazine*, "Taking Charge of Congress," details how, under Lyn Nofziger's direction, the Reagan administration pressured congressmen, especially "boll weevil Democrats" and other wavering representatives, through mobilizing political activists in their own districts to urge their support for specific presidential policies.[49] The Reagan administration carefully nurtured its core supporters, with the President addressing groups in person, on closed circuit television, or on tape, arranging programs in Washington and in home districts, and making sure that political allies let members of Congress know they cared.[50] News commentators may have imagined that the huge response Reagan received to some of his early television addresses was altogether spontaneous, but the White House had not left this to chance or to charisma.[51] Before a television address Reagan provided previews to political allies, several hundred at a time, and instructed them to notify their compatriots to send a message to Congress. The flow of phone calls, telegrams, and letters was primed by this activity.[52] Congress was indeed hearing from its constituents, but far from being a random sample, it was a carefully orchestrated chorus of conservative voices. It should not be forgotten that 1980 saw the defeat of six prominent liberal senators—Birch Bayh, Frank Church, and George McGovern among them—as well as John Brademas and other prominent House liberals. This development enhanced the idea of a general conservative mood, although it, too, probably owed more to a carefully orchestrated and effectively targeted political campaign.

One legislative success led to another, each success impelled by the reputation that prior success afforded. Routines of news coverage in the press amplified the power of prior success, too. The press is more willing to judge a president's skills as a politician and as a marketable image during a term of office than to evaluate the public worth of his policies. Reagan's persona fit remarkably well into the tendency of the news media to judge effective accomplishment stylistically rather than substantively. The result, in the press's coverage of Reagan, was to play down exactly those elements of the Reagan presidency—his policies—that were not, in fact, playing very well in Peoria, and to exaggerate those elements that—whatever their effect in Peoria—were taking Washington by storm.

The press believed, then, that Reagan won his legislative victories because he was a great communicator. To some extent, the reverse is true: his image as the Great Communicator was confirmed because he won the legislative victories. The aura of victory carried with it a kind of protective shield that made both congressional opponents and the media shy of criticizing the President. As Anthony Lewis wrote early in 1982, "He won big in 1980. He won again last year in the Congressional tax and budget battle. He has a political legitimacy that may well make the press shy."[53]

So the perception of Reagan's widespread success with the American people was in some measure a projection onto the American public of his popularity as a politician and a person in Washington, an extrapolation from his effectiveness with the Congress, and an outcome of his effectiveness in mobilizing the active opinion of a new right-wing constituency. The final factor in manufacturing the sense of Reagan's general popularity was the belief in Washington, by now an article of faith, that politics today is in the television age and that a man with Reagan's evident personal charm on the television screen has practically irresistible power to shape public opinion. One need not look too carefully at the polls; one need only turn on the evening news and see what a winning way the President has on television.[54]

In subscribing to this view, the media may have proved too clever by half. Not wanting to mistake image for substance, the news media have grown more and more sophisticated in the past decade in looking behind the scenes at how a president or presidential candidate shapes his image. If television runs the well-crafted photo opportunity and the newspapers follow with the obligatory news photograph, at the same time the commentators in print and occasionally on television as well observe that this was a well-calculated photo opportunity. (That the term "photo opportunity" became common parlance in the Reagan years is not an accident.) All presidents attempt to manipulate the press and control their own image, but Reagan's advisers seemed particularly skillful at this task, and the press seemed particularly awed by their image-making machinery. By the fall of 1981 when Sid Blumental in the *New York Times Magazine* dubbed Reagan the nation's "Communicator in chief," there was plenty of news attention to Reagan's "marketing brain trust." James Baker, David Gergen, Larry Speakes, and others were all given high marks for professionalism and inventiveness in selling the President's image.[55] But the news media assumed too quickly that if a lot of time and money was being spent on something—image-making—that time and money surely would bring results in its direct impact on public opinion.

Laurence Barrett, senior White House correspondent for *Time,* argued in a 1982 book on Reagan that the skill of the Reagan White House in shaping the President's image came to be a "minor myth" in Washington. He attributed what he called the "fairy tale" of White House media omnipotence to the contrast of the smoothly running Reagan White House to the ineffective Carter White House. He also noted that the skill of the President's lieutenants was overrated because the lieutenants themselves were the sources for the "behind the scenes in White House image-making" stories—far from being examples of aggressive, muckraking reporting, these pieces served the self-promotional ends of White House insiders.[56]

Print journalists in particular tended to overrate the power of the television image. Thomas Griffith wrote in a *Time* "Newswatch" column: "The Reagan administration, more than any before it, aims its message to the big television audience and wastes little time on those who want to follow the fine print." This was, he wrote disapprovingly, "a TV presidency and the skillful merchandising of personality."[57] Mark Crispin Miller wrote an angry and in places brilliant column in *The New Republic* that tore into television news reporters. "The press," he asserted, "and TV in particular elected Ronald Reagan . . . Reagan won because his image was a perfect television spectacle . . . television has reduced our political culture to a succession of gestures, postures, automatic faces."[58] But there was no evidence to suggest that Reagan's television brilliance rather than Carter's Iran hostage problem and a faltering economy decided the election.

What evidence is there that everything in American politics follows from the television image—in particular, that public opinion is a pawn of televisual politics? Not, when it comes down to it, very much evidence at all. The news establishment has a delusion not only about the power of the media but about the power of the public. The media, convinced that the story of modern politics is the story of the capacity of candidates and officials to appeal directly to the public, attribute enormous power to "public opinion." However, that "public opinion" is expressly known only through polls or elections. Otherwise, it must be coaxed into existence by leadership of various kinds—articulated by parties and interest groups, mobilized by social movements, sounded by reporters and congressional aides talking to cab drivers or irate constituents. Public opinion is not something that exists bodily. It is not something that storms down doors or barricades streets. Rather, it is a set of beliefs in the heads of key decision makers about what people who are rarely asked to express their opinions publicly believe.

A good illustration of this comes in the frequent assertion in Washington that "the public" or "the people" wanted the President to succeed because they were tired of failed presidencies: Lou Cannon— "Everybody wants our president to be up on a pedestal a little"; Meg Greenfield—"People wanted to break the spell of a series of doomed presidencies"; Haynes Johnson—"Americans do not want to see another failed presidency." John Herbers also reported that people wanted to see this president succeed after a string of failures.[59]

While all of this could plausibly be true, never did the commentators offer any evidence of this popular yearning, and it is at least reasonable to suspect that the Washington community, not "the public," wanted the President to succeed and projected its feeling onto the public. Whatever the general public might have felt, the media had a strong desire to "reverse the trend of failed presidencies," as Laurence Barrett observed.[60] The public did not hesitate to give Reagan low marks for his policies even if the press and the congressional elite were reluctant to do so; and if they tended to rate his personality higher than his policies, they nonetheless rated it lower than the personalities of his predecessors. If the public was rooting for Reagan, they did not mention this to the pollsters. In August 1982, Richard E. Meyer of the *Los Angeles Times* wrote a page one story, "Third of Reagan Voters Wouldn't Back Him Again." This was a conservatively worded headline: fewer than half (49%) of the voters who voted for Reagan in 1980 asserted they would like him renominated, 35% wanted him dumped, and 16% had no opinion.[61]

Conclusion

We believe the evidence indicates that Ronald Reagan came to be described as a Great Communicator in the press not because of his special skills in communicating directly to the American people but because of significant skill in communicating with key elites, including the media itself. In their attempt to evaluate their own personal impressions of Reagan, his series of legislative victories, and the information they were receiving from a fresh set of legitimate conservative sources, the national media determined that Reagan could communicate with the public unusually effectively. There is no evidence from his first two years in office, the period in which the media drew this self-sustaining conclusion, that the public agreed with the assessment. Reagan's honeymoon in the polls was less intense than with previous presidents; his rating on personal likability was high but no higher than for previous presidents; and the percentage of people disapproving his policies (rather than having no opinion) was much higher than for his predecessors.

Is it wise to rely on the polls in these matters? We do not want to argue that they are the only measure of public opinion, or that they are a "true" measure. The polls are a construct, just as is the informed but informal judgment of Washington pundits. They give more credit to the silent and the apathetic than do other measures—and critics of the polls suggest, rightly in our judgment, that this makes them misleading as a measure of "opinion." They evoke "opinions" where people have no opinion or no strong opinion but feel obliged to say something. The polls, for this and other reasons, are far from perfect. Still, if they are not the last word on public opinion, they are certainly the first word. And many of the reports of Ronald Reagan's popularity implicitly or explicitly take the polls to be the benchmark of popularity, the measure of the effectiveness of Reagan as a "communicator" with the general public.[62]

In the past fifty years, the direct relationship between the President and the people has grown enormously. However, the press has overrated the extent to which this communication is, even in the age of television and photo opportunities, "unmediated." Thomas Griffith, writing in *Time* in 1982, noted that President Reagan gave more primetime television speeches than any other president and only a third as many press conferences as Jimmy Carter. "As an actor, Reagan learned that the box office is more important than the critics."[63]

No, that's what it pleased Washington to believe the President learned. But Reagan assiduously curried favor with Congress and the media; the general public was by no means his only or even primary concern. We have argued that just as important in the assessment of a president's image is his ability to communicate directly with key elites, including the media. The White House press corps experiences the President bodily, personally, emotionally. Yet, since the canons of objective journalism prohibit the overt expression of personal impressions in most brands of news, the nature of the unmediated experience must either be held in check or attributed elsewhere. In this case, we believe, the feeling in the press corps that Ronald Reagan was a nice guy, a feeling confirmed by other Washington sources who also judged him from firsthand experience to be a nice guy, was attributed to the wider public.

Indeed, it appears the only community not enamored with the Reagan performance in his first years were the folks in South Succotash, the people with whom Reagan was purportedly communicating on a tribal level. But the press, instead of labeling this president the Great Conservative, a description driven by an analysis of his policies, or calling him one of the most controversial modern presidents, a description driven by his divided poll ratings, dubbed him the Great Communicator, a description based in large part on the experience of congressmen and reporters with an "unmediated" president.

Washington journalism is an oral culture at the center of a national network of print and broadcast culture. Washington reporters use no documents at all in some 75 percent of their stories, apart from press releases. Where they do use them, a third of the "documents" are other newspaper articles. The interview is the mainstay of the Washington reporter, face-to-face, person-to-person. The inhabitants of the world of Washington politics, naturally enough, talk more to one another than to other people, but there is the danger that this practice can become self-enclosed. "The echo chamber of this world," writes political analyst Stephen Hess, "gives a special resonance, like the corridors in a hospital or penal institution."[64] "If you send a reporter to Washington," said Steve Isaacs, former editor of the *Minneapolis Star*, "that reporter tends to be co-opted by the elitist values and nincompoop news sense there."[65] That may be too cruel a judgment, but it is one for which, in this instance, our own research provides support.

7 Watergate
and the Press

Watergate overwhelms modern American journalism. According to one close observer of the press, Watergate "had the most profound impact of any modern event on the manner and substance of the press's conduct."[1] According to another, the *New York Times* publication of the Pentagon Papers and the *Washington Post* coverage of Watergate "inspired a whole generation of young journalists to dig below the surface of events."[2] No other story in American history features the press in so prominent and heroic a role. Students may learn in their history classes that John Peter Zenger bravely dared to attack the royal governor of New York or that the *New York Times* went after Boss Tweed or that "muckrakers" at the turn of the century exposed corrupt politicians, but these tales are scarcely the stuff of enduring legend. If the pen is mightier than the sword in American history, it is more likely the pen of a novelist than the typewriter of a reporter—Harriet Beecher Stowe stimulating antislavery sentiment or Upton Sinclair enlisting citizens in outrage against the food-processing industry. Perhaps the most enduring (but not accurate) story of the American press is that yellow journalism pushed the nation into war against Spain in 1898; hardly a heroic endeavor of struggling journalists yearning for truth, this is recalled as a classic case of unscrupulous capitalists going to any length to make a buck.

The story of Bob Woodward and Carl Bernstein in bold pursuit of the perpetrators of the Watergate break-in is resonant and powerful in both the world of journalism and the culture at large. The *Washington Post* received a Pulitzer

Prize for its reporting on Watergate. Woodward and Bernstein's account of their own role as investigators, *All the President's Men,* became an extraordinary best seller, and the film by the same title became a box-office sensation. The film, even more than the book, ennobled investigative reporting and made of journalists modern heroes. This tale of the press in Watergate developed into a significant national myth, a story that independently carries on a memory of Watergate even as details about what Nixon did or did not do fade away.

At its broadest, the myth of journalism in Watergate asserts that two young *Washington Post* reporters brought down the President of the United States. This is a myth of David and Goliath, of powerless individuals overturning an institution of overwhelming might. It is high noon in Washington, with two white-hatted young reporters at one end of the street and the black-hatted President at the other, protected by his minions. And the good guys win. The press, truth its only weapon, saves the day.

That is the myth in its most general form, but this is only a portion of a larger complex of themes about modern journalism that the Watergate story opens up. The Watergate myth is available for comment and criticism, not just for reverent attention, and the initial romantic construction of the myth has been challenged on at least three points. First, did "the press" as an institution act courageously to keep power in check? Or was it especially one lonely newspaper or even a few lonely individuals within that lonely newspaper who acted in ways *uncharacteristic* of the press in general?

Second, was the press unaided in its battle against the evils of Watergate? Or was it but one institution and one set of individuals among many, with the Congress and the courts standing stalwart at its side while other institutions of investigation, including the FBI, made equally important contributions?

Third, was the press morally pure, which is to say, professionally unbiased, in its pursuit of Watergate, driven only by its sense of responsibility to the public weal? Or was the press partisan, even petty, all too delighted to bring down a man journalists had long abhorred?

On each point, a critical look at the myth of journalism in Watergate forces some telling adjustments. First, "the press" as a whole did not pursue Watergate, at least not in the beginning—the *Washington Post* did. From the break-in in June 1972 until after the election in November, the *Post* frequently felt itself alone on a story that many leading journalists regarded as a figment of active election-year imaginations, no more than the political shenanigans Nixon claimed it to be. *Washington Post* publisher Katherine Graham remembers saying to editor Ben Bradlee, "If this is such a hell of a story, where is everybody else?"[3]

Where indeed? Of all 433 Washington correspondents in 1972, at most 15 worked full-time on Watergate in the first five months after the break-in, and some of these only briefly.[4] The *Washington Post* Watergate stories went out on the *Post* news wire, but few papers picked them up.[5] Even at the *Post* there was plenty of skepticism. *Post* White House reporters discouraged Woodward and Bernstein and their editors from following up the story. The national staff was dismissive.[6] Because the whole thing began so accidentally and grew so unpredictably, it made *Post* executives nervous. The decision in 1971 to publish the Pentagon Papers, Katherine Graham recalls, had been self-conscious and carefully considered. But with Watergate, "there really wasn't a decision." When the story began, "it was small and sort of a farce . . . It just looked sort of lunatic and not very consequential."[7] Although a few other leading papers competed with the *Post* on Watergate, contributing new leads and new revelations—notably the *Los Angeles Times,* the *New York Times,* and *Time* magazine—"journalism" or "the press" as a whole did little investigating and showed little courage.

Second, journalists did not uncover Watergate unassisted. In a mini-classic of press criticism, Edward Jay Epstein asked in *Commentary:* "Did the Press Uncover Watergate?" and answered in the negative. *All the President's Men,* Epstein correctly points out, tells very little about how Watergate was in fact uncovered. The contributions of the FBI investigations, the federal prosecutors, the grand jury, and the congressional committees are "systematically ignored or minimized by Bernstein and Woodward." What they report, instead, are "those parts of the prosecutors' case, the grand-jury investigation, and the FBI reports that were leaked to them." This calls attention to two lacunae in the mythic account of Watergate journalism. First, agencies besides the press were instrumental in pursuing Watergate. The journalistic contribution was one among many, and there would have been no presidential resignation had it not been for Judge John Sirica, the Ervin committee, the existence and discovery of the White House tapes, and other factors. Even the matter of "keeping the story alive" was not exclusively a reportorial function: candidate George McGovern kept talking about Watergate throughout his campaign; the General Accounting Office, Common Cause, and the Democratic National Committee and its lawsuit against the Nixon campaign all forced disclosures that kept the Watergate story in the public eye. Moreover, the journalistic contribution itself was dependent on government officials who risked their jobs or their careers by leaking to the press. Epstein insists that it was less the press that exposed Watergate than "agencies of government itself."[8]

This skeptical view of the Watergate myth has been endorsed by many people in journalism, not least of all Katherine Graham. Graham has observed that the press did not bring down a president. In the spring of 1974, with Richard Nixon still in the White House, she gave a speech at Colby College, where she insisted that Woodward and Bernstein were successful only because some people, including "many inside government and mostly Republicans," were willing to go out on a limb and talk with them and that Judge Sirica, the Senate Watergate committee, the grand juries, and other agencies of investigation produced "many of the key revelations."[9]

Finally, skeptics have argued that it was not journalism's devotion to truth but the *Washington Post*'s or the liberal news media establishment's contempt for Richard Nixon that led it to pursue the Watergate story. The *Post* was a liberal paper and long had been a liberal, if thoroughly establishment, institution. Ben Bradlee had been a Kennedy intimate. "The press," as *Post* reporter Thomas Edsall told me, "is a liberal entity, with a commitment to liberal values and the 'rights revolution.' " This, he said, is "inherent in the press—opening things up."[10] Larry Sabato argues that the press is in fact, whether or not in principle, liberal.[11] Conservative media critics, of course, have been complaining about this for years.[12]

In the view of some conservatives, this is enough to explain the *Post*'s chase after the Watergate story, but no one in journalism I spoke to and no student of journalism I know believes this. "Liberal bias" does little to explain why the *Post* followed up every allegation that came to it of Democratic campaign spying against Republicans, why journalists at the *Post* resented McGovern supporters who told them what a great job they were doing, or why editors working on the Watergate stories were nervous and self-doubting about them. "I had harbored misgivings, story by story, as had the reporters and the editors above me," writes Barry Sussman, Woodward and Bernstein's immediate supervisor. "We all wanted to push our coverage to its proper limit, but not any farther, and we didn't want to be tools in anyone's election campaign."[13] As for Ben Bradlee, he backed up his young reporters and their editors because he was after a good story, not after Richard Nixon. Ben Bagdikian, a media scholar and former *Wash-*

ington Post national editor, recalls Bradlee saying, "I want every fucking cocktail party in Georgetown talking about this." Bradlee "got excited by a story that was going to make a difference."[14]

But the *Post* was also an establishment newspaper, generally cautious at its highest levels. The management struggled over the decision to publish the Pentagon Papers in 1971, finally forging ahead against the counsel of company lawyers.[15] The *New York Times* published the Pentagon Papers first. This rankled Bradlee, and there was a delicious sense of revenge in the *Post*'s pursuit of Watergate. If Bradlee was out to get anyone, it was the *New York Times,* not Richard Nixon. He is said to have walked around the *Post*'s newsroom in the midst of Watergate, shouting, "Eat your heart out, Abe!"[16] Bradlee's counterpart at the *New York Times,* Abe Rosenthal, was Bradlee's real rival.

Nixon long had friends as well as adversaries in the press, and his early career was sponsored by the powerful *Los Angeles Times,* but he felt battered and betrayed by the press in 1960 when it was apparent that reporters were not charmed by him as they were by the Kennedy entourage. (Newspaper management was more favorably inclined: 54 percent endorsed Nixon, 15 percent Kennedy, and the others did not endorse.) After his embarrassing loss in the election for the California governorship in 1962, he lashed out at the press, though some historians doubt that he was treated badly.[17] In his presidential bids in 1968 and 1972, some analysts hold that the press treated him well, perhaps even too well, not probing hard enough and, in 1972, not pushing enough to get him out of his Rose Garden retreat.[18] Sixty-one percent of American newspapers endorsed Nixon to Humphrey's 14 percent, while 71 percent endorsed Nixon in 1972 compared to McGovern's 5 percent.[19] Newspaper endorsement was significantly related to Watergate coverage. In a study of thirty of the country's leading daily newspapers representing 23 percent of newspaper circulation, Ben Bagdikian found that many papers did not carry important Watergate stories available on the wire services, and when they did, the stories typically were not given much prominence. Papers endorsing Nixon put Watergate stories on page one at half the rate of the nonendorsers.[20]

So Nixon may not have had as much cause to damn the press as he believed. He was aware that the leading Eastern establishment press— the *Times,* the *Post,* and even *Time* magazine—was critical of his Vietnam policy and deeply suspicious of government pronouncements on Vietnam. Still, as British journalist Godfrey Hodgson observes, leading journalists did not get where they were "by being quixotic or sentimental. Their job was to get on with those who had access to stories, which meant with those who had power. They were good at that." Nixon could have had a sympathetic press, Hodgson believes: "The price would only have been a little tact, a little openness. It was too high a price for Richard Nixon to pay."[21] Perhaps Nixon longed to be treated with the deference accorded Eisenhower, but he did not have Ike's affability, competent staff, or good luck not to preside over an unpopular and divisive war. Moreover, Nixon followed in office a president whose administration repeatedly lied to the public about the progress of the war. Lyndon Johnson was battered by the press on this, and the term "credibility gap" became common political parlance.

Even if the notion of a "liberal press" is only a weak assault on the myth of journalism in Watergate, it is clear that the myth, in its un-adulterated form, is overblown. Nonetheless, it remains a powerful force in the news media. When I interviewed Leonard Downie, Ben Bradlee's successor at the *Washington Post,* and at the time of Water-gate one of several editors working with Woodward and Bernstein, I distinguished between "what the *Post* did in Watergate and . . . the mythology about it, two lone reporters versus the government." Downie objected:

I want to correct you a little bit about mythology. The movie was fairly accurate but it did overly focus on just the two reporters. There were obviously other people involved, editors who were helping them figure things out and other reporters who were doing other things. But it was a small group of people against the government. And as someone who edited Carl and Bob directly through the second half of that, the question of whether the President was going to fall or not, we felt small. We did not feel big and powerful. We were not swaggering. Our responsi-bilities were huge to us. We didn't really believe the president was going to resign. Most of us were dysfunctional the night that he resigned be-cause the role which we had played in that looked overwhelming to us. We were very concerned about being right all the time. We were very concerned about the judgments we made. And we were a small group of people. As Ben [Bradlee] liked to say, we didn't have subpoena power. We didn't have the FBI. It was a small group of people doing this . . . That's still what this business is about. That's still what makes a dif-ference. That's a lesson of Watergate I want to remind people about. It was hard. It was not glamorous at the time. Later on it was glamorous with movies and movie premieres at the Kennedy Center and so on but at the time it was dirty. People weren't sleeping, people weren't show-ering, Bernstein's desk was a mess, he and Woodward were fighting all the time, they were fighting with their editors all the time, we were all under such great pressure, it was difficult to figure out what was going on because everybody was against us, because people were whispering to Katherine Graham that they'll ruin her newspaper, and that's still what it's about, you know, initiative and bravery and enterprise. That's what makes a difference.[22]

Downie's objection is eloquent, I think, but it only underscores the power of Watergate mythology. "Watergate" is indeed a myth in journalism, and I think its impact on journalism has more to do with the carrying power of this myth than with any specific social changes in the practice of journalism after Watergate. But the myth among journalists is multifaceted. Downie, knowing that he spoke on the record to an outsider, insisted on presenting the full-scale, romantic version of the myth and not a more skeptical revision. Speaking to insiders, Downie was more willing to criticize journalistic practice. Upon being named managing editor, he acknowledged to his colleagues his continuing interest in investigative reporting but added that "there was a period—after Woodward and Bernstein became household names—[in which] a number of journalists lost their perspective. Too many got caught in the thrill of the chase and it was a very, very dangerous period when a lot of people got burned."[23]

A responsible editor might well, as does Downie, emphasize different faces of the Watergate legend, depending on his different purposes and audiences. Indeed, it is fair to say that there are two myths about Watergate and journalism, and Downie is drawing on both. If there is a myth of journalism-in-Watergate, there is also one of Watergate-in-journalism. It is a myth spun about a myth, a set of tales and feelings about how journalism has changed in the past generation expressed as a set of propositions about how Watergate changed journalism. The second myth, Watergate-in-journalism, is that Watergate led to a permanently more powerful, more celebrated, and more aggressive press. This is often supported by reference to a set of presumably empirical propositions: (1) Watergate led to an extraordinary increase of interest among young people in journalism as a career; (2) Watergate created unprecedented bitterness between the President and the White House press corps; (3) Watergate turned journalists into celebrities; (4) Watergate stimulated extraordinary (and, it is often added, excessive) media interest in the private affairs of public persons; and (5) Watergate caused an unprecedented (and, many think, excessive) increase in investigative reporting. These propositions about post-Watergate journalism are widely believed, but are they true? If these changes happened, did they last? If they did, are they attributable to Watergate?

The Rush to Journalism

Watergate did not initiate a wave of interest in journalism among students. The best available data show that the number of students majoring in programs in journalism and communication began shooting upward in the mid and late 1960s.[24] Undergraduate degrees awarded in journalism doubled between 1967 and 1972. The trend continued to move upward through the mid-1970s at the same pace as in the late 1960s. One can always argue that, without Watergate, it might have tailed off more quickly (enrollments plateaued in the late 1970s but picked up again in the 1980s). But Watergate clearly did not start the rush to journalism.

Why, then, does almost everyone think otherwise? Perhaps people remember an *Atlantic* magazine cover story by Ben Bagdikian called "Woodstein U.: Notes on the Mass Production and Questionable Education of Journalists," published in March 1977. It documented the rapid growth in journalism majors at the nation's colleges and universities. But it offered nothing to indicate that Watergate or even *All the President's Men* was a cause. In fact, Bagdikian's article expressed serious concern that the advertising major within journalism schools was growing, accounting for a significant part of the overall rise in journalism and communication enrollments. Bagdikian's essay was never intended to explain increasing journalism enrollments, and the *Atlantic*'s striking cover, showing not Woodward and Bernstein but Robert Redford and Dustin Hoffman, stars of *All the President's Men,* is nowhere justified by the article. The *Atlantic*'s editors were already trading on the currency of the myth of Watergate journalism.[25]

I do not say that Watergate did not affect how young journalists thought about journalism. It did.[26] I recognize, too, that charting journalism majors is not a perfect index of the interest of young people in journalism as a career. Students majoring in history or literature or economics may have sought positions in journalism more than they did before Watergate. But even if this is true, surely any turn toward journalism was caused not by Watergate alone but by the whole context of the moralism of the sixties and the general turn to public affairs. To take Watergate as the sum and substance of what brought young people to journalism is mistaken. But it is a mythic mistake; the mythic attraction of Watergate as a key to modern journalism distracts attention from alternate sources of explaining why contemporary journalism is what it is.

It is impossible to distinguish a Watergate effect on the growing interest of young people in journalism from the vital influence of other forces simultaneously at work: the still-fresh inspiration of John Kennedy's live television press conferences; the growing salience of news to young people subject to the military draft; the growing opportunities for women in journalism; the increasing salaries of journalists, at least in national publications; the increasing profitability of local broadcast news programming; and most of all the continuing influence of national events of the 1960s—John Kennedy's assassination followed by Martin Luther King's and Robert Kennedy's; the succession of shattering reports from Vietnam, not only about the slow progress of the war but about its moral horrors.

The White House Press and the President

Journalists and observers of journalism agree that for a time after Watergate the tone of civility between the White House press corps and the White House staff vanished. Before then, the White House press corps had been a passive press corps; after Watergate it became more angry but not less passive.[27] Ron Nessen, President Ford's press secretary, attributes this to the frustration White House reporters felt at being scooped by Woodward and Bernstein, who "broke that story without ever going inside the gates of the White House." The White House correspondents decided to be investigative reporters, too, but "they thought the way to become an investigative reporter was to bang on the press secretary or ask nasty questions . . . of the president."[28] David Broder writes that White House reporters, outgunned by two unknowns, developed a "professional fury" and a style of questioning at White House briefings that became "almost more prosecutorial than inquisitive."[29]

The appearance of civility began to return to the White House press conference in the Reagan administration, perhaps less because the press grew more civil than because the White House grew more astutely managerial. The "Deaver Rule," named after Reagan aide Michael Deaver, was that reporters jumping up and down and shouting at press conferences would not be recognized. Reporters "would sit in their chairs and raise their hands," Deaver insisted, "or there would be no press conferences."[30] But relations were still not the way they had been before. Former NBC News anchorman John Chancellor recalls, "I grew up in an America where you could win debates in school by reaching in your pocket and reading official government figures. During Watergate that went out the window." (More accurately, during Vietnam it went out the window.) "I think Reagan brought it back to some degree. But not much, and the distrust is still there."[31]

How deep does the distrust go? What Watergate may have produced in the White House press conference was a public relations need of journalists to appear adversarial rather than a motivational drive to actually be adversarial. Leonard Downie insists that Watergate did not reduce the civility between press and government, with the solitary exception of the press conference. "It's misleading," he said, "to see the theater of press conferences as being representative of the actual interaction. Press conferences account for very little information gathering by the press. They're mostly stagey events."[32] But Gerald Warren, deputy secretary to Richard Nixon and now editor of the *San Diego Union*, remembers it differently. He saw a sharp decline of civility not only in White House press conferences but in private press briefings, not only at the White House but at the State Department, where, traditionally, reporters had been more diplomatic than the diplomats.[33]

Ben Bradlee, at the time I spoke with him in 1991, thought the White House press had grown all too civil. "I worry about the lack of *in*civility. The Gridiron Club? That's an embarrassment, the way that the press aspires to the establishment and, in fact, has made it."[34] Civility is not something easy to measure, but it seems clear that Watergate contributed to the uncivil expression of surface tensions between the press and the government, at the White House certainly and most likely beyond, even if the press did not become fundamentally more adversarial.

Celebrification

The proposition that Watergate propelled journalists to fame and fortune is well supported by the experience of Woodward and Bernstein. The book *All the President's Men*, when it appeared in May 1974, was the fastest-selling nonfiction hardback in the history of American publishing. It sold nearly three hundred thousand copies, and paperback rights were auctioned for a record $1,050,000.[35] A few months before the book's publication, Robert Redford, who had acquired the film rights, asked screenwriter William Goldman if he had heard of Carl

Bernstein and Bob Woodward. He had not, but he liked the manuscript Redford showed him, signed on to the project, and kept with it even though his acquaintances assured him that people had heard quite enough about Watergate.[36]

The film *All the President's Men* was released amid much publicity in the spring of 1976, during the presidential primaries. The premiere, at the Kennedy Center in Washington, was picketed by striking *Washington Post* pressmen, but, as CBS News reported, "serious Washington showed up, its men in sincere coats and ties."[37] Like the book before it, the film was critically acclaimed. It was also praised for its realism; as Nat Hentoff wrote, "In some places the gritty familiarity is so compelling that a watching reporter may get hit with the nagging feeling that he's missing a deadline while sitting there."[38] Vincent Canby, film critic for the *New York Times,* found it the most successful work ever by director Alan Pakula and screenwriter Goldman and praised it for its ability "to make understandable to non-professionals the appeal and the rewards of American journalism at its best."[39]

As the film begins, before the credits appear, the screen is white. Has the film in fact started? The audience is entitled to a moment's hesitation. Then a typewriter key vigorously and loudly slaps a "J" on what we now recognize as a blank sheet of paper: "u" "n" "e" follow as a date in June 1972 is written out. Then, suddenly, there is a cut to what appears to be old news footage, with the President's helicopter landing outside the White House and President Nixon entering and being announced at the House of Representatives to a thunderous standing ovation. Then the screen goes black. The next thing we see is security guard Frank Wills finding a taped door; the discovery of the Watergate burglary begins. It is almost as if the film announces itself as myth—white and black, the purity of the page with which the journalists work, the dark night within which the burglars operate.

All the President's Men pushed the David versus Goliath myth of Watergate journalism to its height, but in doing so it also evoked a skeptical response. The journalist as celebrity is a paradox. When journalists are doing their jobs, according to journalists' own professed ideals of objectivity, they are on the sidelines—the transcribers, perhaps the watchdogs, but not the central actors, of society's dramas. CBS news executive Barbara Stubbs Cohen, at the time of Watergate an editor of the *Washington Star,* remembers joking with Carl Bernstein that the problem with *All the President's Men* as a film is that "in most movies, when you get to a climax, somebody punches somebody, or something like that happens, and in this case they would go back and pound furiously on the computer. It didn't quite have the same dramatic impact."[40] But Woodward and Bernstein came out of *All the President's Men* (not out of Watergate itself) as national celebrities. For a journalist in 1976, this was unseemly.

It was all the more unseemly because, just as the film was released, Woodward and Bernstein had the bad taste to publish a second stunning book, *The Final Days,* an extraordinarily detailed and intimate account of Nixon's last weeks in office.[41] Critical comment within the journalistic fraternity came fast and furious. CBS news commentator Eric Sevareid spoke disapprovingly of both book and film the evening after *All the President's Men* premiered. In what seems almost a parody of journalistic "balance," he compared the excesses of Nixon with the excesses of Woodward and Bernstein: "Mr. Nixon and his intimates did not know where to stop in their quest for power; the two reporters did not know where to stop in their quest for fame and money. A pause, at least, was in order. There is something in life called the decent interval." He concluded with the observation that Kennedy and Roosevelt were in the grave before their private peccadilloes were exposed. "Not even the cannibals feasted on living flesh."[42]

Reaction to journalism's heroics in Watergate had in some measure already set in. In March 1974 William B. Arthur, executive director of the watchdog National News Council, warned that "the press must be wary of overkill" in Watergate.[43] Speaking before the Magazine Publishers Association, Katherine Graham worried soon after Watergate about a "new and rather indiscriminate emphasis on disclosure as the index of fitness for public office."[44] But this rivulet of cautionary comment became a torrent of criticism with the appearance of *The Final Days* and the transformation of Woodward and Bernstein, heroes of the myth of journalism-in-Watergate, into Redford/Woodward and Hoffman/Bernstein, the trickster figures of Watergate-in-journalism. In May 1976, a month after *All the President's Men* opened, Associated Press general manager Wes Gallagher complained to the American Newspaper Publishers Association (ANPA) annual meeting that Watergate had let loose "an investigative reporting binge of monumental proportions." He chided his colleagues: "The First Amendment is not a hunting license, as some today seem to think." ANPA chairman Harold W. Anderson criticized journalists who "almost joyously cast themselves in the role of an adversary of government officials."[45]

The Final Days became very controversial. Several people whom Woodward and Bernstein interviewed, including Henry Kissinger and

Nixon sons-in-law Edward Cox and David Eisenhower, disclaimed parts of the work that the book suggested they could confirm. Some fellow journalists were up in arms over a narrative constructed primarily of unattributed statements, including the technique of citing as direct quotations statements from conversations that Woodward and Bernstein had obviously reconstructed from the fallible, and self-serving, memories of their informants. This was, wrote *New Republic* White House correspondent John Osborne, "the worst job of nationally noted reporting that I've observed during 49 years in the business." There were some glowing reviews, ecstatic reviews, but even these mentioned the widespread reservations about journalistic method.[46]

Watergate certainly contributed to the celebrification of journalists and the notoriety of celebrification. However, other factors contributed decisively, too. The development of the Public Broadcasting System, with a new range of news programs, and cable TV's rapidly growing appetite for relatively cheap, easy-to-produce news programs, created a growing *organizational* demand for journalists to appear on television. By the 1980s the call for televisable journalists was enormous, from "Nightline" to "The McLaughlin Group," both of which, as James Fallows observed, "magnify journalists' celebrity and blur the distinction between journalists and politicians."[47] Once celebrified on television, journalists became more and more bankable on the lecture circuit, too.[48]

Celebrification is a part of a larger development, the rising status of Washington journalists. In Washington people are measured by their clout, and after Watergate, rightly or wrongly, the clout of journalists has been judged greater than ever before. Salaries have increased, and educational levels may have risen, too, although the evidence on the latter is more equivocal than popular accounts of journalism generally assume.[49] But there is certainly a widespread perception of rising status. "There are no drunks in this business any more, you know, we really dressed up pretty good," Ben Bradlee remarked.[50]

Ironically, the improving status of journalism as a field may owe more to Richard Nixon than to Woodward and Bernstein. From the beginning of his presidency, Nixon insisted on treating the press as the enemy and identifying it as a distinct power center in American life rather than as a representative of the public or a medium through which other power centers speak.[51] "In all the world of 'us against them,' " William Safire wrote in his memoir of the Nixon administration before Watergate, "the press was the quintessential 'them,' the fount and the succor of other 'thems.' "

In terms of power, the academic "them" was insignificant; the social-cultural elitist "them" was useful as a foil that would help attract workingmen to a Nixon coalition; the liberal, political "them" was in the process of destroying itself by narrowing its base along severe ideological-faddist lines; but the journalistic "them" was formidable and infuriating, a force to be feared in its own right, but even more important, a magnifying glass and public address system that gave strength and attention to all the other "thems."[52]

Nixon came into office with Lyndon Johnson's credibility gap standing between the presidency and the public. At first he proclaimed openness and sought to contrast his administration to Johnson's. His communications director, Herbert Klein, declared: "Truth will be the hallmark of the Nixon Administration . . . We will be able to eliminate any possibility of a credibility gap in this Administration." But Nixon quickly came to treat the press as his enemy. By the fall of his first year in office, he regularly instructed his staff to "get" this or that reporter or news institution.[53] In November 1969, he unleashed Vice President Spiro Agnew for a speech in Des Moines, Iowa, that blasted the television news establishment.[54] Agnew's widely discussed speech was written by Nixon's own speech writer, Patrick J. Buchanan. A week later Agnew struck again with a speech adding the *New York Times* and *Washington Post* to the list of dangerous elite media. Harassing the news media became established White House policy.

For all the importance of Agnew's public attacks, perhaps the more important war went on behind the scenes. White House officials were generally uncooperative with the press. Reporters were frozen out of relations with the President or his aides, often on Nixon's explicit instructions.[55] The White House "press conference" was renamed the "news conference" to emphasize that it belonged to the President, not to the press.[56] Moreover, Nixon's concerns about leaks—a perennial presidential concern—led him to wiretap illegally a number of journalists, including syndicated columnist Joseph Kraft, reporters Hedrick Smith and William Beecher *(New York Times)*, Marvin Kalb (CBS), and Henry Brandon *(London Sunday Times)*.[57] The administration prosecuted the Pentagon Papers case, seeking "prior restraint" of the press—suppressing publication rather than prosecuting after publication—for the first time in American national history. The Nixon-appointed FCC chairman, at the request of the White House, sought to intimidate uncooperative newscasters, while the White House office of telecommunications policy prodded local affiliates to pressure their networks to report on Nixon more favorably. The *Washington Post's*

Florida broadcast stations were challenged in license renewals by known friends of Nixon on advice from the President.[58] The FBI investigated CBS correspondent Daniel Schorr at the request of the White House. White House pressure on CBS executives led CBS just before the 1972 election to cut short a special report on Watergate.[59]

The administration's aim was not only to make the President look good but to make the press as an institution look bad. H. R. Haldeman wrote Herb Klein a memo in early 1970 urging him to get the story out in the media that Nixon had overcome the "great handicaps under which he came into office," namely, "the hostile press epitomized by the NEW YORK TIMES, WASHINGTON POST, TIME, NEWS-WEEK, etc., the hostile network commentators, the generally hostile White House press corps, the hostile Congress, etc."[60] This was a persistent theme in the Nixon White House. Haldeman's assistant Larry Higby wrote to Klein later the same year that an important public relations point to be made was that "RN is the first President in this century who came into the Presidency with the opposition of all . . . major communication powers."[61]

In the heat of Watergate Nixon personally lashed out at the press. After the Saturday Night Massacre, Nixon gave a televised press conference in which he called television news coverage of him "outrageous, vicious, distorted." Asked by CBS correspondent Robert Pierpoint what in particular about the coverage made him angry, Nixon replied that he was not angry. Pierpoint said he got the impression he was. Nixon explained, "You see, one can only be angry with those he respects."[62]

The outcome of the Nixon administration's calculated attacks on the press was just what *Chicago Daily News* reporter Peter Lisagor suggested at the time—that the Nixon administration successfully promoted for the news media an identity separate from that of the public.[63] The very term "the media" was promoted by the Nixon White House because it sounded unpleasant, manipulative, a much less favorable term than "the press."[64] The Nixon administration insisted that the media were not, as they often claimed to be, the voice of the people. Nor were they, as many had traditionally understood them, the voice of wealthy publishers, on the one hand, or the organs of political parties, on the other. Instead, they were an independent and dangerously irresponsible source of power. The aggressiveness of the *Washington Post* in Watergate, then, not only enacted and enlarged an old script of muckraking but at the same time played out a scenario drafted by the Nixon White House.

Not surprisingly, like the myth of journalism-in-Watergate, the myth of Watergate-in-journalism serves two masters: both government, which employs it to portray itself as unfairly besieged; and journalism, which uses it to present itself as a brave and independent social force. Both usages veil the fact that, for the most part, there remains a comfortable and cooperative relationship between public officials and the press in Washington.

The Rise of Prurient Reporting

The private lives of national public figures have been featured more prominently in the news in the two decades since Watergate than in the two decades before. Watergate helped stimulate this, particularly when the White House transcripts produced extraordinary shock and prurient interest in the private language and private attitudes of President Nixon and his top advisers. Later, *The Final Days* renewed this. Still, contemporary journalistic fascination with writing about the private lives of public figures owes more to Edward Kennedy and Chappaquiddick in 1969 than to Richard Nixon and Watergate in 1972–1974.[65] It owes much, too, to the way Jimmy Carter, first among equals in this regard, promoted "character" as a chief criterion for presidential candidates in 1976. It owes something to the women's movement and its insistence that private life is political, and that the dividing line between public and private is a politically constituted boundary. No doubt the newly intimate reporting of politics is indebted also to Theodore White and the new brand of behind-the-scenes political reporting he pioneered, as well as to the face-to-face, close-up approach brought to television news by "60 Minutes."[66]

In any event, prurient reporting has brought down on journalism a tidal wave of criticism. Robert Redford, speaking in 1983 to the American Society of Newspaper Editors about celebrity coverage in the press, questioned whether Watergate's lasting impact on the press was a good one. Ten or twelve years earlier, he wishfully and wistfully claimed, there had been a clear line between privacy and what the public needed to know.[67] But this is not so. Watergate was a factor but not the key factor in creating new patterns of intimate inquiry in political reporting.

The Rise of Investigative Reporting

Did Watergate lead to an increase in investigative reporting? That depends on what "investigative reporting" is. Of course, Watergate was not the beginning of an adversarial relationship between the government and the Washington press corps. The key event was Vietnam, not Watergate, and the "credibility gap" that drew the press toward deep distrust of government voices first came to a head in Johnson's administration, not Nixon's. But the real question is not whether investigative reporting increased—all signs indicate that it did—but when this increase began and whether it was transient. Only a few news institutions devoted significant new resources to investigation, even in the aftermath of Watergate, and many of these began their investment in investigation before that. *Newsday* established an investigative team in 1967, the Associated Press in 1967, the *Chicago Tribune* in 1968, the *Boston Globe* in 1970. The *New York Times* devoted increasing resources to investigative work through the 1960s. Auxiliary institutions appeared to stimulate more critical and investigative journalism: some two dozen journalism reviews (only a few of which survived into the 1980s) beginning with the *Chicago Journalism Review* in 1968; the Fund for Investigative Journalism (1969), which provided small grants to journalists doing investigative work; and Investigative Reporters and Editors (1975), a membership organization to promote investigate reporting.[68]

But investigative reporting is not a priority for most institutions today, nor has it ever been. "A main thing to say about newspaper editors is they're not crusaders," former *Washington Post* editor Barry Sussman told me.[69] Stephen Hess argues that investigative work became fashionable "for a relatively short time." Journalists "took great satisfaction in thinking of themselves as great investigators, but that's not what most of the press is most of the time." After editors assigned reporters to hunt for a new "gate" a few times and they came back not with a "gate" but with a mouse, Hess suggests, only institutions with enormous resources would take that risk again.[70]

The influence of Watergate on investigative journalism was most evident in the immediate aftermath of Watergate, and most devastating, after the brief Ford interlude, for President Jimmy Carter. Carter cooperated in opening up his administration to any charges of hypocrisy or corruption because he had so willingly taken up Watergate as his implicit presidential campaign anthem. In the wake of Watergate, it would have been hard for the press not to take that as a challenge. Journalists in Washington were newly aware of government deceit and newly hungry for investigative work. "One by-product of the Watergate adventure," wrote Charles Seib in the *Washington Post* in 1977, "was a journalistic fad: investigative reporting."[71] As Ben Bradlee put it, reporters, especially young reporters, "covered the most routine rural fires as if they were Watergate and would come back and argue that there was gasoline in the hose and the fire chief was an anti-Semite and they really thought that was the way to fame and glory."[72]

Early in his term, Carter was faced with the Bert Lance affair. That it rocked the administration as badly as it did was in many ways a post-Watergate phenomenon. But Lancegate was just the beginning for the Carter administration. The Carter years were a time, Jimmy Carter himself has noted, "when every reporter thought, well, since they found horrible events in the president's life in Watergate, maybe there's something here. If we dig deep enough, we'll find it."[73] Both Gerald Ford's press secretary, Ron Nessen, and Carter's, Jody Powell, complained that the media saw Vietnam and Watergate everywhere. James Deakin, White House correspondent for the *St. Louis Post-Dispatch*, agreed: "The imprint of catastrophe is slow to fade. When a full realization of disaster sinks into the fabric of 200 million people, it is hard to dislodge. It was a long time before Americans forgot the Depression of the 1930's. It was the same with Vietnam and Watergate. The public had been badly burned and was wary. The reporters, intensely so."[74] Bob Woodward said of the media's pursuit of President Jimmy Carter's chief of staff, Hamilton Jordan, for alleged cocaine use at a New York disco: "You have to remember that our experience for the past ten or fifteen years has been that in the end the government official always ended up being guilty as charged. We just didn't run across people whose defense held up under close scrutiny." And a *New York Times* reporter on the Hamilton Jordan story explained that he believed Jordan was guilty because "in every case that I can remember, the politician turned out to be lying."[75]

By the Reagan years, the investigative binge seemed over. In part, it could not last: no Watergates were turned up after years of digging. Journalists grew discouraged. In part, leaders in journalism came down hard on overzealous investigative work themselves. In part, Ronald Reagan was just terribly good at public relations, at least in his first term.

And, in part, the second myth of Watergate and the media took hold. Where the film *All the President's Men* glorified and popularized the journalism-in-Watergate myth, the second myth, Watergate-in-journalism, received a film presentation in *Absence of Malice*. This 1981 film directed by Sydney Pollack, which brought in Oscars for best actor (Paul Newman) and best supporting actress (Melinda Dillon), announced itself in its opening sequence as the post-

Watergate journalism film. Where *All the President's Men* closes with the soothingly old-fashioned staccato of teletype, *Absence of Malice* opens with shots of the high-tech laying out and printing of a newspaper page with photo-offset technology. *All the President's Men* implied that dubious reportorial tactics may be justified when the press takes out after a powerful public leader (who, indeed, turns out to be guilty of crimes); *Absence of Malice* condemned the tactics of a newspaper going after a private person (who, in fact, turns out to be not guilty). The audience that sees *All the President's Men* from the point of view of Woodward and Bernstein is tutored by the camera in *Absence of Malice* to watch the action from the point of view of journalism's victims. There is a scene in which the victim, Michael Gallagher (Paul Newman), comes to plead his case before the newspaper reporter, editor, and lawyer. In one powerful moment the audience looks up across the table, from Gallagher's view, to see the reporter and editor, impassive, remote, unreachable, and unfeeling about Gallagher and the possibility they may be doing him an injustice. Although the film makes no explicit reference to Watergate, the contrast to *All the President's Men* could not be more pointed.[76]

Despite all the suggestions of Watergate's influence on post-Watergate journalism, there is something remarkably elusive about it. The "null hypothesis," that Watergate did *not* change journalism at all, has some unlikely adherents. Carl Bernstein leaned toward the null hypothesis in remarks he made at the Kennedy School in 1989: "Watergate has not had the effect one would have hoped it would have . . . we haven't seen any truly significant breakthroughs in journalism" since Richard Nixon resigned.[77] Bob Woodward also inclined toward this view in suggesting some years ago that Watergate was a "blip" in the history of journalism, not the defining moment of a new era.[78]

After Watergate Woodward moved onward and upward to an editorial position at the *Post,* producing one book after another of reporting—after *The Final Days* (with Bernstein) there was *The Brethren* (with Scott Armstrong) and *Wired* (on John Belushi), *Veil* (on William Casey and the CIA), and *The Commanders* (on the Pentagon).[79] The triumph of each of these books—all best sellers—was marred by continued criticism of Woodward's methods. Why the unattributed quotations? Why the unnamed sources? What warrant is there for the reconstruction of exact dialogue at meetings that Woodward did not attend and that witnesses were asked to recall days, weeks, or even years later? This kind of questioning was only encouraged by the fact that Woodward was Janet Cooke's editor for the "Jimmy World" story that won a Pulitzer Prize in 1980 but then lost the prize when it turned out that the child heroin addict at the center of the story was the reporter's invention. Cooke was fired, and the *Washington Post,* Bob Woodward included, was red with embarrassment.

Woodward was controversial again as the editor on a story in 1979 concerning William Tavoulareas, chief executive officer of Mobil Oil. When I spoke with Woodward in 1991, he suggested that the Court of Appeals decision in the Tavoulareas libel suit against the *Washington Post* was a more important watershed in the history of journalism than was Watergate.

The *Tavoulareas* decision is indeed extremely interesting, but it, and Woodward's own role in it, may confirm rather than deny the importance of Watergate in journalism. The story described Tavoulareas as "setting up" his son Peter in a firm that did business with Mobil. Tavoulareas sued the *Post* for libel for the story's implication that he had not carried out his obligations to Mobil stockholders in the decisions concerning his son. Tavoulareas won with the jury at the trial court in 1983. The judge overturned the verdict, however, ordering a "judgment notwithstanding the verdict," an option open to federal judges who find that no reasonable jury could have come to its verdict without misapplying the law. This decision was reversed by a three-judge panel of the appeals court in 1985, but this judgment itself was overturned when the full appeals court met to decide the case in 1987.

The myth of Watergate was curiously implicated in *Tavoulareas.* The *Washington Post* hired a private research firm to survey a sample of potential jurors to find if their sympathies would likely lie with the *Post* or with Mobil. They discovered a leaning in their favor; one *Washington Post* source said, "I guess we were associated with the downfall of Nixon, which in D.C. had to help us."[80]

So the *Post* requested a jury trial. In the trial, the *Post*'s attorney never mentioned Watergate. Woodward urged that he be questioned on the witness stand to bring out his role in Watergate, but the attorney said, "No, let them discover you're Robert Redford and that Ben is Jason Robards." He assumed that the *Post*'s role in Watergate would be so well known to District of Columbia jurors that the *Post* would win greater favor without pressing the point. In fact, none of the six jurors had seen *All the President's Men,* only one knew that Woodward or Bradlee had played a role in Watergate, and no one in the jury room mentioned Watergate.

The jurors focused on the question of whether the *Post* story on

Tavoulareas was true or false and neglected the central matter of whether the journalists had pursued their story recklessly and with "actual malice." While the jurors ignored this question, the prosecution did not. It raised issues about malice that were rooted in Bob Woodward's Watergate-related career. Judge George MacKinnon, writing the majority opinion for the divided three-judge panel, leaned heavily on this evidence. MacKinnon argued that the jury could have reasonably considered the *Post*'s general orientation—including Woodward's own reputation for "high-impact investigative stories of wrongdoing"—as placing great pressure on reporters under his supervision to arrive at similar stories.[81]

When the full court reversed the three-judge panel in 1987, Judge Kenneth Starr, writing for the majority, observed that some of the evidence of "malice" that MacKinnon found was nothing more than an appropriately adversarial stance. "It would be sadly ironic for judges in our adversarial system to conclude," he wrote, "that the mere taking of an adversarial stance is antithetical to the truthful presentation of facts." For Judge MacKinnon, it was evidence of malice to say, in the words of the *Post*'s chief reporter on the story, that "it is not every day you knock off one of the seven sisters" (one of the seven largest oil companies). But for Judge Starr, this "is certainly not indicative of actual malice under the circumstances where, as here, the reporter conducted a detailed investigation and wrote a story that is substantially true."

As for the evidence of malice in Bob Woodward's use of the term "holy shit story" to describe the kind he looked for from his reporters, Judge Starr was equally unimpressed. Only if there is managerial pressure to produce "holy shit stories" without regard for their accuracy, he wrote, could this be evidence of malice. At no time did the evidence suggest that Woodward was unconcerned about accuracy. And, indeed, the Tavoulareas story was, Starr repeated, thoroughly researched and "largely accurate." MacKinnon, in dissent, argued that the issue is not whether the *Post* "subjectively desired false stories" but whether "extra-heavy pressure to produce sensationalistic stories could motivate reporters to stretch the truth." But Starr held that, far from providing evidence of malice, pressure for high-impact investigative stories of wrongdoing was laudable: "We agree with the *Post* that the First Amendment forbids penalizing the press for encouraging its reporters to expose wrongdoing by public corporations and public figures. Rather, such managerial pressure is designed to produce stories that serve, as the panel majority rightly stated, 'one of the highest functions of the press in our society.' "[82]

Starr's decision not only backed up the *Washington Post* but provided a ringing defense of the right of the press to engage in aggressive investigative reporting, seeking out wrongdoing in high places. But Woodward places too much weight on the majesty of the law, I think, to suggest that Starr's 1987 opinion will have greater influence on journalism in the long run than Woodward and Bernstein's 1972 and 1973 reporting on Watergate. He overestimates the power of a single judicial decision, especially one that proposes no new legal doctrine.

At the same time, Woodward underestimates the power of a journalistic story become legend. The story about Watergate that has come down to us may matter much more than specific institutional changes that can be attributed to Watergate and Watergate alone. The story is in many respects distorted, overemphasizing the heroism of journalists, underestimating the heroism of bureaucrats, neglecting the role of other agents of investigation, and ignoring the accidents and luck that made the uncovering of Watergate possible. But that does not matter. Even when the revisionists have had their say, the enormity of what began with Woodward and Bernstein remains astonishing. That they did not uncover Watergate alone is true. The press as a whole during Watergate was, as before and since, primarily an establishment institution with few ambitions to rock establishment boats. But that doesn't matter either. What matters is that events, circumstances, and the energy, drive, ambition, competitiveness, and courage of some young reporters and their editors at a liberal Washington daily kept alive a story that eventually drove a president from office for the only time in our history. And that kernel of truth sustains the general myth and gives it, for all of its "inaccuracies," a kind of larger truth that is precisely what myths are for: not to tell us in empirical detail who we are but what we may have been once, what we might again become, what we would be like "if."

In that regard Leonard Downie was right to object to the skepticism implied in my use of the term "myth." Who cares if journalism during Watergate was generally lazy? Or if Judge Sirica or some FBI agents were as vital to Nixon's undoing as were Woodward and Bernstein? It does not matter, because the Watergate myth is sustaining. It survives to a large extent impervious to critique. It offers journalism a charter, an inspiration, a reason for being large enough to justify the constitutional protections that journalism enjoys.

A myth is not always invoked. It is what *Los Angeles Times* reporter Thomas Rosenstiel calls an "institutional memory, sometimes slumbering, sometimes not, and it is kicked in sometimes by events." The journalists "trot out" this memory "on occasions when it's triggered, when it's appropriate, when we think it's safe, when we're not leading public opinion too much, when all the conditions and all the stars line up."[83] And if the myth of journalism-in-Watergate is not invoked, the companion myth of Watergate-in-journalism may be, the latter as antiheroic as the former is romantic.

Myths necessarily have multiple meanings; in fancier terms, they are "polysemous." They do not tell a culture's simple truths so much as they explore its central dilemmas. They can be read many ways, and the myth of Watergate journalism certainly has been. The myth has empowered the enemies of a bold journalism just as it has inspired practitioners of aggressive reporting. The Watergate myth of the independent and irresponsible "media" is as much the willful creation of Richard Nixon as the accidental invention of Woodward and Bernstein. For better and for worse, it is the crystallization of the hopes and fears and confusions of American society about its own increasingly prominent news media.

When I interviewed media analyst Stephen Hess, he interviewed me, too: Could you accept, he asked, the conclusion that Watergate did not affect journalism? I waffled for a moment, then put on my best scientific front and said that of course, if that's where the evidence led me, I would be prepared to come to that conclusion, only I believed that the culture of journalism had changed even if the institutional apparatus had not. What I did not see then, and believe I can argue now, is that myths may themselves become part of an institutional apparatus, like corporate goodwill, like any tradition, like language itself. Although a tradition of muckraking preceded Watergate, Watergate gave it flesh and blood (Woodward and Bernstein), as well as an unforgettable knock-out-punch triumph (Nixon's resignation), however unfairly attributed to journalism. Watergate, by forcing a president to resign, was an exploding supernova in the sky of journalism, blotting out the record of investigative work during Vietnam. It was not only more salient, it was more consensual. Seymour Hersh's work in uncovering the My Lai massacre was too bloody and devastating and divisive a report to hold up as the epitome of American enterprise journalism. Watergate, at least retrospectively, could be widely accepted as a triumph not only of American journalism but of the American system of a free press.

What is most important to journalism is not the spate of investigative reporting or the recoil from it after Watergate but the renewal, reinvigorization, and remythologization of muckraking. The muckraking theme has been powerful in American journalism for a century, even though its practice is the exception, not the rule. It is hard work. It is painstaking. It is expensive. It is often unrewarding. It runs against the ideological grain of professional neutrality. It has official celebrants within the world of journalism, especially in the form of the prestigious Pulitzer Prize for public service. Still, in the time between Lincoln Steffens, Ida Tarbell, and Ray Stannard Baker in 1904, and Woodward and Bernstein in 1972 and 1973, it had no culturally resonant, heroic exemplars. But Woodward and Bernstein did not simply renew, they extended the power of the muckraking image. In the age of Steffens, the symbolically central White House seemed exempt from muckraking. Steffens tried his hand at it, only to be wined, dined, and charmed by Theodore Roosevelt.[84] Indeed, for the turn-of-the-century muckrakers, the federal government was a resource for pressuring state and local government, the primary seat of the corruption Steffens unearthed, not a locus for muckraking itself.

If President Nixon himself had not ultimately been implicated in the Watergate scandal, if the scandal had stopped with Jeb Magruder, no one would remember Watergate. If the scandal had stopped with Mitchell, Haldeman, Ehrlichman, and Dean, Watergate would be remembered as a great journalistic coup, bringing investigation into the White House itself. But it would not be the heart of American journalism mythology. Watergate found a president guilty of crimes, waist-deep in deception, and forced him from office. That makes Watergate, with all of its complexities for the press, the unavoidable central myth of American journalism.

III Citizenship and Its Discontents

8 National News Culture and the Informational Citizen

If being well informed means having at hand reliable information about the community and nation, the international world as it impinges on national interests, the natural world, and the world of the arts, then Americans have never before been so well informed nor so abundantly served by broadcasting, the press, and publishing.

If, however, being well informed means having a world view coherent enough to order the buzz of information around us, and having enough personal involvement with people, ideas, and issues beyond our private worlds to absorb and use information, then there is little reason for self-congratulation. This second sense is more nearly what we mean, or should mean, by "the well-informed citizen." The well-informed citizen is defined not by a consumer's familiarity with the contemporary catalog of available information but by a citizen's formed set of interests that make using the catalog something other than a random effort. The news media increasingly help to provide the materials for the *informational* citizen, but they do not and cannot create the *informed* citizen. The informed citizen appears in a society in which being informed makes good sense, and that is a function not of individual character or news media performance, but of political culture, broadly defined.

Well-reported news, free from censorship, does not a democracy make. Full and accurate reporting of candidates' records and policy positions, even if we had that, would not a well-prepared voter create. What, then, is the impact of all the information around us? What sort of person does it help establish or, at least, set the conditions for? Who are we, these informational people, who daily digest political scandal here and an earthquake there, a crime wave in our home town and a guerrilla movement in El Salvador, a ban on alcohol at the local beach and a surgeon general's report on passive smoking, a protest against local developers and a worried report on Third World debt? Are we disabled by media saturation? Distracted or deadened or at least thrown off stride by the avalanche of information?

I don't think that's what happens. People probably muddle through their lives as well today as people ever did (although that may not apply to the poorest residents of urban ghettos). Indeed, they may muddle along a little better, armed with the view that the world is subject to their control. Fundamental matters of fertility, contraception, sexual satisfaction, pain relief, and contact with other human beings across a distance are all more within human capacity and even individual control than ever before. At the same time, different groups in society feel newly entitled to control over their lives—notably blacks and women—and they have found broad political support for their sense of entitlement.

The growth of the media, the explosion of information, and the pounding headache of hype have not prevented this; on the contrary, they have helped it along. Most anxious and apocalyptic commentators on the media forget these and other fundamental realities. Without firmly planting their feet in sociological soil, they examine the media out of social context, picturing them as self-contained technologies rather than porous social practices, and they often ask unreasonably that "art" or "truth" flow from the media spigot.

Often critics find major cause for alarm in a trend or development of the past year or five years or decade, although, in a somewhat larger compass, our media environment has not changed. The media in the United States in the 1990s, as in the 1960s, are more completely controlled by private corporations than are the media in any other industrialized country in the world. The range of political opinion available in mainstream media in the United States is narrower than in much of Western Europe; this has been true not only for the last generation but for much of American history. At the same time, the freedom of the American media to investigate and to publish is more supported by institutional resources and more protected by constitutional safeguards than in any other country, both today and thirty years ago.

Despite these fundamental continuities in the American media, changes in the past thirty years have significantly altered the ordinary person's experience of popular and public culture and have surely enlarged the role of the media, especially the news media. One sign of change is that the concept of "the media" itself has become inescapable. The term *the media* (meaning, especially, the news media), was not much used before the 1970s. It came into play, I think, in part because the term *the press* began to seem limited as a descriptor of both print and broadcast journalism (although the term survives in this usage). It gained wide exposure thanks to the Nixon administration's vendetta against "the media." Nixon inherited both the Vietnam war and Lyndon Johnson's "credibility gap." He and Vice President Spiro Agnew declared war on the news media, arguing publicly and privately that the nation's leading news institutions were an independent source of political power managed by bleeding-heart liberals and dyed-in-the-wool Nixon-haters. This forceful attack helped create the beast it sought to describe. It certainly helped give the beast a name.

So, too, did Vietnam and Watergate and the events leading up to what Hedrick Smith has described as the "political earthquake" of 1974.[1] As Vietnam tore apart consensus between the executive and the Congress in the conduct of foreign policy, between hawks and doves within the Congress, between parents and children even in families where fathers were Cabinet officers or *New York Times* editors, the media scrambled to represent these divisions. When governing leaders spoke in a single voice, so did the press; when dissent sparked on the floor of the Senate, it fired the media. If the media followed rather than led the breakdown of consensus, they learned from the experience a new style of journalism. In covering Vietnam and Watergate, journalists did not abandon "objectivity" so much as recognize what a poor shadow of objective reporting they had been allegiant to for a generation. Journalism sought, sometimes awkwardly, sometimes irresponsibly, sometimes bravely and brilliantly, to invent the independence it had long claimed to exercise. This, too, helped establish "the media" as a distinct institution.

The present uneasy feeling of media omnipresence and information overload comes in part from this sharp, visible presence of the media as an institution. It comes also from the increasing nationalization of the news media and the identification of the nation itself as an "imagined community," to use Benedict Anderson's phrase, with the national news. It comes as well from other transformations in the character of mass-mediated information—the blurring of the line between news and entertainment, the melding of public and private and the

National News Culture   171

politicization of once-private affairs, and the increasing efficiency of organizations that "target" messages to specialized audiences. All of this makes American citizens informational cousins, even if we are not a particularly close-knit family. These are the features of cultural transformation I want to discuss in the sections that follow.

Nationalization of the News Media, 1960–1990

"Nationalization" did not happen all at once. In fact, Godfrey Hodgson has argued that the "nationalizing of the American consciousness" was the primary trend in the media in the late 1950s and early 1960s.[2] But in 1960 or even 1963, the machinery of nationalization was only partially in place, the political and social consequences of cultural nationalization still on the horizon of consciousness, the sense that citizens know too much about things they can do too little about not so keenly experienced.

A national television news system, present in the 1950s, took on new importance in the 1960s and later. The 30-minute format (instead of 15) became standard in 1963. In that same year the Roper poll found, for the first time, more Americans claiming to rely on television than on newspapers as their primary source of news. To the three network evening news shows were added "60 Minutes" (in 1968) and its imitators, "20/20" (1978) and others. ABC began a late-night news program in 1979 called "America Held Hostage," a daily update of the Iranian hostage crisis. In 1980, its name changed to "Nightline" and it became a regular part of the broadcast news diet.

Only in the 1970s did news on television take on a central role in the thinking of the broadcasting corporations themselves as "60 Minutes" became the most highly rated program in the country and local news began to turn big profits. "60 Minutes" made television news interesting and profitable. This economic maturing of television news coincided with its political coming of age. When President Kennedy began holding live televised press conferences, television as a regular news source gained an official imprimatur (the famous Murrow-on-McCarthy programs of the early 1950s were exceptional; television news was generally superficial, unvisual, and short). It was not until the Vietnam war that television news coverage took on a centrality, both for Washington elites and for the public at large. Then the evening news became the symbolic center of the national agenda and the national consciousness. Political campaigners measured their success as much by seconds on the evening news as by polls; presidents—notably Johnson and Nixon—became obsessed with the television screen.

Within two decades of the time when television network news became ringmaster of the American circus, network dominance was challenged. The networks in 1970 had no competition; only 10 percent of American homes had cable systems. By 1989 the figure was 53 percent. The networks' share of total television viewership has steadily declined, so much so that in 1990 the networks formed their own public relations firm to promote themselves collectively against cable (and other) competition.[3] In news gathering in recent years, new technologies have enabled local television stations to steal a march on the networks. The availability to local stations of vans equipped with satellite dishes, combined with the growing costs of syndicated news programs, has led to several satellite-connected consortiums of local stations that cover national news events on their own. The combined audience for the three evening network news programs has declined by nearly 25 percent since 1980.[4]

In 1979, the cable industry began C-SPAN as a public service gesture. C-SPAN's tiny audience is important, and the presence of C-SPAN in the Congress has affected the conduct of public affairs. The House of Representatives was on C-SPAN from the beginning; the Senate came along in 1986.[5] Cable News Network (CNN) began operations in 1980; it provided news around the clock and quickly established a reputation for responsible reporting. Also unknown in President Kennedy's day was television news on public television; by 1975, the Public Broadcasting System brought the MacNeil-Lehrer program to most communities.

As television news has expanded, radio news has had something of a renaissance. In 1970, noncommercial and educational radio licensees formed National Public Radio and a year later launched their first network news program, "All Things Considered." The NPR audience is relatively small (seven million listeners) but devoted;[6] among academics a reference to a recent "All Things Considered" interview is as likely to be common coin as reference to a current Hollywood hit.

News means money on radio as well as television. There had been some experiments with an all-news format in the 1950s, but only in 1964, when WINS in New York became an all-news station, did the phenomenon attract general attention. WCBS joined as a second all-news station in New York in 1967. Soon dozens of cities had all-news stations. "When you want water," said one station manager, "you turn on the faucet. When you want news, you turn us on."[7]

Equally important, "talk radio" became lively and popular. Larry King's nationally syndicated show made its debut on 28 stations in 1978 but eventually served more than 350. CNN adapted it to television in 1985, and by 1990 the program was running nightly on both radio and television. There were interview programs before Larry King's, but his innovation (begun in Miami in 1960) was to add live call-ins to the interview format.[8] News, or "reality programming," has become a pervasive cultural experience.

In the 1990s, if I want to get a copy of the *New York Times* or the *Wall Street Journal* in my home town of San Diego, I need only open my front door and pick up my home-delivery copy on the driveway. As late as 1971, when Anthony Russo had a strong incentive to read the *New York Times* because it was publishing the Pentagon Papers, which he had helped Daniel Ellsberg photocopy, there were only a few locations in Los Angeles where the paper could be found.[9] Overcoming the vast size of the country, satellite communication technology and computerized printing systems have made the regional and national newspaper a reality.

The *Wall Street Journal* has had a national presence for some time, but in the past generation it has sharply increased its coverage as a general newspaper rather than an exclusively business newsletter. It expanded to a two-section format in 1980. The *Los Angeles Times,* when Otis Chandler became publisher in 1960, had one foreign bureau and two reporters in its Washington bureau. It was a provincial, conservative paper that, within a decade, developed into a distinguished, professional newspaper. The same thing happened at the *Washington Post.* When the late Howard Simons joined the *Post* in the early 1960s, the paper had a single foreign correspondent and a single business reporter. Not until it released the Pentagon Papers in 1971, according to editor Ben Bradlee, did the *Post* make "some kind of ultimate commitment to go super first class."[10]

Another indicator of nationalization is that elite newspaper news services began to compete with the standard Associated Press (AP) and United Press International (UPI) services. The *Los Angeles Times–Washington Post* news service began in 1961 and grew to more than 350 clients by 1980. The *New York Times* news service began during World War I, but as late as 1960 had only 50 clients; by 1980 there were 500 clients. These news services are not so much high-fiber substitutes for the traditional wire services as they are dietary supplements, adding more detailed and analytic news for the local subscriber. So while metropolitan daily newspapers have continued to die, new sources of national news have become available. *Time* and *Newsweek* developed into professional publications, and other magazines provided new sources of public affairs news and comment, too, including the *Washington Post* national weekly edition (1983) and several magazines that reached a mass market—notably *Rolling Stone* and *Mother Jones*.

The largest and most prosperous newspapers exert regional influence well beyond city limits. The *Los Angeles Times* challenges the *Orange County Register* in Orange County. In Santa Cruz, California, the local daily, the *Sentinel* (owned by Ottaway Newspapers, a Dow-Jones company), is only one of several newspapers available by home delivery: there are also the *New York Times*, the *San Francisco Chronicle*, the *San Jose Mercury-News* (a Knight-Ridder paper), and the *Wall Street Journal*.

All this needs emphasis when the most visible national newspaper is the flashy and widely disparaged *USA Today*. Begun in 1982, it had a circulation of more than 1.5 million by 1987. Printed in thirty-two different sites and produced by satellite transmission of copy, it is a technical achievement of considerable proportion. There is some question about the paper's journalistic achievement, though little dispute about its influence on the look and style of other newspapers in the country. It initiated widespread use of color, for example. Its almost pathological focus on the weather has encouraged more comprehensive weather reporting elsewhere.[11]

While an average citizen has access to more, better, more critical, and more diverse sources of national news today than a generation ago, control over news is paradoxically in the hands of fewer and fewer institutions, run more and more by accountants. The chain newspapers are not so much politically conservative as economically risk-averse, which generally comes to the same thing. (In 1986 there were 1,657 dailies, down only slightly from 1,763 in 1960—and the number of cities with a daily newspaper actually increased. But a mere fourteen corporations account for over half of daily newspaper circulation.)[12] Although the quality of journalism may be more often increased than decreased in communities whose independent newspapers are bought out by chains, the chance for an independent-minded publisher or individual eccentric to run his or her own show is dying fast. There is a legitimate concern that chain ownership inevitably precludes diversity. The op-ed page, a development that became a standard practice in the 1970s to increase the diversity of opinion, more and more seems the same from one newspaper to the next. In leading news institutions, the reliance on official government sources is overwhelming, the absence of left-wing critics or commentators consistent, and the inside-the-northeast-corridor orientation hard for a midwesterner, southerner, or westerner to ignore.

National News Culture

Accompanying the nationalization of news institutions is the nationalization of newsroom culture. The managers of small papers or television news shows around the country are aware, as never before, of what goes on on the networks, in *USA Today*, in the *New York Times*. So are their employees. One result has been the ability of blacks and women, and in some instances other minorities (Chicanos in Los Angeles, for example) to press their institutions for better treatment in the newsroom and more appropriate play in the news pages for the groups they identify with.[13] It may be hard to recall how recent these changes are. Before the 1960s, women journalists wrote about fashion and society—and rarely anything else. The National Press Club only admitted women in 1971. In 1966, the Chicago bureau chief for *Newsweek* could turn down a woman reporter from UPI for a job, explaining that "I need someone I can send anywhere, like to riots. And besides, what would you do if someone you were covering ducked into the men's room?"[14] That would be hard to get away with today.

The diversification of the newsroom may be less than it appears, however. In television news, women and minorities are most often seen on weekends, what has been known in the business as the "weekend ghetto." Although Max Robinson and Barbara Walters were among ABC's co-anchors in the mid-1970s, no other women or minorities were regularly assigned as anchors on a network evening news program until Connie Chung in 1993. Still, anecdotal evidence suggests that women (and to a lesser extent minorities) in the newsroom have made a real difference in what gets covered and what emphasis coverage receives. Women staff members at the *Los Angeles Times* spearheaded a major ten-part series on women in the work force in 1984; a woman editorial writer at the *Seattle Times* asserts that almost all the editorials written on subjects concerning children are done "because I'm here."[15]

Journalists at national news institutions are better educated than ever before, more likely than in the past to have come from relatively privileged backgrounds, and more likely to be paid relatively privileged wages. They are more and more likely to get their views from other journalists, not their own editors or publishers. They are likely to share in what Herb Gans calls a "Progressive" outlook—a belief in a two-party system, responsible capitalism, the virtues of small-town life, individualism, moderate measures under all circumstances, and some vague notion of the public interest.[16] The solidity of these values grows as more and more news is reported out of a single location—Washington, D.C. In Washington there is more of a social arena for journalistic culture than ever before. In 1961, there were some 1,500 journalists working in Washington—but more than 5,300 by 1987.[17] Journalists there can, and apparently do, talk mostly to one another.[18]

This is not to say that ours is now a seamless, coherent national journalistic culture. Look, for instance, at the growth of the Spanish-language media. In 1974, there were 55 Spanish-language radio stations; today there are more than 200. In 1970, there were only a handful of television stations that broadcast Spanish-language programming. Today Univision, the largest Spanish-language television network, claims over 600 broadcast and cable affiliates while Telemundo boasts more than 500. There are now several hundred Spanish-language newspapers, with more than 80 concentrated in the "Hispanic Top Ten": Los Angeles, New York, San Francisco, Houston, Dallas, San Diego, Brownsville-McAllen, San Antonio, Miami, and Chicago.

Ethnic and linguistic diversity is well represented in the American media, both print and broadcast. So, too, are the flourishing media that appeal to different religious groups, most visibly with the rise of the "televangelists." The technological capabilities that have made possible a dominant national news culture have also been a key resource for the growing power of more parochial but nonetheless nationally based "consumption communities." The nationalization of the news media has not meant the homogenization of media experience, but the creation of a new set of national arenas for a variety of distinctive subcultural tastes. For instance, thanks in part to computers and desktop publishing, there are (by rough estimate) some 100,000 newsletters in the country that circulate for free or as part of an organization, association, or business. There is even a newsletter industry, with its own trade associations; *Newsletters in Print* catalogs over 10,000 newsletters.[19] Pluralism is not without problems. Such cases as Ku Klux Klan use of easily accessible computer bulletin boards or unscrupulous evangelists on their own cable programs raise difficult issues. The new national media increase the visibility of pluralism more than they insist on homogenization.

In the world of information, the poor grow richer but the rich grow richer more rapidly (the "knowledge gap" hypothesis, as communication researchers call it). The rich have more information and more incentive to get and use information efficiently. Take, for instance, the Republican National Committee's 1984 opposition research group, which started collecting data and quotations on leading Democratic contenders early in the primaries. By the time the Democratic convention opened, the Republican computer had 75,000 items on Walter Mondale, including 45,000 quotes from all through his career. The data base was updated daily during the campaign. The materials were accessible through a computer reference dictionary, and computer links were made to 50 state party headquarters, 50 state campaign headquarters, and Republican spokesmen in all 208 broadcast rating markets. This was impressive. More impressive still was that similar systems were available to all Republican candidates for the House in 1986 through the Republican Information Network. If a candidate was running against a Democrat incumbent, he could instantly learn the incumbent's voting record back to 1974 on any issue. Now, this did not change the outcome of the 1984 election; Republicans remained a minority in the House, even after 1986. But it gives a sense of the sophistication of the new information technologies in matters very close to the heart of the democratic process.[20]

Thanks to the campaign reform acts of the early 1970s, parties have taken to new forms of campaign fund-raising, especially direct mail advertising. With computerized mailing lists and sophisticated targeting of zip code locations most likely to provide names of wealthy contributors, direct mail experts have transformed political fund-raising. One senator had 150,000 names in his computerized lists, divided into a thousand categories according to topic of interest, field, or occupation (117 names appear on the list of people interested in women's issues, 8 on the list of those interested in women in mining).[21] These lists are used for fund-raising and self-promotion so that the right message can be addressed to the right people.

While the disproportionate weight of media and publicity lies, of course, with established powers, guerrilla media use has its brilliant practitioners. The first "Earth Day" (1970), a scheme of Wisconsin Senator Gaylord Nelson's to draw attention, especially through college teach-ins (an invention of the antiwar movement), to environmental issues, was a "patchwork of demonstrations and community activities," though a patchwork that attracted significant media attention and public interest. Planning for Earth Day 1990 was run by two different groups, one with 38 employees, and received backing from labor, business, and the media.[22] Weeks before Earth Day 1990, the *Los Angeles Times* was already covering not only Earth Day but the coverage of Earth Day. As in the 1988 election campaign, the media were as attracted to the story of media coverage as to the stories media coverage was covering.[23] News culture tends to consume itself.

The Newsification of Popular Culture

An important corollary to the nationalization of news has been the nationalization of public problems and the nationalization of an audience for them. Most observers of the media have complained that serious news institutions have been turning news into entertainment, but the larger trend is that entertainment has turned into news. If "60 Minutes" exemplifies a trend to make news entertaining, the "Donahue" program is the model for making entertainment that feeds on the news.

"Donahue" was first syndicated out of Chicago in 1979; the "Oprah Winfrey Show" was syndicated in 1984, and in the last few years several other competitors have entered the fray. These programs are sometimes televised sideshows, parading the American psyche before us with an exaggerated, freakish self-consciousness. At the same time, cheaper than psychotherapy and more readily available than a close friend, they inform people about a wide range of social, psychological, medical, and occasionally (at least on "Donahue") political problems. The producers of "Donahue" conceive of their topics as "serious issues," or more precisely, "serious issues that are in the news." News culture becomes the central storehouse for the various national conversations in American society.[24]

Television unashamedly—in fact, proudly—runs dramatic programs, sitcoms, and soaps that borrow from contemporary controversies for plot material. This is not like the "spy" shows of the early 1960s that reflected a general Cold War ideology; these are programs whose makers frequently engage in careful research to model a plot episode after a recent news event or to mimic in a sitcom the arguments that rage around a contemporary social problem. This began with "All in the Family" in 1971. Over the course of just a few months, that new sitcom dealt with homosexuality, cohabitation, race and racism, women's rights, and miscarriage. By the end of the 1971–1972 season, it

National News Culture   179

was the top show in television, and producer Norman Lear had developed enough clout to retain some independence from network censors. When a group called the Population Institute, a lobbying organization for promoting population control, set up a meeting in 1971 with television executives to encourage them to deal with population issues, Lear became personally interested in doing an episode that would deal with this issue.[25] The "Maude has an abortion" episode on "Maude" (a spin-off from "All in the Family") the next year was the highly controversial result. "M.A.S.H." dealt with the war in Vietnam (through displacement to Korea), and a whole array of made-for-television "problem" movies dealt with issues from child abuse to chemical pollution of the environment to wives murdering abusive husbands. "Lou Grant," a popular drama in the 1970s and early 1980s, was set in a metropolitan newsroom, and it borrowed directly from recent news events. *Mother Jones* took pride in telling its readers that the January 19, 1981, "Lou Grant" show, which dealt with the dumping of hazardous products in the Third World by the United States, drew on a 1979 special issue of the magazine, thereby using television fiction to legitimate its own journalism.[26] In 1989, after a jury found for the defendants in a medical malpractice suit in Florida, the plaintiff's lawyer asked for a new trial because, he claimed, a recently aired "L.A. Law" episode in which the doctors won in a malpractice case was "propaganda" that probably influenced the jury.[27]

This newsification of popular culture is no doubt rooted in a longstanding Puritan temperament that distrusts entertainment unless it is instructional. But the leakage of news into comedy and drama in the past decades has a more contemporary ideological source, too. Critics of popular culture have argued convincingly from the 1960s on that entertainment is a form of instruction, whether it is meant to be or not. It was an old complaint that mass media portrayal of crime and violence encourages crime and violence, and this criticism was renewed in the 1960s with television as the target. It was more novel and more challenging to complain that the subordinate status of women and minorities in contemporary society was encouraged by mass media stereotyping. This criticism was effectively turned into politics by Action for Children's Television in its persistent attacks on children's television programming and by the Ford Foundation's support for Children's Television Workshop and "Sesame Street." "Sesame Street" may look almost painfully self-conscious about racial and sexual stereotyping and, critics charge, not nearly self-conscious enough in its submission to the rapid-fire pace and gleam of commercial broadcasting. But it provides parents a televisual haven of safety from the persistent violence, sexism, and racism of commercials and programming emanating from the commercial stations.

The cultural, rather than political, consequences of newsification may be more important. We live with more vivid, dramatic knowledge of events around the world than ever before. We live our "real" lives bodily, in our homes and workplaces and on our streets. But at the same time we live alongside the hyper-reality on our television screens and radios and in our newspapers. Contemporary life becomes some kind of science fiction, two parallel worlds moving along in tandem, usually disconnected, only occasionally, and then perhaps jarringly, in touch.

Television in the Media System

To tell the story of dominant developments in the news media in the past generation as a story of nationalization, newsification, and the rising symbolic centrality of something called "news" is to differ substantially from some other popular accounts. Perhaps the most common story is that "television" is the simple one-word answer to the question, What has happened to the media in the past thirty years? In this view, television has overwhelmed society, propelling the decline of literacy, the decline of seriousness, and the decline of political participation.

But consider what should be a simple instance: as television news has expanded and as the public's professed reliance on television news has increased, newspaper "penetration" has declined. Newspaper readership among young people is particularly low. What could be a simpler cause-and-effect relationship? Vulgar television does in virtuous newsprint. This has often been cited as incontrovertible evidence of the dangers of television. But in a comparison of twenty Western countries (and Japan) from 1964 to 1984, Leo Bogart found no overall relationship between the spread of television and newspaper penetration.[28] While the number of television sets per capita and the total time spent viewing television are pretty much the same from one Western country to the next, newspaper circulation per 1,000 population differs dramatically from Japan (562 newspapers per 1,000) to Sweden (521) to the United Kingdom (414) to the United States (268) to Canada (220) to Italy (96). During this period, when television penetration increased everywhere, newspaper circulation per capita also increased in Japan and Sweden, declined imperceptibly in Canada (1 percent) and Italy (5 percent), and declined dramatically in the United

States (16 percent) and Britain (21 percent). Television certainly is vital in American news today, yet its centrality can be (and usually is) exaggerated. American journalists underestimate how much time people spend reading newspapers and overestimate how much time they spend watching television news. They mistakenly believe that making print more like television, with shorter news items and more feature stories, will bring in more readers. In fact, in recent years, papers gaining circulation showed no markedly different editorial practices from those losing circulation. Distribution, not content, is the cause of a loss of readership.[29] That is, the main decline in news-paper circulation in large metropolitan areas is in single-copy sales, rather than home delivery, and the problem seems to be not that people find television more satisfying, but that the suburbanization of American life, the decay of urban neighborhoods, and the unemployment, poor health, poor education, and disaffection of the urban poor make engagement in a community through the newspaper an irrelevance. The other side of that coin, as Ben Bagdikian has observed, is also important: the economics of newspaper production has led competing papers in a city to fight for the same upscale consumers in order to attract the same advertisers. This process, leading to more and more monopoly newspaper cities, leads to news content that is less and less relevant to the blue-collar citizens who were once reliable newspaper subscribers. The newspaper, in short, in its upscale move, has significantly authored its own irrelevance.

Television is a centrally important medium in American culture, but it is not in and of itself an explanation for the changing informational environment of American citizens.

Are the News Media Moving Right or Left?

Another story is that the main development in the news media has been a sharp move of news content to the right (a favorite theory on the left) or, alternatively, that the national news media have been captured by a corps of too well paid, too comfortable, too Eastern, too Ivy League, and too liberal journalists (a favorite, naturally, on the right).

In 1969 an economist with the Federal Reserve System, Reed Irvine, created Accuracy in Media, an organization devoted to pointing out every actual, and imagined, left-wing bias in what Irvine calls "Big Media," meaning the networks, the few newspapers of national influence, the news magazines, and the wire services.[30] By 1990 AIM had a membership of more than 25,000, an annual budget of $1.5 million, a speakers' bureau, a newsletter with a circulation over 30,000, a daily 3-minute radio program that appeared on 200 stations nationally, and a weekly column appearing in some 100 newspapers. A variety of other right-wing critics of the media arose in the wake of AIM. For instance, Robert and Linda Lichter, conservative media scholars, founded the Center for Media and Public Affairs in 1986, which surveys media performance and analyzes media impact on public opinion. In 1986, Fairness and Accuracy in Reporting (FAIR), a left-wing counterpart to AIM, was established.

Although the right-wing institutes pushed a view of the left-wing media, their very existence, coupled with the general rightward tilt of elite political thinking in the 1980s, helped promote the idea of a shift to the right in the press. FAIR went over the "Nightline" guest lists for the period 1985–1988 and found an overwhelming preponderance of government officials, almost all of them white and male. What else is new? FAIR also observed the flourishing of political talk shows hosted by conservatives—William Buckley's "Firing Line" being the granddaddy, followed by John McLaughlin, Patrick Buchanan, Rowland Evans, and Robert Novak. No show at the time of FAIR's study was hosted by a liberal.[31]

If there was a shift to the right in the media in the 1980s, it may have had something to do with consternation in the business world in the 1970s over the fact that the media seemed to be tilting against business. Mobil began taking out ads in the 1970s in the *New York Times* (and the new terms *advocacy advertising* and *advertorial* were coined). In 1975 corporations spent $100 million on advocacy advertising, aiming as much as a third of their total advertising expenses toward people as "citizens" rather than as "consumers." Business groups began to seek ways to influence the news media by giving prizes for economic reporting, establishing training programs in business reporting at universities, sponsoring arts and cultural programs on television, creating or supporting new neo-conservative think tanks, and holding roundtables with journalists and complaining loudly that they were being maligned by a "liberal" press.[32]

Perhaps this desire to influence the media had something to do with a loss of direct control over them, notably over television. In the 1950s, sponsors of television programs had significant influence over the content of programming, to the extent of reviewing scripts before broadcast. But following the quiz show scandal in 1959 (when it was revealed that quiz shows were "fixed"), the networks took tighter control of the reins themselves. Moreover, as advertising time grew more and more expensive and competition for television time increased, the program with only a single sponsor disappeared from the screen. Between 1967 and 1981 the number of commercials on the networks per week increased from 1,856 to 4,079, while "spot" commercials increased from 2,413 to 5,300 as the standard length of the commercial declined from 60 seconds to 30 seconds.[33] It is no wonder that recently General Motors, among others, has asked for something new in advertising lingo—"pod protection." That is, GM wants to be the only automobile ad within a group of commercials (or "pod") aired consecutively within a single commercial break in a program.[34]

The decline of direct advertiser control over television was minor compared to the loss of business control over the political agenda. The sixties created the climate for a set of issues and institutions that cast a cold eye on business in the 1970s. Congress, especially the Senate, was influenced beginning in the early 1960s by northern Democrats, who successfully challenged what had been a domain of conservative southern Democrats. This helped the passage of liberal legislation in the late 1960s and 1970s, including the creation of new government agencies to monitor business activity—the Environmental Protection Agency (1970), the Equal Employment Opportunity Commission (1965), the Occupational Safety and Health Review Commission (1970), and the Consumer Products Safety Commission (1973), not to mention a newly militant Federal Trade Commission. The press, devoted as always to covering government, covered the new agencies and so shone a light on business that was necessarily more critical and concentrated than in the past.

Business antipathy to the media was also a response to the success of Ralph Nader, who helped invent a new public opposition to business. Nader used some old-fashioned media methods in his rise to prominence. He first published an article on automobile safety in *The Nation* in 1959. His book *Unsafe at Any Speed* propelled the 1966 legislation that made the federal government a guarantor of highway and automobile safety and led to the "recall" of automobiles with safety defects. In the following years, Nader established a fleet of public interest lobbying and research organizations both in Washington and around the country. The federal government, by establishing new agencies to protect occupational health and consumer safety, and private industry, by getting itself into and mishandling near-disasters (Three-Mile Island) and major disasters (Bhopal), did the rest. Congress, while still the center of Washington legislative activity, was increasingly a consumer of policy initiatives, not only from the White House but from a mushrooming assortment of lobbyists.[35] Although citizens' groups and public interest groups remain a small fraction of the total lobbying effort in Washington, they nonetheless proliferated between 1960 and 1980.

So the media, following Washington, moved left in the 1970s; again following Washington and the coming to power of the Reagan administration, they moved right in the 1980s. Too many media critics, left and right, have overestimated the independence of the media and underplayed the power of media routines, repeatedly documented in studies by Edward Epstein, Herbert Gans, Todd Gitlin, Daniel Hallin, Stephen Hess, Michael Robinson, Leon Sigal, Gaye Tuchman, and others.[36] What changed from the 1960s to the 1970s to the 1980s was the political climate that gave differential legitimacy to different sources. The media, which tend to be in the middle when a polyphony of voices are raining in, have few intellectual resources for independent judgment and no political portfolio for independent polemic.

The 1960s did change the internal culture of working journalists. Television news coverage of election campaigns is more negative than it used to be for both Republican and Democratic candidates.[37] Reporters, like patients seeking medical counsel, are more likely than they used to be to seek second opinions. Institutions well versed in giving second opinions have multiplied rapidly in and around Washington. There is a "social movement industry" now, as Mayer Zald and John McCarthy write, with more resources than ever before.[38] The result, in the national media, is a picture of the world not more left or more right but more muddled and multidimensional (and, if your tastes run to such terminology, more postmodern).

The Survival—and Flourishing—of Print

It remains to say a word about the not negligible medium in which this chapter appears—the book. Little is more important in characterizing the changing contemporary culture than the fact that in 1960 only 41 percent of the adult population (aged 25 and over) had graduated from high school, while in 1988 it was 76 percent. In 1960, 7.7 percent of the adult population had four years or more of college; by 1988 this had jumped to 20.3 percent.[39] Although most college education is largely technical or preprofessional, many institutions stress a "liberal education," and pockets of "liberal education" exist even in technically oriented schools, providing an opening for critical inquiry that high schools rarely afford. Literacy is not on its last legs. In fact, there are more books published by a greater variety of publishers and distributed through more bookstores today than ever before. Despite major mergers and acquisitions in the publishing business, the total number of publishers has increased—to say nothing of the "desktop publishing" that the personal computer has made possible. Where some 15,000 new books and new editions were published in 1960, there were 36,000 in 1970, 42,000 in 1980, and 47,000 in 1990.[40] In 1963, there were 993 book publishing establishments; that number grew to 2,264 in 1987.[41]

Still, books reach the public through an increasingly concentrated distribution network. B. Dalton had more than 500 stores by 1980 and nearly 1,000 when it was bought by Barnes and Noble in 1987; Waldenbooks had more than 700 stores in 1980, 1,100 in 1994. The five largest bookstore chains accounted for 34 percent of all book sales, and B. Dalton and Waldenbooks exercise a significant impact on the industry as a whole.[42]

Books as a category are up against heavy entertainment and leisure competition—not just television, but the new adaptations of the home television set. There are twice as many video rental outlets as bookstores.[43] But the uses of print literacy are still growing. Reports that ours is now a television culture are vastly exaggerated.

Conclusion

It is tempting to suggest that with the present flood of information and the hype that carries the informational load, our eyes glaze over more and more readily, that increasingly we surrender our critical powers or never assume them, accepting that "all politicians are crooks" or that "everything causes cancer." But people keep making sense of their own lives, despite all. People still get irritated, bored, incensed, and mobilized, despite all. We make a mistake if we judge the public mind by the menu for public consumption. There is a tendency to believe that if the television news sound bite has shortened from a minute to 10 seconds (and it has in the space of twenty years),[44] the public capacity for sustained attention has shrunk accordingly. But this does not square with the intensity of careerism in business, the growth of the two-income family, the vitality of the pro-life and pro-choice movements, the return of religious revivals, and even the upturn in SAT scores.[45]

Then what does media saturation mean? Consider a fast food

analogy. Most people I know eat more Big Macs than salmon dinners at fine restaurants. McDonald's is faster, cheaper, more predictable, easier to squeeze into the rest of life. This does not mean that people prefer Big Macs to salmon. It does not mean, aside from economistic tautology, that they greatly "value" Big Macs. It does not mean that their palates are jaded. It means they have made some decisions about their priorities and, then and there, eating a good meal is lower on the list than quickly reducing hunger. I do not think the growing success of *USA Today* necessarily indicates anything different: it does not mean that people judge McPaper the "best" meal or the only meal they seek; simply that they find in it what they need from a newspaper at a given moment, given the constraints of daily life. With world enough and time, or with an important local issue, or with a hot presidential race, their choices might be different. Their choices, in any event, at any given moment, include an array of other sources of information.

If we cannot infer individual tastes from public menus, can we nonetheless observe something about how available cultural repertoires limit or shape opportunities for consciousness? Yes, but carefully. The flourishing of McDonald's forces other restaurants to change and still others to close up. The prevalence of McDonald's tutors citizens, particularly the young, in what food is good, what food *is*, what a meal is supposed to feel like. This may not be the tutor we would most like to have for our children. At the same time, Americans eat less beef today than they did when McDonald's was only a gleam in Ray Kroc's eye; McDonald's is not the only tutor in the culture. Nor is McDonald's itself untutored by larger social and cultural change; witness the availability of salads and the declaration that french fries will no longer be fried in animal fat. Again, judging American habits or structures from the most visible elements of public consumption is something to undertake only with great care.

American citizens have more information today than they had a generation ago. More credible information. More national sources of information. More authenticated conflicts of information and opinion, thanks to the proliferation of expert lobbying groups and the changing habits of the media to seek out a variety of sources. More information coming to the laity through the media rather than through expert intermediaries. If the *New England Journal of Medicine* publishes research of possible interest to the laity, it does not percolate down through family physicians but goes straight to the newspaper, magazine, and broadcast science reporters, and gets picked up soon thereafter in women's and consumer magazines, too. At least for the middle-class citizens who read the women's magazines or Jane Brody's column in the *New York Times* and are empowered by their education and social standing to instruct their friends and families and talk back to their doctors, this kind of information is useful and gets used.

I do not conclude from this that we have the right information at the right time or that available information is distributed equitably or that the informational citizen is well informed. Our increasingly dazzling library of information provides only an illusion of knowledge and a false promise of citizenly competence if the social order does not equip people to use it, if young people are cynical, if the poor have no hope, if the middle class is self-absorbed, and if forays into public life are discouraging and private pursuits altogether more rewarding than public enterprise.

9 Was There Ever a Public Sphere?

Critiques of American politics and culture are sometimes phrased as if contemporary life represents a decline from a great and golden age. Christopher Lasch, for instance, bemoans "the transformation of politics from a central component of popular culture into a spectator sport." What once existed but has been lost, in Lasch's view, is "the opportunity to exercise the virtues associated with deliberation and participation in public debate." What we are seeing is "the atrophy of these virtues in the common people—judgment, prudence, eloquence, courage, self-reliance, resourcefulness, common sense."[1] Different images of the good old days appear without any consensus about just when the good old days happened. George Anastaplo, among many others, has blamed much of the recent decline on television, and he successively offers two datings of the golden age. First, impressed that people would stand in the hot sun for several hours listening to "tight, tough arguments," he suggests the Lincoln-Douglas debates as a contrast to the TV era. He argues that the trouble with television is not only that it fails to inform but also that it deceives people into believing they are informed. In contrast, "a generation ago"—not, I note, an era when people listened to hours of tight, tough argument in any forum—"you would know that if you had not read certain things, you were not able to talk about issues properly, and you might defer to those who had taken the trouble to inform themselves."[2]

If liberals see atrophy, so too do conservatives. Allan Bloom is the most celebrated to discuss a straight-line decline of civility in an age characterized by lack of character, lack of seriousness, lack of discipline, lack of nerve by those in positions of authority, the advance of a superficial and relativistic democratic ethos ultimately inimical to a good society. Both liberals and conservatives often see television as the cause, or at any rate the chief symptom, of the decline of a public sphere. It is an almost reflex-like, parenthetical explanatory catchall, as in the claim of *New York Times* media and politics reporter Michael Oreskes that "the first generation raised with television is a generation that participates less in the democracy than any before it."[3]

In fact, Oreskes is referring to the second generation raised with television, not the first, and he is wrong that it participates less in the democracy than any before it. Voting rates were just as miserable in 1920 as in 1984, and they were worse in the 1790s. But let me offer as the main foil for this discussion an observation of the political scientist Walter Dean Burnham. In a 1974 essay he offers the example of the Lincoln-Douglas debates as evidence of the character of the mid-nineteenth-century American voter. He infers, from the fact that rational campaigners seeking election would engage in what seem to us unusually sophisticated and erudite debates on national issues before rural publics and the fact that party newspapers with similar rational inclinations to advance the interests of their candidates would reprint these debates in their entirety, that mid-nineteenth-century voters were literate, attentive, and interested in issues of transcendent importance.[4]

Are these safe inferences to make? I do not think so. Burnham himself all but declares them faulty in his next paragraphs. For he goes on to hold that nineteenth-century American politics was characterized by what he terms "political confessionalism." That is, mid-nineteenth-century Americans were devoutly attached to political parties. They tended to live in "island communities" surrounded by other people like themselves. Ethnic and religious communities provided the basis for political allegiances and very often were closely connected to the ideological content of political parties.[5] Political campaigns were, in a sense, more religious revivals and popular entertainments than the settings for rational-critical discussion. It is true that the voters who attended or read about the Lincoln-Douglas debates in their party newspapers were literate. It is true that they attended, but it is not at all apparent what in those debates they attended to. It is true that they participated, but it is not clear that they were "interested in issues of transcendent importance" (or that even if they were in 1858, a moment of particularly heightened political conflict, this has any bearing on their political interests in 1848 or 1868).

A point of comparison may help clarify this. Lawrence Levine has shown that Shakespearean drama was enormously popular in nineteenth-century America. But do we know from this how audiences related to it? No. What Levine's research suggests is that audiences enjoyed Shakespeare because they could read him as a creator of just the sorts of melodramas to which they were most partial. They saw Macbeth and Lear as rugged individualists up against the dangers of time and nature, warring against fate with all the larger-than-life energy Americans liked to see on the stage. Audiences saw Shakespeare's plays as a set of moral lessons: Thomas Jefferson saw *Lear* as a study of the importance of filial duty; Abraham Lincoln saw *Macbeth* as a study of tyranny and murder; John Quincy Adams saw *Othello* as a tale cautioning against interracial marriage. In popular American ideology and in the Shakespeare that Americans enjoyed, the individual bore responsibility for his own fate; if he failed, it was only through lack of inner discipline and control. All of these lessons came draped in the kind of expansive oratory that Americans liked in both their theater and their politics.[6]

What does this say of Lincoln-Douglas? It reminds us, as does a great deal of contemporary literary theory, that what the audience receives from the texts it approaches is not obviously encoded in the texts themselves. Did the Lincoln-Douglas audiences attend the debates because they sought to follow the arguments rationally and critically? Did they attend because they were thinking through the questions of slavery and states' rights? Were they out for a good time? Were they connoisseurs of oratory who admired the effectiveness of Lincoln and Douglas at skewering each other but lacked much concern for whether their arguments were right or wrong? Did they simply enjoy the spectacle of solitary combat? Had they already made up their political minds and come out only to show support for their man?

The longing of contemporary critics of our political culture to stand in the sun for three hours to listen to political speeches is selective. If there is nostalgia for the Lincoln-Douglas debates (not that they left any words, phrases, or ideas anyone can recall), there is no hankering for dramatic readings of Edward Everett's hours-long address at Gettysburg. Instead, it is Abraham Lincoln's sound-bite-length address that has left a lasting impression. (As it happens, not long ago people did listen to literally hours of political addresses, interspersed with music, at antiwar rallies in the 1960s. If it is any measure, I can say from personal experience that there is a big difference between attending a rally and actually listening to the speeches.)

This is not to deny that the Lincoln-Douglas debates were an impressive exercise of democracy. But it is well to remember that they were strikingly unusual even in their own day. The idea that a public sphere of rational-critical discourse flourished in the eighteenth or early nineteenth century, at least in the American instance, is an inadequate, if not incoherent, notion. Its empirical basis, in the American case, seems to me remarkably thin. When we examine descriptions of what public life was actually like, there is not much to suggest the rational-critical discussion that Jürgen Habermas posits as central to the public sphere. Perhaps more distressing, for some periods there is not much to indicate even very general interest, let alone participation, in public affairs.

What I want to focus on in the rest of this chapter are two defining features of the political public sphere. First, what is the level of participation in the public sphere: who is legally eligible for political activity and what portion of those eligible actually participate? Second, to what extent is political participation carried out through rational and critical discourse? This is a vital part of the concept of the public sphere as Habermas has presented it. No plebiscitary democracy, for instance, would qualify for Habermas as having a functioning public sphere; not only does participation need to be widespread, but it must be rational. One of the great contributions of the concept of a public sphere is that it insists that an ideal democratic polity be defined by features beyond those that formally enable political participation. It is not only the fact of political involvement but its quality that the concept of the public sphere evokes. There are, certainly, other conditions or preconditions of a public sphere, but these two are undoubtedly central, and I will limit my discussion here to these alone.[7] This discussion is inspired by Habermas more than it is directly responsive to his work. That is, I am not engaged in criticizing the historical evidence he adduces for the emergence (and later disintegration) of a public sphere. His historical account concerns European affairs, and I do not presume that the American case either confirms or contradicts European developments. I am concerned with Habermas's model of the public sphere not so much as "a paradigm for analyzing historical change," as Peter Hohendahl put it, but more as "a normative category for political critique."[8] That is, I think historians should examine as a central question of political history the rise or fall, expansion or contraction (the appropriate metaphor is not clear) of a public sphere or, more generally, what the conditions have been in different periods that encourage or discourage public participation in politics and public involvement in rational-critical discussion of politics.

Citizens' Participation in Politics

The more people participate as citizens in politics, the closer one comes to the ideal of a public sphere. By this criterion, in American history the period since 1865 is an improvement upon all prior periods, with the enfranchisement of Negroes; the period since 1920 is better than any prior period, with the enfranchisement of women; and the period since 1965 is better still, with the civil rights laws that made the Fifteenth Amendment a substantial reality.

But the question is not only what segments of the population are legally eligible to participate in politics (I am taking the franchise as a reasonable, though certainly incomplete, index of inclusion in the political world) but also what percentages of those groups actually exercise their political rights. Contemporary commentators regularly observe that present voting participation rates are significantly lower than they were in the mid-nineteenth century. This is so. There was a sharp decline in voter turnout from the 1880s to a low in the 1920s; during the New Deal and after, voting rates increased, but there has been a striking decline again from 1960 to the present. This should be viewed, however, in the longer perspective of American history.

Jane Mansbridge found in her study of a New England town meeting in the 1970s that only some 35 percent of eligible voters turned out for this archetype of democratic decision making. How did this compare, she asked, to the New England town meetings of the seventeenth and eighteenth centuries? In Dedham, Massachusetts, where records are quite complete for the mid-seventeenth century, attendance varied. From 1636 to 1644, 74 percent of eligible voters typically attended the meeting. While this turnout is much higher than in town meetings today, its significance is mitigated by the facts that every inhabitant lived within one mile of the meeting place, there were fines for lateness to town meeting or absence from town meeting, a town crier visited the house of every latecomer or absentee half an hour into the meeting, and only some sixty men were eligible in the first place. In Sudbury, a town that did not impose fines, attendance averaged 46 percent in the 1650s. In many towns for which we have good evidence, attendance in the eighteenth century was lower still. Mansbridge estimates that 20 to 60 percent of potential voters attended town meetings in eighteenth-century Massachusetts. The figures for the nineteenth century are similar except for periods of particularly intense conflict, when turnout rose to as high as 75 percent. In the town Mansbridge studied, nineteenth-century attendance was 30 to 35 percent, while in the current period it is around 25 percent or as high as 66 percent in times of special conflict.[9]

John Adams told a friend while visiting Worcester in 1755, "This whole town is immersed in politics." Yet as the historian Robert Zemsky concludes, "The average provincial seldom engaged in political activity. He had little desire to hold office; his attendance at town meetings and participation in provincial elections was sporadic; and when he did join in political campaigns, he rarely lent more than his moral support to the cause."[10] In revolutionary America, 10 to 15 percent of white adult males voted at the beginning of the Revolution, 20 to 40 percent during the 1780s.[11] In Massachusetts the first Congressional elections of 1788 and 1790 brought out 13 percent and 16 percent of eligible voters. The high point of turnout in state elections in the decade came in 1787 after the "near civil war" of Shays' Rebellion—a 28 percent turnout.[12]

In eighteenth-century New England, the most democratic culture in colonial North America, people participated in politics occasionally at best. "Apathy prevailed among citizens until they perceived a threat to their immediate interests," according to Ronald Formisano's analysis of eighteenth-century Massachusetts.[13] The nineteenth century, before party mobilization began in the 1840s, was no better. "In the 1820s the vast majority of citizens had lost interest in politics. They had never voted much in presidential elections anyway, and now they involved themselves only sporadically in state and local affairs."[14] There is not much to be said in favor of any time in America's past before the 1840s in terms of political participation and political interest. William Gienapp characterizes American political life before the 1820s as follows: "Previously deference to social elites and mass indifference characterized the nation's politics; despite suffrage laws sufficiently liberal to allow mass participation, few men were interested in politics, and fewer still actively participated in political affairs. Politics simply did not seem important to most Americans."[15]

With the rise of mass-based political parties in the Jacksonian era, political participation took a new turn. Voting rates shot up dramatically. For example, the percentage of the potential electorate that voted in Connecticut was 8 percent in 1820 and 15 percent in 1824. By 1832 this rose to 46 percent, and by 1844 to 80 percent.[16] Turnout figures of around 80 percent were common outside the South until the turn of the century, when they began to decline, reaching a lower point in the 1920s than at any time since before Andrew Jackson. If we take voter turnout as the measure (and it seems to me a good one), there is no question that in terms of political participation, there *was* a golden age of American political culture, the period from 1840 to 1900. This period, then, merits close consideration. What was the character of political culture in this period? What was the nature of political discourse? What features of the era supported mass political involvement? And was this involvement of a type or quality we might reasonably long for, or at least learn from, today?

Rational-Critical Political Discourse

It is difficult enough to determine voter turnout rates for the nineteenth century. To try to learn how eighteenth- or nineteenth-century voters conceived of politics, came to political views, and arrived at political choices and actions is substantially harder. There are so many things we would need to know, and we never will know them in any complete way. Did people talk about politics in their homes? Was the talk of politics at taverns or coffeehouses "rational-critical," or was it gossipy, incidental background to sociability rather than its center? What connection did people feel to politics? Was voting a proud act of citizenship or a deferential act of social obligation to community notables? When people read about politics, what did they look for? What frameworks of meaning did they possess for absorbing new information? Did they have coherent ideologies, or patchwork sets of beliefs with little connection among the pieces? None of this is easy to discover. Still, there are some important clues available. In the following discussion I will distinguish between the internal resources of citizens for participation in political discourse and the external resources available for their use—specifically, parties, the press, and electoral procedures.

Internal Resources of Citizens

American colonists of the eighteenth century were not well read. If they owned a book at all, it was the Bible. If they owned a second book, it was likely to be a collection of sermons or possibly John Bunyan's Christian allegory, *Pilgram's Progress,* or some other religious work. Where we have comprehensive inventories of communities, it appears that, even in New England, 50 to 70 percent of households owned no books at all. The most active bookseller in Virginia in the mid-eighteenth century sold books to 250 customers a year in a colony with a white population of 130,000.[17] In New England, where literacy rates were somewhat higher than elsewhere in the colonies, popular reading was severely restricted and was almost entirely religious. Works of science or literature reached only a small audience made up almost entirely of the very small group of people who were college graduates.[18]

The one class of deeply literate people, the clergy, almost exclusively read religious literature and played relatively minor roles (judging, for instance, from their insignificance at the Constitutional Convention) in the great political debates of their time.[19] Benjamin Franklin's and Thomas Jefferson's wide reading in contemporary philosophy was not a trait they shared with many others. That Franklin read books at all was itself a social calling card; he reports in his autobiography that when he first journeyed to Philadelphia, he met a physician at an inn who "finding I had read a little" became sociable and friendly. Readers were relatively rare birds, not participants in a broad, ongoing, and institutionalized rational-critical discourse. The best-seller success of Thomas Paine's pamphlet *Common Sense* in 1776 was due, in Paine's own estimation, not only to its being issued at a time of intense political conflict but also to its being addressed to the common republican reader. Political pamphlet literature in the colonies was ordinarily addressed to the small, educated elite and was written in a florid style full of classical references that had meaning only to a few. Paine purged his writing of the classics, used as reference primarily the biblical tradition, and sought "language as plain as the alphabet."[20]

In the nineteenth century the intellectual resources of the population expanded. Literacy shifted from being intensive to being extensive; schooling became much more accessible; and the secularization of culture, along with the democratization of religion, spread a wider range of ideas to more and more people. This is not to say that the growth of literacy and the growing market for printed literature, including political literature, always represented a force for liberation. Harvey Graff, among others, has argued that literacy was equally a form of social control designed to keep people in their place and that it was often successful in its aim.[21] Still, nineteenth-century Americans were more educationally equipped for participation in a public sphere than their eighteenth-century forebears. And despite concerns about a "decline" in American educational achievement in recent years (a decline that, by the measure of test scores, began in the 1960s and ended by the early 1980s), basic literacy skills and educational attainment have become more widely available in the twentieth century than in the nineteenth.[22]

All of this is a relatively poor measure of the internal resources of American citizens for political participation. It may be that the notion of internal resources is one that cannot be taken very far. At least, however, this thumbnail sketch suggests little reason for nostalgia about the educational qualifications of any prior era in American history.

External Resources of Political Culture

The Press. One critical feature of the bourgeois public sphere is the availability of public media for carrying on and informing public discussion. There is a distinction to be made between "carrying on" and "informing." Habermas distinguishes between an early press devoted to political controversy and a later, commercial press that pursues the commodification of news. While the commercial press is not without its virtues, actively engaging the public in political debate is not one of them. The contemporary mainstream press in a sense prevents the political activity of its readers because in some situations it avoids publishing what James Lemert calls "mobilizing information." That is, it will report about a political demonstration after the fact but it will not announce it the day before and provide a phone number or other information on how to reach the organizers. Where there is a celebration or demonstration that unites the community (the Fourth of July parade), in contrast, "mobilizing information" is ready at hand, with parade routes and locations for watching fireworks.[23]

Tocqueville's notion of a newspaper as a creator of associations accurately described the reform journals of the 1830s and 1840s, has some application to the party papers that remained strong into the late nineteenth century, and also describes a large number of newsletters of voluntary associations even today. But the commercial model of journalism that dominates general, public discourse today and grew out of the penny press of the 1830s seeks a market, not an association or a community. A leading early editor of a penny paper, James Gordon Bennett, boasted that his press was "subservient to none of its readers—known to none of its readers—and entirely ignorant who are its readers and who are not."[24] This market ideal of the new journalism is the antithesis of association or community.

That journalism shifted toward a more fully commercial model during the nineteenth century should not lead us to romanticize the early press. As Stephen Botein has argued, the colonial newspaper scrupulously avoided controversy on almost all occasions up to the decade before the Revolution, when the printers were dragged, sometimes kicking and screaming, into taking sides with the loyalists or the patriots. When news was printed, it was generally chosen because it avoided controversy. In fact, the more remote the news, the better. News of other colonies was more useful, because it was regarded with greater indifference, than news of one's own colony; news of European affairs was better still, because it had even less connection to local affairs.[25]

So the colonial press was not, generally speaking, a press of political conversation except when political drama dragged it into the arena. Politics sometimes made of newspapers and pamphlets a public forum, but it was rare indeed that editors of their own volition created a public forum that stimulated political action. This is not to diminish the importance of the press at moments of heightened political activity, as during the Stamp Act crisis of 1765 or in the years leading up to the Revolution. But the colonial press was not a permanent resource for political discussion; its politicization was a sometime thing. By the early nineteenth century the politicalness of the American press receded just as party competition evaporated in the Era of Good Feelings. The relevance of the press to political discourse rose and fell with the fortunes of formal political organization, close electoral competition, and intense community conflict.

In any case, there were limits to what the press could provide. Eighteenth-century colonial assemblies conducted much of their business in secret. In Massachusetts the House began publishing a journal of its proceedings annually in 1715, though it was published twice a week after 1717. But the journal only rarely published roll-call votes (17 between 1739 and 1756), which made it difficult to know the policy stands of one's own representative. Any newspaper or other commentator who revealed business of the House not printed in the journal was subject to fine. Boston's half-dozen newspapers and its pamphleteers therefore usually just paraphrased what the journal had already published. In times of crisis, enough information might percolate out to enable rational voting; in ordinary times, this was rarely the case.[26] One could reasonably argue that Massachusetts towns were sufficiently homogeneous that the legislator "ordinarily voiced his community's aspirations and grievances because he shared its prejudices."[27] If this was democracy, it was nonetheless far from a democracy based on rational-critical discussion. And Massachusetts was not unusual. From the 1740s to the Revolution, the New York Assembly regularly restated its right to prohibit the publication of its proceedings. Only two state constitutions drafted in the years after the Revolution opened the doors of the legislature to the public. In Congress, reporters were forbidden until 1800. Even when reporters did gain access, few newspapers took advantage of this. Until the 1820s no newspaper outside Washington maintained a regular Washington correspondent.[28]

In contrast, the press of the heyday of American political participation, from 1840 to 1900, was of a different color altogether. These papers were typically loyal to political parties; they served as information-promoting boosters of a particular political organization. American politics saw its highest level of participation begin just as party organizations moved self-consciously away from ideological stances. As Richard Hofstadter documents, from the 1840s on political parties shifted from ideological institutions within an elite to organizational combat units competing for masses of voters.[29] They sought voter loyalty on the basis of program but even more on the basis of social and communal solidarity. American politics in this era has been described as divided along ethnocultural lines—people voted in solidarity with their ethnic and religious communities, not in allegiance to a political theory or philosophy and not with careful discussion or consideration of alternatives. People did not normally choose a political party or political philosophy any more than they chose a religion. On election day, most voters did not conceive of their having a choice between alternatives any more than the Methodist imagined he had a choice on Sunday morning between the Methodist Church and the Congregational Church across the street. (If people *had* sought to make rational choices among parties, it would not have been an easy matter. Parties in the nineteenth century showed relatively little ideological consistency. By the 1890s, Ballard Campbell reports, the most consistent separation of Republicans and Democrats on the state level in midwestern legislatures was over the liquor issue. This was the kind of "quasi-confessional" matter, to recall Burnham's terms, that parties did clearly present with some consistency, but no major party represented a coherent political program or philosophy.)[30]

Correspondingly, newspapers boosted the parties they represented. The press, in Michael McGerr's terms, "imposed a coercive cultural uniformity" on its readers. It encouraged citizens to see politics in partisan terms. While this helped citizens to understand politics, it also helped them to see politics in the most simplified light: "By reducing politics to black-and-white absolutes, the press made partisanship enticing. The committed Republican or Democrat did not need to puzzle over conflicting facts and arguments; in his paper he could find ready-made positions on any candidate and every issue."[31] Later, when more than one position could be found in a single newspaper, editors feared that readers would find this bewildering. In the median political paper for the mid-nineteenth century, if one can imagine such a thing, a one-sided view of the political battleground was maintained not only by attacking the opposition party and its candidates but, for the most part, by failing to mention them altogether. The aggregate of political newspapers, read side by side, might well have approximated some form of rational-critical discourse, or at least the kind of cari-catured, zany "Point/Counterpoint" that "Saturday Night Live" used to lampoon. But there is nothing to indicate that papers were read in this way, any more than one would expect the Baptist to peruse the church newsletter of the Presbyterian.

Party. In any event, without some way of limiting debate, defining issues, and restricting alternatives, no debate can be rational. To be sensible, political debate cannot be a set of simultaneous equations that only a computer could handle. It has to be a small set of identi-fiable, branching alternatives that can be examined reasonably enough one at a time. The political party helped make that possible. "Parties," as Maurice Duverger put it, "create public opinion as much as they express it; they form it rather than distort it; there is dialogue rather than echo. Without parties there would be only vague, instinctive, varying tendencies dependent on character, education, habit, social position and so on."[32] Parties do not distort raw opinion but make possible real opinion. Critics, as Duverger wrote, "fail to realize that raw opinion is elusive, that formed opinion alone can be expressed, and that the method of expression necessarily imposes on it a frame which modifies it."[33] If this is so, then modern democracies owe a great deal not only to the bourgeoisie in general but to the United States in particular for its invention of the mass-based party in the 1840s.

At the same time, party politics does not necessarily mean rational, informed voting. In William Gienapp's description of politics from 1840 to 1860 there is more evidence of participation than of serious discussion. Gienapp notes the widespread popularity of campaign songs whose purpose was to "provide entertainment and generate en-thusiasm while lampooning the opposition."[34] Political barbecues were popular in Western states, and politics provided relief from social isolation. Was this also good political education? That would be harder to affirm. "Campaign hoopla generated popular interest, but at times this pageantry took precedence over the dissemination of political in-formation."[35] If that is the kind of politics as popular culture that

Christopher Lasch fondly looks back on, not all contemporaries felt the same. Edward Everett Hale, for one, complained that the 1856 Republican campaign with a tent, traveling blacksmith orator, and glee club "is putting politics on just the level of Circus Riding."[36]

It should be noted that the Lincoln-Douglas kind of campaign had its critics in Lincoln's day. Hale felt that stump speaking was "one of the downward tendencies" of the age, favoring the young and able-bodied over more seasoned, and presumably wiser, leaders and giving too much room to mere adventurers.[37] Today, in an era suspicious of television—and suspicious in part because television seems to favor certain superficial traits of good looks and the ability to invent a catchy sound bite—it is important to remember that an era of oratory had related problems. Being a winning public speaker was no guarantee that one could be a wise leader in office. The public speech before a live audience uses a "medium" with special properties just as much as the interview before a camera. (As it happens, live public speeches by the candidates were not very common, at least in presidential campaigns, in the nineteenth century. The campaign of 1888, for instance, had an incumbent president, Grover Cleveland, who made exactly one speech, to accept his nomination, and a challenging candidate, Benjamin Harrison, who gave quite a number of speeches, but every one of them from the front porch of his home in Indiana.) In any event, it is also true that in a day of intensely strong party loyalties, the people who listened to Lincoln and Douglas were not listening to make up their minds. They were there to rally for their candidate, whatever he might say. It was neither a personality contest nor a debate whose winner would be declared by people weighing the best arguments.

Electoral Procedures. Stanley Kelley wrote in a 1960 study of political campaigning that the basic assumption of his work is that "campaign discussion should help voters make rational voting decisions."[38] That seems a useful assumption. Can we characterize when during American history campaign discussion most closely approximated that ideal?

Michael McGerr examines this subject in *The Decline of Popular Politics,* where he studies political campaigning in the American North from the middle of the nineteenth century through the 1920s. In short, he chronicles campaigning from the era of the greatest participation of citizens in American politics through its rapid decline to the low levels of the 1920s that it had not reached since before 1840 and would not reach again until the 1970s. While McGerr recognizes a variety of factors that contributed to the decline of voter turnout, he draws attention to the influence of a conception of politics among an elite of reformers that disparaged the party-dominated and emotionally extravagant campaigns of the Civil War era. These reformers decried "spectacular" politics and sought to replace it with "educational politics." Pamphlets, not parades, was their idea of the rational way to run a campaign.

In the spectacular style of politics, local party organizations created special clubs, marching groups, and civic organizations that engaged in parades, demonstrations, picnics, and other outdoor forms of political entertainment. These forms were widely participatory, more so than any other form of American politics before or since, but this does not mean they were altogether democratically participatory. Members of the upper class held the most important local offices, and parades, as Michael McGerr observes, "stopped at the homes of the wealthy to serenade them and to hear their wisdom."[39] The spectacle of nineteenth-century politics helped establish, McGerr argues, "the upper class's right to rule."[40]

Politics, then, was more a communal ritual than an act of individual or group involvement in rational-critical discussion. This extended all the way to the ballot box. Ballots were drawn up by parties, not by a common state agency, and voters would very often deposit them in separate ballot boxes. Until the late nineteenth century there was no secret ballot in the United States, and the act of balloting was relatively public. Your neighbors knew not only if you voted but also which party you voted for. The party-printed ballots made it difficult for individuals to split their tickets; they also made it easy for bribery to be effective, since the party leaders could determine whether the bribed voter did or did not follow through on his voting pledge. The election, as a form of political communication, was itself a very different experience than it is today. It was organized much less with the rational choice of the individual voter in mind. The voter, in a sense, was not conceived of as an individual but as an entity enveloped in and defined by social circumstance and party affiliation.

The transformation of the election campaign from a communal ritual to a political marketplace, a transformation that took place primarily in the period from 1880 to 1920, was in part a self-conscious effort of reformers to root out the corruption of the party system—bribery and multiple voting—and to improve upon the election as a voice of people rationally seeking their interests on the basis of informed judgment. The reformers promoted what they called "educational" campaigns that replaced parades with pamphlets and outdoor rallies with in-home newspaper reading. The reformers, who were remarkably successful, helped to create of the electoral campaign an institution that pictures as the ultimate object of its efforts the isolated individual. This lonely but rational citizen gathers information from different sides, evaluates it, and conscientiously makes up his mind. The irony about contemporary longing for nineteenth-century politics is that it seeks the realization of an ideal that itself was formulated only on the funeral pyre of participatory, communal, ritualistic politics.

Conclusion

It does not appear that, in any general sense, rational-critical discussion characterized American politics in the colonial era. The politically oriented riot was a more familiar form of political activity than learned discussion of political principles. If some modern authors write with fondness of the spontaneity of such political expression,[41] others doubt that these riots were very often spontaneous at all.[42] In the nineteenth century, when political participation increased substantially, political discourse did not become markedly more rational and critical. To infer eighteenth-century politics from the fact that the Federalist papers appeared in the newspapers or to infer nineteenth-century politics from the Lincoln-Douglas debates would be something like characterizing American politics of the 1970s by the fact that the impeachment debates in the House Judiciary Committee in 1974 were broadcast live on television and discussed widely and fervently among people of all walks of life. All these events were extraordinary; none of them represents the normal political discourse of its era.

I find the concept of a public sphere indispensable as a model of what a good society should achieve. It seems to me a central notion for social or political theory. I think it is also enormously useful as a model that establishes a set of questions to ask about politics past and present. What I have tried to do here is just that and, in the process, to raise questions about how well a model of the public sphere was approximated in earlier periods of American history. If I have used my questions more as a club than a beacon, I have done so to dispel the retrospective wishful thinking that beclouds too much contemporary political and cultural analysis. Our place in the world is different from that of eighteenth- or nineteenth-century Americans, but not, I think, fallen. In thinking through the conditions and possibilities for more rational and critical, fair and fair-minded, political practices in our own day, we will not profit from maintaining illusions about the character of the public sphere in days gone by.

10 The News Media and the Democratic Process

Can the news media help create a more democratic society? To people who frequent journalism awards banquets or American Society of Newspaper Editors' conventions or journalism school commencement exercises, this question will be familiar, tired, and worn. *Of course* the news media can contribute to a more democratic society. The job of the press is to help produce a more informed electorate. A more informed citizenry will create a better and fuller democracy.

That is the answer in journalism. To outside observers, it may seem a naive answer to a simple-minded question. Most social scientists and social critics who diagnose the ills of American democracy do not see the media as a major source of democratic disease but as heir to an anemic body politic. Real improvement in our political affairs, they assert, must come from outside the media. Some eminent political thinkers would go further to argue that the problem of modern democracy is that there is too much participation, and probably too much information, not too little. If the media were to do something salutary, they might say, it would be to discourage people from taking an interest in politics.

I believe the news media *can* contribute to a more democratic society and should try to do so. The question is, how? More precisely, how—in light of the view of skeptics who deny the capacity of the media to make much of a political difference at all—can there be a plausible political mission for news institutions?

This is not to assume that the sole aim of the media is or should be to help create a better democracy. The media aim to make money for owners, provide jobs to employees, establish prestige among colleagues, entertain consumers—and these are all legitimate aims. But the media claim also to have a special mission of informing the citizenry to make democratic government possible, and the media claim special rights (First Amendment rights) and privileges (for instance, special postal system rates) based on their unique status as the "fourth branch of government." Suppose, hypothetically, that making American society more democratic were the sole or primary aim of the news media. What, then, should the media do to advance this aim most effectively?

Leading lines of thought in political science and political theory concentrate on democracy without ever centering on the media. Yet this work has substantial implications, which I will seek to analyze here, for a journalism that takes its role in democracy seriously.

Classical and Realist Models of Democracy

Twentieth-century theorists of democracy have attacked what they call the "classical" view of democracy, a view that takes democracy to be composed of "rational and active citizens who seek to realize a generally recognized common good through the collective initiation, discussion, and decision of policy questions concerning public affairs, and who delegate authority to agents (elected government officials) to carry through the broad decisions reached by the people through majority vote." This view, I should say, still has its defenders. They argue that only in this model does democracy find a justification—not as the least bad form of government, but as one with positive attributes. The role of "education in public responsibility," which the classical model requires, contributes to an ideal of human dignity and development. In this model, the process of decision making and its benefits for the individual, as well as the outcomes of decision making and their consequences for the collective good, are evaluated and found humane. This classical notion of democracy, its modern defenders suggest, is "informed by an exceedingly ambitious purpose: the education of an entire people to the point where their intellectual, emotional, and moral capacities have reached their full potential and they are joined, freely and actively, in a genuine community."[1]

That is all very well, say the skeptics and realists, but if it bears some resemblance to a New England town meeting, it bears none to the functioning of any known large modern state. If we are looking for a model to serve as a practical goal and not as a fantasy, then it is necessary to define more narrowly what democracy means—what democracy can *possibly* mean.

One of the first and most prominent thinkers to adopt a "realist" model of democracy in relation to the news media was Walter Lippmann. Lippmann is still paid obeisance as the premier theorist of American journalism. Nevertheless, during World War I he abandoned the belief that the press could do very much to improve American democracy. His key works on the press, *Public Opinion* and *The Phantom Public,* both declare that elites rule in a democracy, that we cannot expect otherwise, and that journalism cannot reform itself to change matters. The press, Lippmann argued, is entirely dependent on outside forces to record the activities of the political system: "It can normally record only what has been recorded for it by the working of institutions." Where there is what he calls a "good machinery of record," as with the stock market, the news can be full and accurate. Where there is not a good machinery of record, news must be gathered from press agents, from a "nose for news," from luck, and all of this without appropriate organizing frameworks. The best hope lies in establishing independent bureaus of intelligence and a corps of independent experts whose job would be to gather and transmit information to the press regarding the governing forces of society.[2]

This chastened view of the possibilities of the press in *Public Opinion* grew still darker in *The Phantom Public.* There Lippmann argued that the citizen is not sovereign but "lives in a world which he cannot see, does not understand and is unable to direct." And there is no solution. We can only scale down our expectations of what a democracy is supposed to be and what role public opinion can conceivably play. The public, Lippmann writes, is not the mass of citizens or the mass of voters: "It is merely those persons who are interested in an affair and can affect it only by supporting or opposing the actors." If individuals are not interested in an affair, then they are not, with regard to that affair, the public. If they are interested and can affect it by shaping policy, then they are insiders, not outsiders, an elite with regard to that affair, not a public. The public is an interested body whose power is limited to supporting or opposing a leadership.

And that, Lippmann says, is all a modern democracy is or can be:

> We must abandon the notion that the people govern. Instead we must adopt the theory that, by their occasional mobilization as a majority,

people support or oppose the individuals who actually govern. We must say that the popular will does not direct continuously but that it intervenes occasionally.[3]

Lippmann held out no hope that the public could be educated to fuller participation. He did not believe the role of the press was to inform citizens to make rational and informed judgments. The best that could be done would be to provide simple, clear signs to serve as "guides to reasonable action for the use of uninformed people." The task for democracy was to find ways for people to act "intelligently but in ignorance."[4]

One trouble with views of democracy like those Lippmann inherited and argued against is that they picture a government at one end, a mass of citizens at the other end, and nothing in between except perhaps the press as a conduit of information. Social scientists have been arguing for a long time, however, following in the footsteps of Tocqueville, that what sustains a democracy are the intermediary groups or associations that bring people together, that formulate, articulate, and crystallize opinion, and that provide collective bases for political action. This includes a large variety of organizations, from the National Rifle Association to the Students for a Democratic Society, from the local Lion's Club to the League of Women Voters. But most of all, it includes the political parties—and these have been faltering badly as avenues of citizen involvement in governing.

There is now a vast literature on the decline of American political parties, summed up in the title of David Broder's book, *The Party's Over.* The parties have failed to articulate distinct policies and positions. They have lost their hold on the public as organizations. Citizens no longer find it in their interest to give the parties loyalty, time, or attention. If the media appear to be powerful, this has as much to do with a vacuum left by the disintegrating parties as with the self-aggrandizement of the press and the television networks.[5]

Classical democratic theory did not pay much attention to parties; indeed, the founding fathers objected to parties, and there was strong anti-party sentiment during the first fifty years of the American republic. But more recent observers have taken parties to be a decisive index of "the existence of democracy itself."[6] Parties stand between the governors and the citizens, enable the coherent aggregation and articulation of popular views, and insist on responsiveness by the governing officials to those views. This point is well made by James Gazlay:

The great mass seldom or ever see more than one political object at a time, and that not very distinctly. They are enlisted from accident or promise of favor, on the side of some one of the office-hunters; and as it is much easier and indeed safer in some instances to support the man than his real principles, and as this course saves one the trouble of much thinking, people are apt to become the zealous advocates of men, at the very time when they suppose they are advocating principle: But if it be principle alone at which they aim, there must be strict organization, or they will become the humble tools of men in power, when they least expect it.

It may be useful to know that Mr. Gazlay wrote this in 1826.[7] The postwar era is not the first in which American political parties have been notably weak, though it is the first time since Mr. Gazlay's day. Today, one political scientist has argued, "the American political party is little more than one of many groups, not greatly disparate in their influence, which participate in elections. The party has been reduced from a quasi-public agency to a private association. Once a source of power, it has become another contestant for power in the pluralistic system."[8]

Specifically, the party has lost its power in presidential recruitment: personal organizations backing individual candidates have become rivals to party organizations. Primary elections have replaced party caucuses for nominations in many states. The mass media have stepped into the void, too, with national political reporters acting as a kind of "screening committee" for presidential aspirants. Campaign finance laws have weakened the resources of parties. Federal subsidies go to candidates, not to the parties. Further, the laws insist that groups (the now famous and fabulous Political Action Committees) may raise whatever funds they like, so long as they do not link up with political parties. All of this reinforces the already powerful trend of voters away from party identification. The number of voters who can be described as pure partisans has declined from 42 percent in 1960 to 23 percent in 1972. New and younger voters are especially likely to describe themselves as independents.[9]

The result, says Gerald Pomper, is "the loss of popular control over public policies and the consequent inability of less privileged elements to affect their social fate."[10] It may come as a shock to some to see the political party as the patron of the less privileged, but the parties have provided, in Western Europe especially but even in the United States, an avenue of group mobility for the working class and minority groups.

The decline of the party is one reason why Lippmann's assessment of American democracy, dark though it was, was perhaps not grim enough for viewers of the contemporary scene. But there are still two other reasons offered by contemporary observers for the sad state of democratic politics: the declining governability of society and the increasing influence of corporations.

Neo-conservative political scientists and sociologists have argued that the "problem of democracy" today is not how to increase democratic participation but how to govern societies overrun by participants. The task is not to make liberal democracy more participatory but to make increasingly participatory democracy minimally governable. They worry about a breakdown of traditional forms of social control, "a delegitimation of political and other forms of authority," and "an overload of demands on government." As Samuel Huntington put it, the vitality of democracy in the 1960s "produced a substantial increase in governmental activity and a substantial decrease in governmental authority." Like Joseph Schumpeter before him, Huntington believes that every democratic society requires a large amount of apathy on the part of citizens in order to function effectively. When marginal groups become effective voices in the political system, the system must handle demands it cannot satisfy. Huntington fears the brownout or blackout of the whole democratic way, quoting John Adams as saying, "There never was a democracy yet that did not commit suicide."[11]

Charles Lindblom's concern is something very different. He is doubtful enough about the prospects of democracy to have given up on the word "democracy" altogether. He prefers "polyarchy," rule of the many, rather than "democracy," rule of the people. He notes the low level of citizen participation in government, and he cites relevant survey data. Only 28 percent of Americans have ever tried to persuade others to vote as they did, only 26 percent have ever worked for a candidate, only 20 percent have ever contacted a local government official about a problem or issue, only 13 percent have ever contributed money to a political campaign, and a mere 8 percent are members of a political club or organization. But the main concern in his sober *Politics and Markets* is the disproportionate influence of business in the political system.

In market-oriented "polyarchies" like the United States, there are two rival forms of control over political authority. There is, obviously, the electoral system. But there is also, Lindblom argues, a separate system of privileged business controls. Businessmen perform functions in market societies that are governmental functions in other systems—decisions about what is to be produced, who is to be employed, how products are to be allocated. And leading corporate executives have considerable discretion in these matters. Government delegates these decisions to business: "Businessmen thus become a kind of public official and exercise what, on a broad view of their role, are public functions." They gain, correspondingly, semi-official public privileges, too. They have special access to government officials. They have the attention of public leaders as no other group in society does. Presidents, recognizing the public service business provides, will sometimes try to shield business from the uncertainties of the mainstream political process. Both Johnson and Nixon suppressed reports of their own committees on antitrust so as to keep a "business" matter out of the normal political arena.

Not only does business have its own separate sphere of influence and separate door to the White House and halls of Congress, legislatures, and governors' mansions, but it has increasingly powerful sway in the mainstream political arena as well. Although political observers have tended to equate business and labor as counterbalanced political pressure groups, the two are not commensurate. In House and Senate races, wealthy individuals still make up a large proportion of campaign contributions—in 1990, 43 percent of campaign income for House incumbents and 53 percent for challengers; 69 percent for Senate incumbents and 60 percent for challengers. Political Action Committees have increased their influence in the past decades. Their number has exploded from around 600 in 1974 to more than 4,100 in 1991. Thier contributions have grown more vital, amounting to 48 percent of campaign income for House incumbents in 1990, up from 34 percent in 1980. PAC money comes predominantly from business, trade organizations, and professional PACs, although they tend to spread their funds across well-placed incumbents of both parties while labor PACs concentrate on supporting Democrats. The consequences of PAC growth and the new world of campaign finance for democracy are not yet clear, but nowhere in the blizzard of suggestions for reform are proposals to weaken significantly the reliance of government on private business. Lindblom concludes his book by saying: "The large private corporation fits oddly into democratic theory and vision. Indeed, it does not fit."[12]

This is no wild-eyed radical. This is a mainstream political scientist, in 1981 president of the American Political Science Association. He is no fan of other possible political systems, but his indictment of our own is stinging.

What is the role of the mass media in all this? Lindblom, like Huntington writing about governability and like the theorists of political parties, does not put the media at center stage. He pays the media little attention, noting only that the voice of business dominates the media overwhelmingly. Not that there is no bad news about businesses in our press, not that business does not grit its teeth at the way it is sometimes pictured in the media, but the controversies around business in the media invariably concern secondary issues where leading businessmen themselves disagree. Although corporations and big business leaders are not often positively portrayed in popular films or TV entertainment, still, fundamental queries about the role of private enterprise and the delegation of power from government to business lie largely outside the realm of legitimate political discussion.

So where do these different—but all dismal—assessments of American democracy leave us? And where do they leave the news media that, hypothetically, want to improve the democratic process?

The News Media's Role

If one has read Walter Lippmann on public opinion, Gerald Pomper and others on political parties, Samuel Huntington and others on the ungovernability of modern liberal democratic states, and Charles Lindblom on the disproportionate role of business in the system of political authority in the United States, it is not easy to take seriously the platitudinous thinking about democracy that is the coin of the realm in and around journalism. Journalists and journalism educators still adhere to a loosely sketched classical ideal of democracy. This, in itself, is not bad. The more "realistic" assessments of democracy define the situation so grimly that they begin to foreclose conceptually the possibility of change. They seem almost to delight in making political science, not economics, the "dismal" discipline.

Indeed, the blindness of journalism to current thinking in political science about democracy has a certain advantage. It may be useful for the media to act *as if* they were instruments of popular education in a rich, vitalized democracy. After all, despite political science, this is sometimes true. In certain states or cities, regarding certain issues or campaigns, during certain moments of heightened political awareness, this *is* a living democracy—there is an approximation to political equality, there is relatively effective participation of large numbers, and public discussion is active and avid enough for participants to arrive at an adequate understanding of the issues.

I propose that the news media should be self-consciously schizophrenic in their efforts to perform a democratic political function. They should both champion the kind of democracy that the political scientists say we have little chance of achieving and, at the same time, they should imaginatively respond to the realities of contemporary politics that the scholars have observed. I will take up each strategy in turn, discussing both the general philosophy it entails and some of the changes in journalistic practice it might call for.

Toward Classical Democracy: Providing the Rational Citizen Better Information

Suppose that citizens are rational, interested in public affairs, and have access to effective participation in politics. Classical democratic theory takes this for granted. Classical thinking about journalism also takes this for granted and then assumes that the job of the news media is to help citizens achieve what Robert Dahl calls an "adequate understanding" of political issues. Helping citizens toward "adequate understanding" has long been and still should be a leading aim of the news media.

What does this entail? When Dahl takes "adequate understanding" as a criterion of democracy, he stresses that, in a democracy, citizens must have adequate understanding to "discover" their own preferences. He does not assume that people have their own preferences built in or that they necessarily know what their preferences are. Political education, then, is not simply a task of making the political scene clear enough for people to match their own predetermined preferences with the appropriate political actors who share those preferences. It is also a task in shaping the citizens' political tastes and preferences.

It is odd how often we forget this. We tend to assume that the wealthy will oppose taxes on high incomes, that blacks will vote for Democrats, and that the pinched middle class will prefer policies aimed at curbing inflation, not those aimed at reducing unemployment. These assumptions are largely—but not entirely—correct. Sociologists and political marketing consultants can show and explain the extent to which such assumptions are correct. Politics—the art of building coalitions, making compromises, persuading people that their own interests may be redefined—enters at the margin; it exists only where the powers of the sociologists and political marketers stop. If people always and only vote their pocketbooks, their race, or their party, then we will know the outcome of elections ahead of time. Then there is no point to politics, as such, at all. But there *is* politics and it does have point, and this is because people's preferences are not foreordained: people are capable of shifting to one side or another; they can be persuaded (and they can be fooled); they are open to political education. Indeed, what is at issue in politics is not manipulating predetermined tastes but shaping morally constituted values and value choices.

This is the faith upon which a democratic polity rests. It is a faith reinforced by the experience of anyone who has succeeded at one time or another in persuading another person to change his or her mind or by the experience of having changed one's own mind under the influence of someone else's concerted efforts at political sway. It is, however, a faith with a powerful foe—the foe of determinism, insisting that people have identifiable interests, know those interests, and vote them, period. There are two ways in which the press can combat this stance.

First, it combats the stance every time it prints news that it hopes will inform the public and lead some members of the public to see the world in a different way. Second, it combats the stance if it refuses to give blind support to the strongest allies of determinism. In recent years, one of determinism's most reliable allies has been public opinion polling. Not that there is anything wrong with public opinion polling in itself. But it is invariably reified, made to take on a permanence and authority it does not deserve. This has dangerous consequences. For one thing, political leaders misunderstand public opinion polls. They take the polls to mean that people have predetermined preferences and that political education or political leadership can have no power against the will of the people. This, of course, is nonsense. When Nixon ordered ground troops into Cambodia in 1970, only 7 percent of the public favored the move. After the President went ahead anyway, 50 percent favored the move. Citizen "volitions," as Charles Lindblom puts it, change "quickly and substantially in response to leadership's acts or advice."[13]

Furthermore, if politicians misunderstand polls, so do ordinary citizens. They, too, are subtly affected, we must imagine, by the reporting of polls as if the "opinion" they captured had some permanence. One thing the press can do is to report polls more wisely. For instance, there should be efforts to place the polls in historical context, to provide not just the most recent poll but comparable results from previous times. And the tone should not be the reverent tone with which the Dow-Jones is reported or the sports scores. The opinion polls simply are not as substantial or accurate a report of the world, not so final—even for a day—and not so trustworthy as a guide to action. The press should take special care not to stunt political education by providing poll data carelessly.

This is a small point, however. The major point is that there is much the press can do to improve its conventional function of providing citizens with the information that will enable them to gain an adequate understanding of politics, including their own preferences, and to participate effectively in political life. Take, for instance, the especially crucial problem of covering elections. How well does the press cover elections? How might election coverage be improved?

Obviously, this issue could require a chapter or a book or several books in itself. I note just one point here. Every social scientific study of the press of the past ten or fifteen years has found that the press overrepresents the views of government officials. To some extent this is inevitable, since the main focus of political news is necessarily government, and since most information about government necessarily comes from government officials. Nevertheless, this leads to certain consequences that arguably work against the media's intention of improving democratic governance.

A study of congressional elections by Peter Clarke and Susan Evans finds that incumbents receive far more press coverage than challengers. Incumbents are almost all reelected; since 1968, over 90 percent of incumbent congressmen running for reelection have been successful, and their margin of victory keeps growing. There are any number of explanations for this "incumbency" phenomenon. Congressmen have more resources—the franking privilege, a travel allowance, computer time, and so forth; this comes to a $100 million edge every election year for incumbent congressmen. Moreover, as federal activities expand and the ordinary citizen comes to have more contact with federal agencies, congressmen increasingly act as and are judged as brokers for local citizens with federal institutions and so develop records with their constituents as providers of public service. Moreover, with party identification growing weaker among voters, the simple fact of familiarity gained by two years or more in office is an increasingly significant advantage. But another factor is worth considering: newspapers provide incumbents much more election coverage than they do challengers.

This is not the result of some direct policy choice. The newspapers spend just as much effort, in terms of reporting assignments, on challengers as on incumbents. But the incumbents wind up with much greater news coverage. Attention to personal characteristics of the candidates and to discussions of their political organizations tends to be even-handed. But incumbents get much more coverage of their political views. Why? In part, as Clarke and Evans say, it is simply that "challengers do not have the raw material—past experience in office, legislative skills, constituent services." In part, it is that reporters avoid issue coverage and disparage issues as critical in election outcomes, even though mounting an "issue" campaign is one of the few key resources available to challengers.

Then what of cases where an incumbent does not run for reelection, what of open contests? This should be a great opportunity for the press to treat candidates equally and to stress political issues. But, Clarke and Evans find, "Open races are almost invisible in public print." In open races, *neither* candidate has a public, legitimated track record. Neither, very often, has the legitimacy of being a government official. As a result, neither gets covered.[14] As for television, it scarcely figures at all. Network news, because it is national, pays hardly any attention to congressional races. Local television news in most communities is unashamedly show business, not journalism, and devotes only the slightest amount of air time to local electoral candidates and issues.

Thus the media's usual attention to public officials, however beneficial or harmful it may be in ordinary circumstances, has the effect in congressional elections of promoting the incumbent when the incumbent is running and of minimizing attention to open races. In this, one of the most vital opportunities for democracy to work, the routines of daily journalism do not help but stand in the way of democracy. The press does not do a good job of aiding the "adequate understanding" of the citizens.

There is much the press could do to improve this performance. Simply to recognize the problem might, in itself, galvanize the press to better work. Special efforts to ask challengers for position papers on political issues and to print stories about the positions would help. So might other simple activities. Where in the paper, for instance, is a citizen to find news about the candidates in his or her district? In large metropolitan areas, citizens are at something of a loss. It is not easy to know where in the paper to look—or whether it will be worth looking, since coverage of the different races tends to be episodic. A more simple, clean format might make a big difference. This would standardize news coverage of local races, make it seem less "newsy" and more like box scores—what's happening in the fourth district, what's happening in the sixth, and so on. The newspapers already provide this kind of service so that readers can monitor their world in other ways—the sports scores, the stock market quotations. Why not do something similar for local elections, by district? Major news stories could still be played more dramatically. Perhaps there could even be a part of the paper organized as a separate election section every day during the weeks before an election.[15] Local television could, but probably will not, do the same, adding a regular "election" segment to its general news, sports, and weather in the weeks before an election.

These changes would not transform the world. But if journalists begin to ask seriously the question I have asked here—what can the media do to improve the American democratic process, assuming an intelligent and interested electorate—they will find ways, these ways or others, to make a difference.

Journalists, like people in other professions, get lazy, fall into ruts, and too often forget what they are there for in the first place. Journalism convention slogans about the First Amendment or the right to know are generally oriented to defending the press from attackers, not to thinking through what the press might do to serve democratic politics better. Most journalists do not find time for serious thought about journalism. Those who do, Clarke and Evans find, do better work; there is some evidence that journalists who read the *Columbia Journalism Review* do a better job of covering challenger candidates in congressional campaigns.[16]

It is not much of a platform to recommend that journalists should think more than they do. However, thinking does not happen in a vacuum; it requires some institutional underpinning. To make thinking more likely in journalism, there is much that news institutions can do. Staff retreats can be useful. Sabbatical policies would be an excellent idea. Sending a reporter off to Harvard for a Nieman fellowship is probably a good way to lose that reporter to a more prestigious publication. But establishing short-term sabbatical relationships with local universities might be a way to provide the time reporters need for reflection and, incidentally, to make contacts (which are generally lacking) with scholars who might be useful news sources.

These are small, practical suggestions for some continuing in-service training for journalists. I do not think that the news media have done all they can to provide more and better political information to citizens. Nor have they invested enough resources in thinking in practical ways about how this might be done.

Confronting Political Realities: Serving Democratic Aspirations in Unfavorable Conditions

There is much, then, that can be done if news institutions assume a rational, intelligent, interested citizenry eager to inform itself. Again, this sometimes is a fair description of the public—perhaps more often than we suspect.

At the same time, it is by no means a complete picture of how the political system works, or fails to work. What is the role or responsibility of the press if the democratic doubters and skeptics are right? If Lippmann is right that the public inevitably lies far from the center of activity? If the many commentators are right that the political parties are practically moribund? If Lindblom is right that business has a disproportionate influence in American politics? If Huntington is right that governability has become a central problem of democracy? Let me take up each question in turn.

Lippmann's Skepticism. If Lippmann is right that the best the public can do is to express its preferences of "ins" or "outs" every few years, and do that on the basis of relatively scant information, then the press cannot perform its classical function. But it could well perform other functions. If the press cannot communicate effectively about government to the people at large, it can nonetheless hold the governors accountable to the relatively small number of other informed and powerful people. The press can serve as a stand-in for the public, holding the governors accountable—not to the public (which is not terribly interested), but to the ideals and rules of the democratic polity itself.

What I mean is not complicated. The Pulitzer committee each year makes an award for newspaper activity that demonstrates excellent work of public responsibility. Very often this goes to a paper that has shown unusual enterprise in muckraking or investigative reporting. That is, the newspaper took it upon itself to define an issue and to create a story. More often than not, these stories do not take some arbitrary value that the journalists care about to report on. Rather, they take some public statute (a law or legitimated social norm) or public statement (a campaign promise) and see if the political actor on the scene has lived up to it. The press, in this regard, has relatively little power to disseminate new values, but it has great opportunity to see that existing values are kept alive in practice. One investigative reporter, David Burnham, has said that his strategy as an investigative reporter was to hold government agencies and other groups he covered to their own stated goals.[17] The question was not: are they doing right or are they doing wrong? It was: are they living up to what they have committed themselves to do? That is a question one may approach in traditional journalistic ways, clinging to the rules of objectivity. At the same time, it is a question that asserts the responsibility of the press as an institution for public accountability.

Political Party Decay. The decline of political parties seems largely beyond the power of the media to influence. That is so. However, it is not *entirely* beyond the power of the media. David Broder has observed that in those relatively rare moments where the press has reported on party congresses and mid-term conferences, the coverage has enlivened interest in party activity.[18]

The extent to which the press actively *avoids* covering political parties may not be clear to journalists. The press, and television especially, have clearly taken a stand in favoring popular primaries over party caucuses as a way to select delegates to national nominating conventions. In 1968, for instance, CBS News ran only one feature story on non-primary delegate selection procedures despite the fact that 60 percent of the delegates chosen that year were chosen by non-primary means. Primary elections may be more democratic—certainly they are on the surface. But I do not believe that that is the judgment the press has made. The press has made a professional, not a political, judgment that elections are more snappy as news than are party caucuses. The press did not initiate the spread of popular presidential primaries but, as Richard Rubin observes, "finding primaries professionally beneficial, they subsequently promoted them as the proper, democratic, and 'American way' to deal with intra-party representation."[19]

The press cannot by itself reverse the decline of parties. It can, however, examine the ways in which it has unintentionally adopted an anti-party stance itself—not on the editorial page, but in the pattern of news coverage. The press regularly takes value positions without even knowing it. An anti-party stance is probably one such position. Recognizing this would be a first step in changing it and providing party structures a more respectful and more active news coverage.

The Privileged Position of Big Business. What might the press do regarding what Lindblom argues is the privileged position of big business? There are no ready answers to this question. The news media are increasingly big businesses themselves, and they enjoy some of the special access to government policymaking available to other large corporations. They also are financially supported by businesses—local businesses of modest size, very often, in the case of the print media;

large national corporations, for the most part, in the case of television. One cannot expect the news media to go after big business with a hatchet.

Nor, I think, would that satisfy the concerns that Lindblom raises. He does not say that business performs its delegated responsibilities badly, nor does he argue that business is undeserving of some of the privileged access to power that it has. What he says is that the current governmental system in the United States does not fit conventional understandings of democracy and that a large extra-electoral arena of decision making in which business plays a disproportionate role goes largely unrecognized and unpublicized.

Could this be changed? The job of the press would not be to assert that business has too much or too little or just the right amount of power; the job of the news media is to cover the news of political life. The job in this instance would be to recognize and report on the ways in which business is a partner in government.

Consider, for a moment, the reporting of congressional legislation— a measure for environmental protection, a bill for a tax increase or decrease. The way this is now reported, the main "scene" is one in which 500-odd representatives make up their minds about how to vote. There may be some attention in feature articles or in news analysis about what happens "behind the scene"—how active lobbyists are, who they are, what their views are. Though this is a part of the career of any legislation, it receives little notice in the press. Why? Not, I think, because reporters want to protect lobbyists from public scrutiny. But simply because, ultimately, the story is about how the legislators vote. Their decisions, in the final analysis, will determine if the tax proposal, say, becomes law or does not. This is reasonable. It identifies the legislators and their top aides as the appropriate news sources. However, it leaves a major part of the legislative process in the shadows.

There may be some simple remedies. One task, clearly, is to report more fully and on a regular basis about decision making in the private sphere that directly affects public policy. Even in the public sphere, however, there may be ways of reporting that more accurately indicate the interconnections of public and private power. Newspapers might identify a certain number of key bills in each session of Congress or of a state legislature and keep a running tab on them. The tab would include where the bill is—in hearings, in committee, on the floor, in conference. It would include a list of different pressure groups—not just business but other interest groups as well that have taken public stands on the bill—and it would summarize the stated positions of those groups. It might even identify sections of the intended legislation that have been more or less "written in" at the behest of a particular interest group. Obviously, this is not going to be possible or worthwhile on every piece of legislation. But on key legislative matters, it would be an important way to keep the electorate informed and to make lobbyists to some degree responsible to the public.

Would everyone read such dull stuff? Of course not. But remember, this is the schizophrenic news media that I am proposing. In this part of my recommendations, it is not required that journalists assume that their readership is entirely intelligent, rational, and active in the political process. They need assume only that there is a small, interested body of readers who will indeed pay attention to such news. And the group can be very small indeed. In theory, it could be just the reporters and their editors themselves. For if we put aside the classical view of rational and interested citizens, then the news media can be viewed not as communicators to the public but as guardians of the public, stand-ins for public scrutiny, gatekeepers who monitor the political process on behalf of the public.

When the matter is viewed this way, the press may have a larger variety of goals and standards than it ordinarily is aware of. In this respect, David Burnham's injunction to hold government agencies to their own goals is a good one. He need not assume a large, active, interested reading public; he need only assume that public standards and civic norms have been written into the enabling legislation for the agency in question or have been restated in public speeches of the agency's leaders. This then sets a standard in relation to which investigative reporting can proceed in the public interest.

The Surfeit of Democracy. Finally, let us consider Samuel Huntington's position that the problem of democracy today is too much, rather than not enough. Government outcomes will be better, Huntington says, if people are not too interested in government. An educated population, he feels, is likely to be too interested in political participation for governing agencies to avoid political stalemate. He writes, "The effective operation of a democratic political system requires some measure of apathy and non-involvement on the part of some individuals and groups."[20]

It is not easy to reconcile this position with a genuine regard for the democratic process. It is easy enough to recognize that the representation of varied interests in the policymaking process will slow things down. We all know how committees work—or fail to work. There is a great concern in recent years that single-issue interest groups—the anti-abortion group or the National Rifle Association or some of the wilderness preservation groups—can thwart legislation or policy that most constituencies find in their interest. While the representation and protection of minorities is a vital part of democratic society, the possibility that splinter minorities have increasing power to stymie majority will is disturbing.

But Huntington's recommendation that we encourage indifference to politics is not acceptable. If participants in the political process are too uncompromising for the system to work, the first line of defense, I should imagine, is not to urge participants to leave the system but to educate them in the arts of compromise. Huntington, like too many others, worries that people are becoming more highly educated and thus more likely to participate in politics, but he then turns around to deny that they are educable. He gives up the possibility of genuine political education. I do not think there is yet reason enough to abandon this hope of democracy.

The rise of single-issue constituencies is related to the decline in older forms of political participation. Unions, churches, and parties—hierarchical organizations with a small number of leaders and a large mass of followers—are losing out to groups that express the citizen's preferences "with far greater precision." The new groups are issue-oriented, and they rely on "a heightened ideological sensitivity among the electorate." More people today have and use "the skills needed to manipulate political abstractions." There is what Ronald Inglehart calls a "cognitive mobilization" taking place in the advanced industrial democracies.[21]

Albert Hirschman has offered an intriguing explanation of the rise of single-issue constituencies. He argues that the main form of political participation in liberal democracies, voting, is an unduly *tame* mode of participation. It does not give most people sufficient scope to "express their feelings about public issues with the intensity with which they experience them." Hirschman argues that the establishment of the vote as the main mode of participation "leads to disappointment with the limited opportunities for civic involvement and hence to its decline." He sees the rise of single-interest groups as a response to the political underinvolvement of voting:

It is possible that people join these movements not so much because they believe in the overriding importance of the particular issue, as because they want to make manifest, to the world, their friends, and themselves, that they are able to work up very strong feelings about *some* public issue. In this manner, a political system in which electoral politics is supposed to be the only politics can engender quite another kind of politics that carries a new, insidious menace to the proper functioning of democracy.[22]

Whatever the explanation, there does appear to be an important new pattern of political involvement that the political system will have to accommodate. The task of the press is neither to encourage nor to discourage these single-issue groups but to report about them. *And* to report on the pattern of political involvement that they represent.

Further, the news media can serve as political educators. This does not mean slogans or sermons. It means that the media can either, by their own actions, promote a more comprehensive view of politics than many of the single-issue groups have or, unconsciously and unintentionally, disseminate and reinforce the view of the interest groups. What the media cannot do is to stand aside, objectively. That is simply impossible. The news media necessarily incorporate into their work a certain view of politics, and they will either do so intelligently and critically or unconsciously and routinely.

For instance, most members of single-interest pressure groups have, in fact, political opinions that are a good deal more complicated than the stands of the groups they adhere to. From most reporting about the public's views, there is no way to learn this. Again, there is emphasis on opinion polls, which tend to suggest fixed, predetermined, and hardened attitudes. In the 1980 presidential campaign, the *Wall Street Journal* developed a simple but important alternative way to study opinion, and they and others have continued this. The *Journal* followed the lead of market researchers who employ not only big national surveys but small, seminar-sized "focus groups" to arrive at a more intimate understanding of what consumers think and how they arrive at their views. It assembled separate groups of white-collar and blue-collar citizens and conducted general discussions with them about politics. One cannot read these stories without being forced to relax stereotyped views of middle-class or working-class people. It is not that "everyone is just the same"—patterns do emerge, but they are more complex and suggest more thoughtfulness than one is ordinarily led to expect.

"Focus groups" are, of course, "unscientific"—but marketers find them a vital supplement to survey research if they are to understand their potential audience. They are an excellent alternative for the news media, too, if the media seek to arrive at, and help their readers arrive at, a more subtle understanding of politics—and one that shows the range of thinking and the room for compromise that, in fact, characterize most citizens.

Conclusion: The Virtues of Schizophrenia

Psychologists tell us that people who set no goals do not achieve much—but neither do people who set lofty goals. Those who set high but *reachable* goals do better. Hitch your wagon to a star, they advise, but one that draws you on and does not dazzle you into immobility.

It may be the same with institutions. Too often, journalists—like people in every other field—set no goals. They just want to get through the day, to meet the deadline. But from that perspective they sometimes shift to the other extreme and think that their goal should be to educate the people to be shrewd observers of politics and enthusiastic participants in the political process. They try to create the world in which a classical notion of democracy would make sense.

I have tried to argue that this lofty goal, while unreachable, is still in many ways an excellent guide for journalistic practice. At the same time, I have suggested that journalistic practice should *also* accommodate itself to the reality that not all citizens are or ever will be rational, intelligent, active, and constant participants in the political process. In cases where an informed and involved electorate does not exist, the news media still have available to them alternative models of their democratic obligations. They can act as stand-ins for the public, holding authority (constituted—in the case of government; unconstituted—in the case of business, lobbies, and interest groups) responsible to its own stated aims and other publicly agreed-upon goals. They can do this simply by the power of the searchlight of publicity and by making that searchlight more constant.

As I have said, this may call for a kind of schizophrenia on the part of the news media—to act as if classical democracy were within reach and simultaneously to work as if a large, informed, and involved electorate were not possible. The virtue of schizophrenia is that *both* things are true under different circumstances. Journalists would do well to be of two minds because the world they report is of two (or more) possibilities. And in this fact, I think, lies not only complication but opportunity.

Notes

Introduction: News as Public Knowledge

1. There is a cottage industry of journalism history with its own professional associations and journals, but it operates almost entirely in journalism schools, outside history departments, and tends to be far removed from important lines of inquiry in historical studies generally. A "political communication" section of the American Political Science Association formed a few years ago and is a promising development, but like the relatively recent "sociology of culture" section of the American Sociological Association and studies of symbolic or expressive culture in any of the social sciences (apart from anthropology), it has had little influence on the core concerns of the discipline as a whole.

2. For a fascinating analysis of the confrontation of American journalists and leaders of the East European "velvet revolution," see Janos Horvat and Jay Rosen, "Singlethink: Thoughts on the Havel Episode," *Gannett Center Journal* 4 (1990): 31–52.

3. Noam Chomsky and Edward Herman, *Manufacturing Consent: The Political Economy of the Mass Media* (New York: Pantheon, 1988). In this work Chomsky and Herman explicitly compare American news institutions to *Pravda* on half a dozen occasions, intending to provoke outrage at so sacrilegious a metaphor. Nowhere do they suggest that there might be important differences, but since they provoke the question, it seems well to answer it directly.

4. Stephen E. Bornstein, "The Politics of Scandal," in *Developments in French Politics,* ed. Peter A. Hall, Jack Hayward, and Howard Machin (London: MacMillan, 1990), pp. 269–281, observes that the French media "are relatively poorly equipped to serve as detectors of, and deterrents to, scandal." The press in France "lacks a tradition of effective, non-partisan investigative journalism," and the French public seems to be characterized by a "short attention span, cynicism and moral indifference" that make French audiences less receptive to scandalous revelations than are the British or Americans.

5. Daniel C. Hallin, "The American News Media: A Critical Theory Perspective," in *Critical Theory and Public Life,* ed. John Forester (Cambridge, Mass.: MIT Press, 1985), reprinted in Daniel C. Hallin, *We Keep America on Top of the World* (London: Routledge, 1994), pp. 32–53.

6. James Houck, 1989, cited in Phyllis Kaniss, *Making Local News* (Chicago: University of Chicago Press, 1991), p. 59.

7. For the distinction between "statist" and "civil" discourse, see Robert Manoff, "Covering the Bomb: The Nuclear Story and the News," *Working Papers* 10 (Summer 1983): 19–27.

8. W. Lance Bennett, "Toward a Theory of Press-State Relations in the United States," *Journal of Communication* 40 (1990): 103–125.

9. Peter Viles, "Dan Rather Blasts TV News," *Broadcasting & Cable*, October 4, 1993, p. 12. See also a useful review of the consequences of "narrowcasting" and the FCC's 1987 abandonment of the fairness doctrine for the broadcast of political information in Austin Ranney, "Broadcasting, Narrowcasting, and Politics," in *The New American Political System*, Second Version, ed. Anthony King (Washington: AEI Press, 1990), pp. 175–201.

10. J. Herbert Altschull, *Agents of Power* (New York: Longman, 1984), p. 298.

11. S. Robert Lichter, Stanley Rothman, and Linda Lichter, *The Media Elite* (Bethesda, Md.: Adler and Adler, 1986), p. 28. For a critique, see Herbert Gans, "Are U.S. Journalists Dangerously Liberal?" *Columbia Journalism Review*, November/December 1985, pp. 29–33.

12. David H. Weaver and G. Cleveland Wilhoit, *The American Journalist*, 2nd ed. (Bloomington: Indiana University Press, 1991), find, for 1982, virtually the same percentage of people identifying themselves as left-of-center among journalists (22 percent) and in the general population (21 percent). More people in the general population identify themselves as right-of-center (32 percent) than among journalists (18 percent), with more journalists seeing themselves as middle-of-the-road (58 percent) than in the general population (37 percent).

13. See Stephen Hess, *The Washington Reporters* (Washington: Brookings Institution, 1981), p. 115, and Herbert J. Gans, *Deciding What's News* (New York: Pantheon, 1979), p. 184.

14. William Greider, *Who Will Tell the People?* (New York: Simon and Schuster, 1992), p. 306.

15. Howard Kurtz, *Media Circus* (New York: Times Books, 1993), pp. 70, 71.

16. America Rodriguez, "Made in the USA: The Construction of Univision News," Ph.D. diss., Department of Communication, University of California, San Diego, 1993.

17. William Grimes, "Randy Shilts, Author, Dies at 42; One of First to Write About AIDS," *New York Times*, February 18, 1994, p. C19 (National Edition). See also Jeffrey Schmalz, "Covering AIDS and Living It: A Reporter's Testimony," *New York Times* (Week in Review), December 20, 1992, section 4, p. 1, for an account of how Schmalz, who later died of AIDS, tried to hold to his identity as a news professional while covering an issue that directly concerned his identity as a member of the gay community.

18. This is where I began my own study of journalism two decades ago, writing a doctoral dissertation and then a book to explore the evolution of "objectivity" as a professional ideal among journalists. Why, I asked, should objectivity ever have emerged as a guiding ideal in journalism? (See Michael Schudson, *Discovering the News*, New York: Basic Books, 1978). Now I return to the question, recognizing anew how central it is but re-visiting it in a broader framework.

19. Among the most important of these works is Leon Sigal, *Reporters and Officials* (Lexington, Mass.: D. C. Heath, 1973); Gaye Tuchman, *Making News*

(New York: The Free Press, 1978); Gaye Tuchman, "Objectivity as Strategic Ritual: An Examination of Newsmen's Notions of Objectivity," *American Journal of Sociology* 77 (1972): 660–679; Edward Epstein, *News from Nowhere* (New York: Random House, 1973); and Herbert Gans, *Deciding What's News* (New York: Pantheon, 1979).

20. Michael Robinson and Margaret Sheehan, *Over the Wire and On T.V.* (New York: Russell Sage Foundation, 1983), pp. 97, 111, 212.

21. Thomas Patterson, *Out of Order* (New York: Alfred A. Knopf, 1993), p. 6. It must be added that campaign reporting has grown substantially more negative over the past thirty years. See Patterson, p. 20. This has to do with journalists' shifting ideology, their efforts not to be patsies, their post-Vietnam, post-Watergate, post-Reagan/Deaver/Ailes efforts not to be taken in.

22. Ibid, p. 206.

23. Steven R. Weisman, "Reagan Pledges Aid to Louisiana Flood Area," *New York Times,* January 3, 1983, p. 7, and George Skelton, "Reagan Pitches In to Help Flood Victims," *Los Angeles Times,* January 3, 1983, I-4.

24. Both reporters graciously commented on a draft of this passage. George Skelton defended his analysis as a close reflection of the views and motives of the White House staff; there was no question, he wrote, that national public relations rather than local morale-boosting and flood relief explained "what the President of the United States was doing in Monroe, La., on a Sunday afternoon." He added that he wrote the story "straight" for the first five paragraphs; the analysis came later. Weisman's story, he added, may have been as different from his own as it was because of constraints of space and deadline. "There's usually much less to these things than meets the eye," he concluded. Steven Weisman replied that he remembered thinking that it was "so obvious" that the Louisiana stop was a ploy to boost the President's image that he did not have to do much to point it out. "In writing, for example, about how the President waited for the cameraman to film him, I probably thought I was making it clear. To me it is much better to present the evidence for a conclusion than to club the reader over the head with the conclusion myself."

25. This whole issue, recurrently discussed among journalists, is most recently elaborated, with plenty of interesting anecdotes but no consistent analysis, in Daniel Schorr's 1993 Theodore H. White lecture, "Press and Politics: Who's Using Whom?" and the discussion that followed; see Daniel Schorr, *Press and Politics: Who's Using Whom?* (Cambridge, Mass.: Joan Shorenstein Barone Center, Kennedy School, Harvard University, 1993).

26. Leon Sigal, *Reporters and Officials* (Lexington, Mass.: D. C. Heath, 1973) is an early study documenting the overwhelming reliance of Washington reporting on government officials.

27. For some outstanding examples of a cultural study of news, see Barbie Zelizer, "Where Is the Author in American TV News? On the Construction and Presentation of Proximity, Authorship, and Journalistic Authority," *Semiotica* 80 (1990); Theodore L. Glasser and James S. Ettema, "Investigative Journalism and the Moral Order," *Critical Studies in Mass Communication* 6 (1989): 1–20; Michael Cornfield and David Yalof, "Innocent by Reason of Analogy: How the Watergate Analogy Served Both Reagan and the Press During the Iran-Contra Affair," *Corruption and Reform* 3 (1988); and the influential essay, both charming and insightful, by Robert Darnton, "Writing News and Telling Stories," *Daedalus*

104 (1975): 175–194. In two other essays, I have elaborated the distinction among "political economy" approaches to the study of news, which take patterns of ownership of news organizations as the primary determinant of news content; "sociological" or "social organizational" approaches, which take the competitive interactions between sources and reporters, reporters and editors, and editors and editors to be the primary determinant; and "cultural" approaches that see the taken-for-granted ideas and beliefs of journalists, both those borrowed from the broader culture and those specific to the culture of journalistic professionalism, to be the primary determinant. See "Why News Is The Way It Is," *Raritan* 2 (Winter 1983): 109–125, and "The Sociology of News Production Revisited," in *Mass Media and Society*, ed. James Curran and Michael Gurevitch (London: Edward Arnold, 1992). In both essays I argue that all three approaches are necessary but I call particularly for more attention to cultural explanations, which I think have generally been neglected by social scientists studying the news.

28. Daniel C. Hallin, *"The Uncensored War": The Media and Vietnam* (New York: Oxford University Press, 1986), pp. 116–117.

29. Soviet journalists had one advantage over Western journalists in their day—they could cover business with the same access they had to government because business was government-owned and managed. They had access to the shop floor that a reporter in the West could only gain with difficulty. See Dean Mills, "The Soviet Journalist: A Cultural Analysis," Ph.D. diss., University of Illinois, 1981.

30. James Carey, "Why: The Dark Continent of American Journalism," in Robert K. Manoff and Michael Schudson, eds., *Reading the News* (New York: Pantheon Books, 1986).

31. Kaniss, *Making Local News*, pp. 65–68.

32. Ben Bradlee, personal interview, February 27, 1991.

33. Jeff Greenfield, "Presidential Politics and Myths of Media Power," in *Covering Campaign '88: The Politics of Character and the Character of Politics* (New York: Gannett Center for Media Studies, 1988), p. 5. From an address delivered January 26, 1988, at the Gannett Center for Media Studies.

34. Michael Kelly, "David Gergen, Master of the Game," *New York Times Magazine*, October 31, 1993, p. 64.

35. Recent essays by two of our most searching culture commentators are scathingly critical of some of the prominent media critics, from Noam Chomsky to Senator Paul Simon to Catharine MacKinnon to Dan Quayle. See John Leonard, "TV and the Decline of Civilization," *The Nation*, December 27, 1993, pp. 785, 801–804; Todd Gitlin, "The Imagebusters," *American Prospect* 16 (Winter 1994).

36. Nancy Gibbs, "Angels Among Us," *Time*, December 27, 1993, p. 61.

37. See, for instance, Joshua Meyrowitz's account of how the press systematically avoided covering Democratic presidential candidate Larry Agran in 1988: "The Press Rejects a Candidate," *Columbia Journalism Review*, March/April 1992, pp. 46–48.

38. Clifford Geertz, *The Interpretation of Cultures* (New York: Basic Books, 1973), p. 14.

39. Thanks to Daniel Bell for this story.

40. I borrow here some language from an essay of mine that explores this question in much greater detail, "How Culture Works: Perspectives from Media Studies on the Efficacy of Symbols," *Theory and Society* 18 (1989): 153–180.

41. *San Diego Union,* October 8, 1993. AP, "Three Featured on 'America's Most Wanted' Captured in One Day."

42. *Newsweek,* July 29, 1985, pp. 17, 20.

43. Herbert J. Gans, "Reopening the Black Box: Toward a Limited Effects Theory," *Journal of Communication* 43 (1993): 32–33.

44. Alice Walker, *In Search of Our Mothers' Gardens* (San Diego: Harcourt Brace Jovanovich, 1983), p. 124.

45. Amartya Sen, "Freedoms and Needs," *The New Republic,* January 10 and 17, 1994, p. 34. See also Jean Drèze and Amartya Sen, *Hunger and Public Action* (Oxford: Clarendon Press, 1989), pp. 159, 212–215, 262–264.

46. I was a partial exception. See my respectful but critical review in *Columbia Journalism Review,* January/February 1988, pp. 55–57.

47. See a similar point in Jack M. McLeod, Gerald M. Kosicki, and Zhongdang Pan, "On Understanding and Misunderstanding Media Effects," in *Mass Media and Society,* ed. James Curran and Michael Gurevitch (London: Edward Arnold, 1992), p. 257.

48. *Public Opinion,* January/February 1988, p. 18.

49. On the lack of knowledge about how attorneys should behave to win jury trials, see Michael J. Saks, "Flying Blind in the Courtroom: Trying Cases without Knowing What Works or Why," a review of Robert H. Klonoff and Paul L. Colby, "Sponsorship Strategy: Evidentiary Tactics for Winning Jury Trials" (Charlottesville: The Michie Company, 1990), in *Yale Law Journal* 101 (1992): 1177–1191. On the lack of knowledge about how (or if) advertising works, see Michael Schudson, *Advertising, the Uneasy Persuasion* (New York: Basic Books, 1984).

50. Bob Goodman, quoted in Larry J. Sabato, *The Rise of Political Consultants* (New York: Basic Books, 1981), p. 17. The political scientist Larry Bartels concludes that electioneering efforts in recent presidential campaigns "have not seemed to produce many large, unaccountable changes in electoral support." For the 1988 campaign, "the wizardry of Roger Ailes and the ineptness of Michael Dukakis together produced a residual vote shift of less than 1 per cent." Larry M. Bartels, "The Impact of Electioneering in the United States," in *Electioneering: A Comparative Study of Continuity and Change,* ed. David Butler and Austin Ranney (Oxford: Clarendon Press, 1992), p. 266.

51. The key work is Daniel C. Hallin, *The "Uncensored War": The Media and Vietnam* (New York: Oxford University Press, 1986). See also Michael Mandelbaum, "Vietnam: The Television War," *Daedalus* 111 (1982): 157–170.

52. George D. Moss, *Vietnam: An American Ordeal* (Englewood Cliffs, N.J.: Prentice-Hall, 1990), p. 274.

53. Lewis L. Gould, *The Spanish-American War and President McKinley* (Lawrence: University Press of Kansas, 1982) dismisses the "yellow press" as a significant factor in leading the country to war (pp. 23–24). So do most authorities. The best account of how American history textbooks and journalism historians came to perpetuate a view resting on little evidence and less logic is to be found in Mark Matthew Welter, "Minnesota Newspapers and the Cuban Crisis, 1895–1898: Minnesota as a Test Case for the 'Yellow Journalism' Theory," Ph.D. diss., University of Minnesota, 1970. Of course, Minnesota papers do not provide a test case. That these papers did not adopt the jingoism of Pulitzer's *New York World* and Hearst's *New York Journal* does not mean that the giant New York "yellows" could not have influenced public opinion or Washington opinion. But the fact is

that there is little indication that they did influence decision-making in Washington or public opinion broadly. Welter's real contribution is to trace the "yellow journalism" theory of the Spanish-American War to the post–World War I revisionists.

54. Kevin O'Keefe, *A Thousand Deadlines: The New York City Press and American Neutrality, 1914–1917* (The Hague: Martinus Nijhoff, 1972).

55. Matthew McCubbins, "Introduction," in *Under the Watchful Eye: Managing Presidential Campaigns in the Television Era,* ed. Matthew D. McCubbins (Washington, D.C.: Congressional Quarterly Press, 1992), p. 50.

56. Richard Beeman, "Deference, Republicanism, and the Emergence of Popular Politics in Eighteenth-Century America," *William and Mary Quarterly,* 3rd series, 49 (1992): 430.

57. *Los Angeles Times,* November 8, 1984. Sara Fritz, "Mondale: Is He Victim of the Electronic Age?" I:1, 26.

58. *New York Times,* April 22, 1990.

59. So do corporations. See Edward H. Bowman, "Strategy, Annual Reports, and Alchemy," *California Management Review* 20 (1978): 64–71, and James R. Bettman and Barton A. Weitz, "Attributions in the Board Room: Causal Reasoning in Corporate Annual Reports," *Administrative Science Quarterly* 28 (1983): 165–183.

60. Xiaoguang Shi, "Communism and Communication: News Media and Political Communication in China," Ph.D. diss., University of California, San Diego, 1992. See also Judy Polumbaum, "Professionalism in China's Press Corps," in *China's Crisis of 1989: Chinese and American Reflections,* ed. Roger V. Forges, Luo Ning, and Wu Yen-bo (Albany: State University of New York Press, 1993), pp. 295–311; Jennifer Grant, "Internal Reporting by Investigative Journalists in China and Its Influence on Government Policy," *Gazette* 41 (1988): 53–65.

61. Michael Robinson, "American Political Legitimacy in an Era of Electronic Journalism: Reflections on the Evening News," in *Television as a Social Force,* ed. Douglass Cater and Richard Adler (New York: Praeger, 1975), p. 106.

62. Recent research by Kathleen Hall Jamieson and Joseph Cappella provides some empirical evidence that there may indeed be an effect of strategy-and-tactics focused political reporting on citizen disaffection. See "The Effects of a Strategy-Based Political News Schema: A Markle Foundation Project Report," paper presented to the American Political Science Association, September 1993.

63. Todd Gitlin, *The Whole World Is Watching* (Berkeley: University of California Press, 1980).

64. There can be very different versions of the goal of fair and full information. In an ambitious version, the media would provide "forward-looking" information, enabling citizens to make up their own minds about public issues and advise their representatives of their views before decisions are made. In a more modest approach, the press would provide only backward-looking information, reporting to the public about decisions that representatives have made and assessing their consequences. Here citizens participate not by contributing to decision making but by voting out of office legislators who make choices they do not approve.

65. Herbert J. Gans, *Deciding What's News* (New York: Pantheon, 1979), pp. 304–305.

66. See James S. Ettema, "Discourse That Is Closer to Silence Than to Talk:

The Politics and Possibilities of Reporting on Victims of War," *Critical Studies in Mass Communication* 11 (1994): 1–21.

67. Debra D. Durocher, "Radiation Redux," *American Journalism Review* 6 (March 1994): 34–37.

68. Jay Rosen, "Politics, Vision, and the Press: Toward a Public Agenda for Journalism," in Jay Rosen and Paul Taylor, *The New News v. The Old News* (New York: Twentieth Century Fund, 1992), pp. 3–33.

69. Cass Sunstein, *Democracy and the Problem of Free Speech* (New York: Free Press, 1993).

70. Ellis Krauss, "Portraying the State in Japan: NHK Television News and Politics," in *Media and Politics in Japan,* ed. Susan J. Pharr and Ellis S. Krauss (Honolulu: University of Hawaii Press, forthcoming).

71. "Newspaper News and Television News," in *Television as a Social Force,* ed. Cater and Adler, p. 292.

72. William James, *Talks to Teachers* (New York: Henry Holt, 1916), pp. 188–189. (From 1892 lectures.)

73. Alexis de Tocqueville, *Democracy in America* (Garden City, N.Y.: Doubleday Anchor, 1969), p. 642.

74. Donald R. Matthews and James A. Stimson, "Cue-Taking by Congressmen: A Model and a Computer Simulation," in *The History of Parliamentary Behavior,* ed. William O. Aydelotte (Princeton: Princeton University Press, 1977), p. 258.

1. Three Hundred Years of the American Newspaper

This essay was presented on November 12, 1990, as the American Antiquarian Society's eighth annual James Russell Wiggins Lecture in the History of the Book in American Culture, and as the fourth lecture in the series "Three Hundred Years of the American Newspaper," a program made possible by a grant from the Gannett Foundation.

1. *The Journals and Miscellaneous Notebooks of Ralph Waldo Emerson,* ed. William H. Gilman et al., 16 vols. (Cambridge, Mass: Harvard University Press, 1973), vol. 10, p. 353 (journal entry of 1848).

2. Richard D. Brown, *Knowledge Is Power* (New York: Oxford University Press, 1989), pp. 273, 184.

3. Others suspect this goes very much too far. See Mitchell Stephens, *A History of News* (New York: Viking, 1988), p. 4, and Martin Mayer, *Making News* (Garden City, N.Y.: Doubleday, 1987), p. 21.

4. Walter Lippmann, *Public Opinion* (New York: Macmillan, 1922).

5. John M. Blum et al., *The National Experience,* 7th ed. (San Diego: Harcourt Brace Jovanovich, 1988).

6. Stanley Kutler, *The Wars of Watergate* (New York: Alfred A. Knopf, 1990).

7. James Carey, *Communication as Culture* (Boston: Unwin Hyman, 1989).

8. See Donald Shaw and Maxwell McCombs, *The Emergence of American Political Issues: The Agenda Setting Function of the Press* (St. Paul: West, 1977), and a valuable critique in Michael Robinson, "News Media Myths and Realities: What Network News Did and Didn't Do in the 1984 General Campaign," in *Elections in America,* ed. Kay Lehman Schlozman (Boston: Allen & Unwin, 1987), pp. 158–162.

9. Shanto Iyengar and Donald Kinder, *News That Matters* (Chicago: University of Chicago Press, 1988).

10. I borrow this insight from an unpublished paper by Elliot King, Department of Sociology, University of California, San Diego.

11. Benjamin Franklin, *Autobiography* (New York: New American Library, 1961), p. 133. Franklin did not confine himself to newspaper writing to "prepare the minds of the people." He uses the same phrase to refer to writing a paper for his literary club, the Junto, and circulating the paper to other clubs in the city, to advocate a reorganization of the night watch. He saw these actions as "preparing the minds of people for the change" (p. 115).

12. Gunther Barth, *City People* (New York: Oxford University Press, 1980), p. 59.

13. William J. Gilmore, *Reading Becomes a Necessity of Life* (Knoxville: University of Tennessee Press, 1989), p. 97.

14. Ibid., p. 112.

15. Ibid., p. 349. These generalizations do not flow directly from Gilmore's evidence but seem to be conclusions Gilmore found inescapable from his immersion in the print culture of the period.

16. Quoted in Richard Kielbowicz, *News in the Mail: The Press, Post Office, and Public Information, 1700–1860s* (Westport, Conn.: Greenwood Press, 1989), p. 49.

17. Ibid.

18. *Autobiography of Will Rogers*, ed. Donald Day (Boston: Houghton Mifflin, 1949), p. 118.

19. Kielbowicz, *News in the Mail*, p. 63.

20. Ibid., p. 98.

21. Ibid., p. 99.

22. On associational journalism, see David Paul Nord, "Tocqueville, Garrison, and the Perfection of Journalism," *Journalism History* 13 (1986): 56–64; on Bennett, see Michael Schudson, *Discovering the News* (New York: Basic Books, 1978), p. 21; and on consumption communities, see Daniel Boorstin, *The Americans: The Democratic Experience* (New York: Random House, 1973).

23. Frank Luther Mott, *American Journalism* (New York: Macmillan, 1962).

24. Charles Clark, " 'Metropolis' and 'Province' in Eighteenth-Century Press Relations: The Case of Boston," *Journal of Newspaper and Periodical History* 5 (1980): 5.

25. Ibid., p. 11.

26. Stephen Botein, " 'Meer Mechanics' and an Open Press: The Business and Political Strategies of Colonial American Printers," *Perspectives in American History* 9 (1975): 196.

27. Ibid., p. 194.

28. Brown, *Knowledge Is Power*, p. 38.

29. Thomas Leonard, *The Power of the Press* (New York: Oxford University Press, 1986), p. 65. This whole paragraph relies on pp. 64–70 of his text.

30. Ibid., p. 78.

31. Stephens, *A History of News*, p. 5.

32. Edward Dicey, in *Spectator of America*, ed. Herbert Mitgang (Chicago: Quadrangle Books, 1971), p. 29.

33. John Bigelow, *Retrospections of an Active Life,* 5 vols. (Garden City: Doubleday, Page, 1913), vol. 4, p. 318. The editorial appeared in the *New York Times,* August 3, 1869.

34. *New York Tribune,* August 20, 1859.

35. Paschal Grousset (pseud., Philippe Daryl), *Public Life in England* (London: George Routledge, 1881), p. 37.

36. On the Pope, see Kevin J. O'Keefe, *A Thousand Deadlines* (The Hague: Martinus Nijhoff, 1972), p. 76; on the German minister of marine, see ibid., p. 73; on British cabinet officers, see Forrest McDonald, *Insull* (Chicago: University of Chicago Press, 1962), p. 185. American industrialist Samuel Insull, an adviser to the British propaganda office in the United States beginning in 1914, was a key figure in encouraging the British to allow newspaper interviews with cabinet ministers.

37. *New York Evening Post,* January 28, 1897 (story by Lincoln Steffens).

38. F. J. Mansfield, *The Complete Journalist* (London: Sir Isaac Pitman, 1935), pp. 85–86.

39. For a full discussion of the development of the summary lead, see Chapter 2.

40. Richard Reeves has suggested this last effect, holding that, when television was through with us, "we would not be able to tell fact from fiction, we would not know what was real and what was true." See Richard Reeves, *Jet Lag* (Kansas City: Andrews and McMeel, 1981), p. 127. This is a prominent theme in the work of Joshua Meyrowitz, *No Sense of Place* (New York: Oxford University Press, 1985).

41. Charles Beard, *American Nervousness: Its Causes and Consequences* (New York: G. P. Putnam's, 1881), p. vi.

42. Report of Department of White Shield and White Cross, Women's Christian Temperance Union of Iowa, Proceedings of the Sixteenth Annual Meeting (October 1–4, 1889), p. 66.

43. Thomas Jefferson to John Norvell, June 11, 1807, in *The Writings of Thomas Jefferson,* ed. Andrew A. Lipscomb and Albert E. Bergh, 20 vols. (Washington, D.C.: Thomas Jefferson Memorial Association, 1905), vol. 11, p. 222.

44. David Paul Nord, "Readership as Citizenship in Late Eighteenth-Century Philadelphia" (paper presented at the Library of Congress conference on Publishing and Readership in Revolutionary France and America, May 1989), p. 27.

45. James McHenry, writing on Oliver Wolcott, July 22, 1800, cited in David Hackett Fischer, *The Revolution of American Conservatism* (New York: Harper & Row, 1965), pp. 133–134, 361.

46. Jacob Bronowski, *Magic, Science, and Civilization* (New York: Columbia University Press, 1978), p. 49.

2. The Politics of Narrative Form

For their interest in this research and for their criticism of earlier drafts, I want to thank Bennett Berger, Aaron Cicourel, Michael Cole, Daniel Hallin, Robert Meadow, and Frank Webster. I am also grateful to Kenneth Burke and to my colleagues who discussed my paper at a seminar in honor of Kenneth Burke at the University of California, San Diego, in May 1982.

1. *The Powers That Be* (New York: Knopf, 1979), p. 250.

2. See Arthur N. Applebee, *The Child's Concept of Story* (Chicago: University of Chicago Press, 1978), pp. 36–37.

3. The data for this study come from an examination of reports of State of the Union messages in the following newspapers: *New York Times*, every fourth year from 1854 to 1978, and every year from 1900 to 1910; *Chicago Tribune*, every fourth year from 1854 to 1954, and every other year from 1900 to 1910; *Washington Post*, every fourth year from 1878 to 1954, and every other year from 1900 to 1910; Washington *Evening Star*, every fourth year from 1854 to 1954, and every other year from 1900 to 1910. Also examined were the *Boston Gazette*, 1791–1797; *Connecticut Courant*, 1799, 1801, 1802, 1816, 1818; *New-York Evening Post*, 1801, 1802, 1810, 1822, 1826, 1850; *Albany Argus*, 1826; *True Sun* (New York), 1845; *Morning Herald* (New York), 1838; *Philadelphia Daily News*, 1866; *Omaha Daily Republican*, 1886; *San Diego Union*, 1886, 1900, 1908; *Iowa Citizen* (Iowa City), 1894, 1900, 1910.

4. In 1934 the *New York Times* related Franklin Roosevelt and his message to the Democratic party, the memory of Woodrow Wilson, and the spirit of war: "Speaking from the rostrum in the House Chamber, where his democratic predecessor, Woodrow Wilson, delivered his war Message in 1917, President Roosevelt unmistakably affirmed the permanence of the ideal if not the form of the National Recovery Administration." More recently, Hedrick Smith's *Times* story on Jimmy Carter's 1979 annual message characterized it this way: "Evoking the New Freedom of Woodrow Wilson, the New Deal of Franklin D. Roosevelt, and the New Frontier of John F. Kennedy, he settled for the first time in his Presidency on an epigrammatic theme—the New Foundation—to symbolize his effort to restructure the nation's economic priorities, foreign policy, and Federal programs for the future."

5. By 1954, the press was aware not only that the President spoke through the broadcast media, but that he knew that he did so. The *Washington Post* reported that President Eisenhower wore a shirt of "television blue" and stood behind a lectern designed for him by the actor Robert Montgomery. There was also an effort to play down Eisenhower's military standing, and so for the first time since 1919 no honor guard of soldiers was at the Capitol to salute the President.

6. Christine Ogan, Ida Plymale, D. Lynn Smith, William H. Turpin, and Donald Lewis Shaw, "The Changing Front Page of the *New York Times*," *Journalism Quarterly* 52 (Summer 1975): 340–344. For related changes toward a more interpretive journalism in the 1920s, see my book *Discovering the News* (New York: Basic Books, 1978), pp. 121–159.

7. Wilson is quoted in Wilfred E. Binkley, *President and Congress*, 3d ed. (New York: Vintage Books, 1962), p. 258. The growth in presidential power beginning around the time of Theodore Roosevelt is noted by many observers. See James McGregor Burns, *Presidential Government* (Boston: Houghton Mifflin, 1965), p. 55; Marcus Cunliffe, *American Presidents and the Presidency*, 2d ed. (New York: McGraw-Hill, 1972); Arthur Schlesinger, Jr., *The Imperial Presidency* (Boston: Houghton Mifflin, 1973), p. 83. On Wilson's revival of Federalist precedent, see also Schlesinger, "Introduction," in *The State of the Union Messages of the Presidents, 1790–1966*, 3 vols., ed. Fred L. Israel (New York: Chelsea

House, 1966). For careful attention to the development of media-President relations in this period, see George Juergens, *News from the White House* (Chicago: University of Chicago Press, 1981).

8. Larry Berman, *The Office of Management and Budget and the Presidency, 1921–1979* (Princeton: Princeton University Press, 1979), p. 3. Rexford G. Tugwell cites the establishment of the Budget Bureau as a major event in the growth of presidential authority in *The Enlargement of the Presidency* (New York: Doubleday, 1960), pp. 396–397.

9. The social sciences and humanities have been converging in the past decade in their interest in "narrative." See, for instance, the special issue of *Critical Inquiry* on narrative (vol. 7, Autumn 1980). Of related interest is the work of the Russian linguist Mikhail Bakhtin. An exposition of some of Bakhtin's ideas can be found in Michael Holquist, "The Politics of Representation," in *Allegory and Representation*, ed. Stephen J. Greenblatt, selected papers from the English Institute, new series no. 5 (Baltimore: Johns Hopkins University Press, 1981), pp. 163–184. Holquist's phrase, "the politics of representation," suggested to me my own phrase, "the politics of narrative form," and hence the title of my chapter.

10. David Riesman, Nathan Glazer, and Reuel Denney, *The Lonely Crowd* (New Haven: Yale University Press, 1950), pp. 197–198.

11. On Progressivism, see Samuel P. Hays, *The Response to Industrialism 1885–1914* (Chicago: University of Chicago Press, 1957), and Robert H. Wiebe, *The Search for Order* (New York: Hill and Wang, 1967).

12. Wiebe, *The Search for Order*, p. 129.

13. Anthony Smith, *Goodbye Gutenberg* (New York: Oxford University Press, 1980), p. 186. For more about the rise of the reporter after 1880, see my book *Discovering the News*, pp. 61–87.

14. The often overlooked role of the telegraph in American culture is discussed in James Carey, "Technology and Ideology: The Case of the Telegraph," in Carey, *Communication as Culture* (Boston: Unwin Hyman, 1989), pp. 201–230.

15. Anthony Smith, "Britain: The Mysteries of a Modus Vivendi," in *Television and Political Life*, ed. Anthony Smith (London: Macmillan, 1979), p. 28.

16. New York: Dell Publishing, 1977, p. 3.

17. This is not to suggest that television has not had an influence in stabilizing and extending the conventions of print that emphasize the presidency. Researchers have found growing emphasis on the President in newspaper reports (Elmer E. Cornwell, Jr., "Presidential News: The Expanding Public Image," *Journalism Quarterly* 36 [Summer 1959]: 275–283, and Alan P. Balutis, "The Presidency and the Press: The Expanding Presidential Image," *Presidential Studies Quarterly* 7 [Fall 1977]: 242–251), but others observe that television network stories place even *more* emphasis on the President. See Stephen Hess, *The Washington Reporters* (Washington, D.C.: Brookings Institution, 1981), p. 98.

18. Kenneth Burke, "Semantic Meaning and Poetic Meaning," in Burke, *Philosophy of Literary Form* (Berkeley: University of California Press, 1973), p. 140.

19. Herbert Gans, *Deciding What's News* (New York: Pantheon Books, 1979), pp. 204–206.

20. Theodore White, *The Making of the President 1960* (New York: Atheneum, 1961), p. 335.

3. Question Authority: A History of the News Interview

I am grateful to the Joan Shorenstein Barone Center on the Press, Politics, and Public Policy of the Kennedy School, Harvard University; the Center for Advanced Study in the Behavioral Sciences; the Spencer Foundation; and the Academic Senate of the University of California, San Diego, for financial support in the preparation of this essay.

1. Stephen Hess, *The Washington Reporters* (Washington, D.C.: The Brookings Institution, 1981) pp. 18, 52.

2. Edwin A. Perry, *The Boston Herald and Its History* (Boston, 1878), p. 23.

3. Francis A. Richardson, "A Glance Backward," *Baltimore Sun,* February 11, 1902, p. 2.

4. Donald Ritchie, *Press Gallery: Congress and the Washington Correspondents* (Cambridge, Mass.: Harvard University Press, 1991), p. 81.

5. Carol Frost, personal communication, 1993.

6. Esther Goody, *Questions and Politeness* (Cambridge: Cambridge University Press, 1978).

7. Brian Winston, " 'The Most Perfect Contrivance': Interviewing as an Unnatural Act," *The Independent* (April 1983): 11–12; Mark Benney and Everett C. Hughes, "Of Sociology and the Interview," *American Journal of Sociology* 62 (1956): 139.

8. Turnbull favors Greeley; Nilsson favors Bennett; Hudson and Grady favor Bennett but for a later—1859—instance; Richardson favors McCullagh; but Pollard locates an earlier—1865—interview with Andrew Johnson by Col. Alexander K. McClure. See George Turnbull, "Some Notes on the History of the Interview," *Journalism Quarterly* 13 (1936): 272–279; Nils Gunnar Nilsson, "The Origin of the Interview," *Journalism Quarterly* 48 (1971): 707–713; Frederic Hudson (James Gordon Bennett's managing editor), *Journalism in the United States* (New York: Harper, 1872), p. 563; Henry W. Grady, "On Interviewing," *Atlanta Constitution,* August 16, 1879, p. 1; Richardson, "A Glance Backward," p. 2; James E. Pollard, *The Presidents and the Press* (New York: Macmillan, 1947), pp. 413–428.

9. *New-York Daily Tribune,* August 20, 1859, p. 6.

10. Charles M. Pepper, *Every-Day Life in Washington* (New York: Christian Herald, 1900), p. 408.

11. Hutchins Hapgood, "A New Form of Literature," *The Bookman* 21 (1905): 424.

12. Hugh Mehan, "The Structure of Classroom Discourse," in *Handbook of Discourse Analysis,* vol. 3, ed. Teun A. van Dijk (London: Academic Press, 1985), pp. 119–131, and Hugh Mehan, "Understanding Inequality in Schools: The Contribution of Interpretive Studies," *Sociology of Education* 65 (1992): 1–20.

13. This crucial point was clarified for me by Steven Clayman (personal communication). He writes that what is distinctive about the news interview is "not that there is a neutral third-turn response; there is no third-turn response whatsoever . . . Interestingly, some manuals of interviewing technique actually counsel reporters to withhold all 'yeahs' and 'uh huhs' during and after the interviewee's answer." See also John Heritage, "Analyzing News Interviews: Aspects of the Production of Talk for an Overhearing Audience," in *Handbook of Discourse Analysis,* ed. Teun A. van Dijk, vol. 3, pp. 95–117.

14. Goody, *Questions and Politeness*, p. 42.

15. Ibid., p. 23.

16. *New York World*, January 31, 1871.

17. William T. Stead, *The Americanization of the World* (New York: Garland reprint edition, 1902, 1972), p. 111.

18. Hugo Munsterberg, *The Americans* (Garden City, N.Y.: Doubleday, Page, 1914), p. 149.

19. E. L. Godkin, "Interviewing," *The Nation*, January 28, 1869, pp. 66–67.

20. Paschal Grousset, *Public Life in England* (London: George Routledge, 1884), p. 39. Published under pseud. Philippe Daryl.

21. Cited in Marion Marzolf, "American 'New Journalism' Takes Root in Europe at End of 19th Century," *Journalism Quarterly* 61 (1984): 531.

22. Alan J. Lee, *The Popular Press in England 1830–1914* (London: Croom Helm, 1976).

23. Cited in Ritchie, *Press Gallery*, pp. 82–83.

24. Richardson, "A Glance Backward."

25. Henry Grady, "On Interviewing," *Atlanta Constitution*, August 16, 1879, p. 1.

26. Frederic William Wile, *News Is Where You Find It* (Indianapolis: Bobbs-Merrill, 1939), p. 152.

27. Ibid., p. 216.

28. James D. Startt, *Journalism's Unofficial Ambassador: A Biography of Edward Price Bell, 1869–1943* (Oberlin: Ohio University Press, 1979), pp. 59–60.

29. Bell to Charles Dennis, December 15, 1919, Edward Price Bell Papers, Newberry Library, Chicago.

30. Isaac Marcosson, *Adventures in Interviewing* (London: John Lane, 1919), p. 72.

31. J. Frederick Essary, *Covering Washington* (Boston: Houghton Mifflin, 1927), p. 147.

32. Willis J. Abbot, *Watching the World Go By* (London: John Lane, The Bodley Head, 1933), p. 270.

33. Lucy Brown, *Victorian News and Newspapers* (Oxford: Clarendon Press, 1985), p. 163.

34. *New York World*, January 29, 1871.

35. *New York Journal*, March 2, 1897, p. 5.

36. *New York World*, April 11, 1915.

37. Marzolf, "American 'New Journalism' Takes Root in Europe," p. 533.

38. *New York Evening Post*, January 28, 1897. The story has no by-line, but it is among the scrapbooks in the Lincoln Steffens papers, Columbia University.

39. Wile, *News Is Where You Find It*, p. 43.

40. Cited in Jim Allee Hart, "The McCullagh-Johnson Interviews: A Closer Look," *Journalism Quarterly* 45 (1968): 132.

41. Charles Hemstreet, *Reporting for the Newspapers* (New York: A. Wessels, 1901), pp. 50–52.

42. Grant Milnor Hyde, *Newspaper Reporting and Correspondence* (New York: D. Appleton, 1912), p. 171.

43. Ibid., p. 170.

44. John L. Given, *Making a Newspaper* (New York: Henry Holt, 1907), pp. 182–183.

45. Charles G. Ross, *The Writing of News: A Handbook* (New York: Henry Holt, 1911), p. 116.

46. Julian Ralph, *The Making of a Journalist* (New York: Harper, 1903), p. 46.

47. Edward Price Bell, "The Interview," *Journalism Bulletin* 1 (1924): 16.

48. Marcosson, *Adventures in Interviewing*, p. 74.

49. Walter Williams and Frank I. Martin, *The Practice of Journalism* (Columbia, Mo.: E. W. Stephens, 1911), pp. 210–211.

50. Walter Williams and Frank I. Martin, *The Practice of Journalism* (Columbia, Mo.: E. W. Stephens, 1922), pp. 170–171.

51. Carl N. Warren, *Modern News Reporting* (New York: Harper, 1934).

52. F. J. Mansfield, *The Complete Journalist* (London: Sir Isaac Pitman, 1935), p. 86.

53. Cited in ibid., p. 86.

54. *New York World,* January 20, 1868, p. 1.

55. John Swinton, "John Swinton's Travels," *The Sun* (New York), September 6, 1880, p. 1.

56. *Chicago Tribune,* August 12, 1896.

57. *Chicago Tribune,* August 13, 1896.

58. *Baltimore Sun,* November 3–6, 1914.

59. *Baltimore Sun,* November 1, 1924, p. 1.

60. Archibald F. Hill, *Secrets of the Sanctum: An Inside View of an Editor's Life* (Philadelphia: Claxton, Remsen, and Haffelfinger, 1875), p. 56.

61. Richardson, "A Glance Backward," p. 2.

62. Charles W. Thompson, *Presidents I've Known and Two Near Presidents* (Indianapolis: Bobbs-Merrill, 1929), p. 118.

63. Wile, *News Is Where You Find It,* p. 203.

64. William C. Hudson, *Random Recollections of an Old Political Reporter* (New York: Cupples and Leon, 1911), pp. 80–81.

65. Charles M. Dana, *The Art of Newspaper Making* (New York: D. Appleton, 1895), p. 19.

66. Marcosson, *Adventures in Interviewing,* p. 83.

67. Bell, "The Interview," p. 16.

68. See Startt, *Journalism's Unofficial Ambassador,* p. 186, and Morrell Heald, *Transatlantic Vista: American Journalists in Europe, 1900–1940* (Kent, Ohio: Kent State University Press, 1988), p. 53.

69. Chauncey M. Depew, *My Memories of Eighty Years* (New York: Charles Scribner's, 1922), p. 347.

70. O. O. Stealey, *Twenty Years in the Press Gallery* (New York: Publishers Printing, 1906), p. 7.

71. Thompson, *Presidents I've Known,* p. 231.

72. *Time,* June 16, 1961, p. 37, and Karl von Wiegand, "Autobiography" (n.d.), Karl von Wiegand Papers, Hoover Institution Library, Stanford, California.

73. Maurine Beasley, *Eleanor Roosevelt and the Media* (Urbana: University of Illinois Press, 1987), p. 42.

74. Marcosson, *Adventures in Interviewing,* p. 73, and Kent Cooper, *Kent Cooper and the Associated Press: An Autobiography* (New York: Random House, 1959), p. 118.

75. Cooper, *Kent Cooper and the Associated Press,* p. 118.

76. Grousset, *Public Life in England,* p. 38.

77. Hyde, *Newspaper Reporting and Correspondence,* p. 170.

78. Joseph I. C. Clarke, *My Life and Memories* (New York: Dodd, Mead, 1925), p. 114.

79. Von Wiegand, "Autobiography," p. 75.

80. Karl von Wiegand, "The Pope, in Interview Granted to the World, Urges America to Work for Peace of Europe, and Pledges the Support of Holy See," *The* (New York) *World,* April 11, 1915, p. 1.

81. Stewart Robertson, *Introduction to Modern Journalism* (New York: Prentice-Hall, 1930), pp. 154–158.

82. Given, *Making a Newspaper,* p. 182.

83. William Salisbury, *The Career of a Journalist* (New York: B. W. Dodge, 1908), p. 279.

84. Paul Lancaster, *Gentleman of the Press: The Life and Times of an Early Reporter, Julian Ralph of the Sun* (Syracuse, N.Y.: Syracuse University Press, 1992), p. 135.

85. G. K. Chesterton, *What I Saw in America* (London: Hodder & Stoughton, 1922), pp. 6, 62.

86. Emil Dovifat, *Der Amerikanische Journalismus* (Berlin: Deutsche Verlags-Anstalt Stuttgart, 1927), p. 111. Thanks to Steven Staninger for the translation.

87. Ishbel Ross, *Ladies of the Press* (New York: Harper, 1936), pp. 373–374.

88. Henry Watterson, *The Editorials of Henry Watterson,* compiled by Arthur Krock (New York: George H. Doran, 1923), p. 240. From *Louisville Courier-Journal,* February 19, 1908.

89. Chesterton, *What I Saw in America,* p. 47.

90. Ben: Perley Poore, *Perley's Reminiscences of 60 Years in the National Metropolis* (Philadelphia: Hubbard Brothers, 1886), vol. 1, p. 400, and vol. 2, p. 525.

91. Charles Nordhoff, letter to Edward Atkinson, July 29, 1893. Edward Atkinson Papers, Massachusetts Historical Society.

92. Edward Shils, *Center and Periphery: Essays in Macrosociology* (Chicago: University of Chicago Press, 1975), p. 319.

93. Ralph, *The Making of a Journalist,* p. 193.

94. Michael Schudson, *Discovering the News* (New York: Basic Books, 1978).

95. As discussed in Chapter 2.

96. Janet Malcolm, *The Journalist and the Murderer* (New York: Knopf, 1990), p. 3.

97. Steven E. Clayman, "From Talk to Text: Newspaper Accounts of Reporter-Source Interactions," *Media, Culture and Society* 12 (1990): 97.

98. Barbie Zelizer, " 'Saying' as Collective Practice: Quoting and Differential Address in the News," *Text* 9 (1989): 369.

4. What Is a Reporter?

I want to thank Dan Martin for research assistance on this essay and Helene Keyssar for a careful and critical reading of an earlier draft. Harrison Salisbury also provided very helpful comments on an earlier draft. I am grateful to William May for providing the occasion and the encouragement for this essay, through a forum on the public role of the news media at Southern Methodist University.

1. Harrison E. Salisbury, *A Journey for Our Times* (New York: Harper & Row, 1983), p. ix. All further references to Salisbury's writing are to this book unless otherwise indicated and are identified by page numbers in the text.

2. George Gusdorf, "Conditions and Limits of Autobiography," in *Autobiography: Essays Theoretical and Critical,* ed. J. Olney (Princeton, N.J.: Princeton University Press, 1980), p. 48.

3. Somewhere the anthropologist Victor Turner remarked that "making is not faking," but I cannot locate the source. The general point, for newspapers, is developed in a number of recent studies of the media, including the essays in *Reading the News,* ed. Robert Manoff and Michael Schudson (New York: Pantheon, 1986).

4. Lincoln Steffens, *The Autobiography of Lincoln Steffens* (New York: Harcourt Brace, 1931), p. 44. All further references to Steffens's writing are to this book unless otherwise indicated and are identified by page numbers in the text.

5. Robert Sayre, *The Examined Self: Benjamin Franklin, Henry Adams, Henry James* (Princeton, N.J.: Princeton University Press, 1964), pp. 23–25.

6. Allen Nevins, ed., *The Letters of Lincoln Steffens,* vol. 1 (New York: Harcourt Brace, 1938), p. 129.

7. Ibid., p. 177.

8. Harrison E. Salisbury, personal communication, September 26, 1986.

9. I am grateful to Helene Keyssar for drawing my attention to "scenes of recognition" in tragedy.

10. Ronnie Dugger, "The Administration's Long Knives and the Hazards of Nationalism," *Deadline* (September/October, 1986): 4.

11. David Halberstam, *The Powers That Be* (New York: Knopf, 1979), p. 534, and Daniel C. Hallin, *The "Uncensored War": The Media and Vietnam* (New York: Oxford University Press, 1986), p. 147.

5. Trout or Hamburger

1. Michael Arlen, *Thirty Seconds* (New York: Penguin, 1980).

2. Hedrick Smith, *The Power Game* (New York: Ballantine Books, 1988), p. 409; David Broder, *Behind the Front Page* (New York: Simon & Schuster, 1987), p. 182; Martin Schram, *The Great American Video Game: Presidential Politics in the Television Age* (New York: William Morrow, 1987), pp. 23–27; and Kathleen Hall Jamieson, *Eloquence in an Electronic Age* (New York: Oxford University Press, 1988), pp. 60–61.

3. Shanto Iyengar and Donald Kinder, *News That Matters* (Chicago: University of Chicago Press, 1984), pp. 36–42.

4. See D. Roderick Kiewiet, *Macroeconomics and Micro-politics: The Electoral Effects of Economic Issues* (Chicago: University of Chicago Press, 1983).

5. *Broadcasting* 59 (November 7, 1960): 27–29. When I originally published this chapter, I was unaware of a very good paper criticizing the conventional wisdom on the Kennedy-Nixon debate by David L. Vancil and Sue D. Pendell, "The Myth of Viewer-Listener Disagreement in the First Kennedy-Nixon Debate," *Central States Speech Journal* 38 (1987): 16–27. Vancil and Pendell nicely dem-

onstrate both how pervasive the myth about the Kennedy-Nixon debate is and how meager is the evidence to substantiate it.

6. Peter Braestrup, *Battle Lines* (New York: Priority Press, 1985), pp. 68–69.

7. Daniel C. Hallin, *"The Uncensored War": The Media and Vietnam* (New York: Oxford University Press, 1986), p. 131.

8. Calculated from Gallup polls reported in "Reagan and His Predecessors," *Public Opinion* (September/October 1987): 40.

9. *The Gallup Poll 1982* (Wilmington, Del.: Scholarly Resources, 1983), pp. 107, 243.

10. *Washington Post,* November 22, 1981.

11. Laurence I. Barrett, *Gambling with History: Ronald Reagan in the White House* (Harmondsworth, England: Penguin Books, 1984), p. 443.

12. *Time,* August 16, 1982.

13. Mary McCarthy, *The Mask of State: Watergate Portraits* (New York: Harcourt Brace Jovanovich, 1974), p. 5.

14. Barry Jogoda, quoted in William Lunch, *The Nationalization of American Politics* (Berkeley: University of California Press, 1987), p. 79; John J. O'Connor, *New York Times,* April 14, 1977, quoted in Joshua Meyrowitz, *No Sense of Place* (New York: Oxford University Press, 1985), p. 273; David Halberstam cited in Meyrowitz, *No Sense of Place,* p. 297.

15. *San Diego Union,* January 31, 1988, p. C-8.

16. *Los Angeles Times,* November 8, 1984, p. 1.

17. W. Phillips Davison, "The Third-Person Effect in Communication," *Public Opinion Quarterly* 47 (1983): 1–15.

18. Frederick T. Steeper, "Public Response to Gerald Ford's Statements on Eastern Europe in the Second Debate," in George F. Bishop, Robert G. Meadow, and Marilyn Jackson-Beeck, *The Presidential Debates: Media, Electoral, and Policy Perspectives* (New York: Praeger, 1978), pp. 81–101.

19. Michael Robinson, "Where's the Beef? Media and Media Elites in 1984," in *The American Elections of 1984,* ed. Austin Ranney (Durham, N.C.: Duke University Press, 1985), pp. 198–199.

20. Stephen J. Wayne, "Congressional Liaison in the Reagan White House: A Preliminary Assessment of the First Year," in *President and Congress: Assessing Reagan's First Year,* ed. Norman J. Ornstein (Washington, D.C.: American Enterprise Institute, 1982), p. 55.

21. Charles W. Ostrom, Jr., and Dennis M. Simon, "The Man in the Teflon Suit: The Environmental Connection, Political Drama, and Popular Support in the Reagan Presidency," *Public Opinion Quarterly* 53 (1989): 353–387.

6. The Illusion of Ronald Reagan's Popularity

1. *Los Angeles Times,* January 21, 1981, p. 1.

2. *Time,* October 7, 1966, p. 31.

3. Jules Duscha, "Reagan: Not Great, Not Brilliant, But a Good Show," *New York Times Magazine,* December 10, 1967, p. 28.

4. *Time,* August 2, 1976, p. 10.

5. Alvin Sanoff, "Silver Tongue Pays Off for Reagan," *U.S. News and World Report,* March 2, 1981, p. 28.

6. *National Journal,* March 14, 1981, p. 456.

7. On August 2, 1981, Lou Cannon wrote in the *Washington Post* (p. A1) that it is fashionable to call Reagan the "Great Communicator." On August 20, 1981, Richard E. Vatz and Lee S. Weinberg in a *Baltimore Sun* op-ed column entitled "Reaganspeak and the New Imperial Presidency" also make it clear that the term "Great Communicator" is a common appellation for Reagan. On June 5, 1981, Stephen Rosenfeld's column in the *Washington Post* (p. A17) refers to Reagan as the "Great Non Communicator." See also Sid Blumenthal, "Marketing the President," *New York Times Magazine,* September 13, 1981, p. 43, where he refers to Reagan as "Communicator in Chief," and the February 21, 1981, *New Republic* "TRB" column that refers to Reagan as "our first communicator-executive." Other notable coinages came later. The term "Teflon President" was coined by Patricia Schroeder (Democratic representative from Colorado), who referred to Reagan as "Teflon-coated" in a House speech on August 2, 1983. (See the *New York Times,* August 9, 1983, p. 18.)

8. *Time,* July 7, 1986, p. 14.

9. *New York Times,* July 18, 1987, p. 26.

10. *Los Angeles Times,* January 4, 1987, pt. V, p. 1.

11. Mark Green, "Amiable Dunce or Chronic Liar?" *Mother Jones* 12 (June/July, 1987): 10.

12. Gallup Organization, *The Gallup Poll 1981* (Wilmington, Del.: Scholarly Resources, 1982), p. 59.

13. We are not the first to note this misperception. Within the political science profession, the phenomenon we point to now—and which appears to be startling news even today to many people—has been widely recognized. Fred Greenstein observed it early on. In a 1983 book he noted that members of Congress had apparently bought the Reagan administration's claim that the 1980 election was a mandate for Reagan's policies. "Although experienced politicians discount such presidential claims, members of Congress, bolstered by near uniformity in mass media accounts and by partially engineered constituency pressure, clearly were persuaded at the time of the 1981 Reagan tax and expenditure cuts that the president was riding high." Greenstein adds that they found it hard to believe "that such an effective communicator had not won the public over." But he then cites the Gallup Poll evidence that, in fact, he had not. See Fred Greenstein, *The Reagan Presidency: An Early Assessment* (Baltimore: Johns Hopkins University Press, 1983), p. 174. William C. Adams reported in 1984 that, contrary to widespread belief, Reagan was not more popular than his policies. See William C. Adams, "Recent Fables about Ronald Reagan," *Public Opinion* 7 (October/November 1984): 6–9. Everett C. Ladd noted some of the evidence about Reagan's poll ratings in 1985. See Everett C. Ladd, "Reagan Ratings: The Story the Media Missed," *Public Opinion* 8 (June/July 1985): 20, 41. So did George C. Edwards in the same journal, calling Reagan "the least well-liked" president in three decades. See George C. Edwards, "Comparing Chief Executives," *Public Opinion* 8 (June/July 1985): 50–51, 54. Edwards found the polls revealed that Reagan, far from magnetically uniting the public, had polarized the polity "along partisan, racial, and sexual lines." Another political scientist, Martin Wattenberg, working from the National Election Studies data rather than the Gallup polls, convincingly arrived at the same conclusion a year later: "Overall, Reagan was the least popular candidate to win election to the presidency since the election studies began in

1952," he wrote. "Never before had a candidate come to office with such luke-warm backing from his followers." Far from being overwhelmingly popular, Reagan had proved an "extremely polarizing" chief executive. See Martin Wattenberg, "The Reagan Polarization Phenomenon and the Continuing Down-ward Slide in Presidential Candidate Popularity," *American Politics Quarterly* 14 (1986): 219–245 at 243. Thomas Ferguson and Joel Rogers debunked both the myth of Ronald Reagan's popularity and the myth of a general "turn to the right" in American public opinion in *Right Turn* (New York: Hill and Wang, 1986). Robert Entman and David Paletz had early on noted that the prevailing wisdom that America had turned to the right was not supported by public opinion polls. See their "Media and the Conservative Myth," *Journal of Communication* 30 (1980): 154–165. We first reported our own findings in "The Myth of the Great Communicator," *Columbia Journalism Review* 26 (November/December 1987): 37–39, and later in "Reagan's Mythical Popularity," *Psychology Today* 22 (September 1988): 32–33 and "By Charming the Washington Crowd, Reagan Put a Lock on His Popularity," *Los Angeles Times*, September 14, 1988.

14. "Reagan and His Predecessors," *Public Opinion* 10 (September/October 1987): 40.

15. *Newsweek*, May 4, 1981, p. 22.

16. Gallup Organization, *The Gallup Poll 1982* (Wilmington, Del.: Scholarly Resources, 1983), pp. 107, 243.

17. *Newsweek*, May 11, 1981, p. 22.

18. *Newsweek*, May 18, 1981, p. 38.

19. Hedrick Smith, "Taking Charge of Congress," *New York Times Magazine*, August 9, 1981, p. 14.

20. *Washington Post*, June 21, 1981, p. A4.

21. *New York Times*, September 29, 1981, p. A-22.

22. *New York Times*, January 10, 1982, p. 1.

23. Burns Roper, "Presidential Popularity: Do People Like the Actor or the Actions?" *Public Opinion* 6 (October/November 1983): 42–44.

24. *Washington Post*, January 23, 1982, p. A-15.

25. Cited in Christopher Hanson (under pseud. William Boot), "Iranscam: When the Cheering Stopped," *Columbia Journalism Review* (March/April 1987): 29.

26. *Los Angeles Times*, December 4, 1986, pt. II, p. 7.

27. *Time*, September 12, 1983, p. 45.

28. *Time*, March 2, 1981, p. 10.

29. *Time*, February 9, 1981, p. 22.

30. *Newsweek*, June 29, 1981, p. 20.

31. *Newsweek*, March 1, 1982, p. 28.

32. Hanson, "Iranscam," p. 20.

33. *U.S. News and World Report*, March 2, 1981, p. 28; *Newsweek*, March 29, 1982, p. 77; *Time*, July 11, 1983, p. 63; and Steve Weisman, "A Test of the Man and the Presidency," *New York Times Magazine*, April 26, 1981, p. 80.

34. *Newsweek*, November 17, 1980, p. 30; *Newsweek*, December 1, 1980, pp. 30–32; Mark Hertsgaard, *On Bended Knee* (New York: Schocken, 1989), p. 43; John Herbers, "The President and the Press Corps," *New York Times Magazine*, May 9, 1982, p. 96; and Michael Robinson and Margaret Sheehan, *Over the Wire and On TV* (New York: Russell Sage Foundation, 1983), p. 137.

35. Herbers, "The President and the Press Corps," p. 96; Hedrick Smith, *The Power Game: How Washington Works* (New York: Random House, 1988), p. 316; Morton Kondracke, "Running Reagan," *The New Republic*, December 31, 1983, p. 11.

36. *Washington Post*, November 8, 1981; *Time*, February 22, 1982, p. 12.

37. Tip O'Neill (with William Novak), *Man of the House: The Life and Political Memoirs of Speaker Tip O'Neill* (New York: Random House, 1987), p. 345.

38. *Congressional Quarterly*, May 18, 1981, p. 19.

39. *New York Times*, March 18, 1981, p. A27; *Newsweek*, May 18, 1981, p. 40; Lou Cannon, *Reagan* (New York: G. P. Putnam's, 1982), p. 333.

40. *Newsweek*, October 27, 1980, p. 15, and November 17, 1980, pp. 27–32.

41. See D. Roderick Kiewiet and Douglas Rivers, "The Economic Basis of Reagan's Appeal," in *The New Direction in American Politics*, ed. John E. Chubb and Paul E. Peterson (Washington: The Brookings Institution, 1985), pp. 69–90, and Douglas A. Hibbs, *The American Political Economy* (Cambridge, Mass.: Harvard University Press, 1987), pp. 186–187.

42. Congressional Quarterly, *Reagan's First Year* (Washington, D.C. Congressional Quarterly Press, 1982), p. 15.

43. *National Journal*, November 8, p. 3295, and November 15, p. 1943.

44. *Newsweek*, May 18, 1981, p. 38.

45. Marc A. Bodnick, " 'Going Public' Reconsidered: Reagan's 1981 Tax and Budget Cuts, and Revisionist Theories of Presidential Power," *Congress and the Presidency* 17 (1990): 13–28. See also Sam Kernell, *Going Public: New Strategies of Presidential Leadership* (Washington, D.C.: Congressional Quarterly Press, 1986).

46. O'Neill, *Man of the House*, pp. 344, 349.

47. Norman Ornstein, Thomas Mann, and Michael Malbin, *Vital Statistics on Congress, 1987–1988* (Washington, D.C.: Congressional Quarterly, 1987), p. 175.

48. Tina Rosenberg, "How the Media Made the Moral Majority," *Washington Monthly*, May 1982, pp. 26–34.

49. Hedrick Smith, "Taking Charge of Congress," *New York Times Magazine*, August 9, 1981, pp. 12–20, 47–50.

50. Hertsgaard, *On Bended Knee*, p. 120.

51. The big response to the Reagan television appearances that Congress noticed did not normally translate into increased popularity judged by the polls. A recent analysis argues that, over his career in office, Reagan's popularity in the polls was affected most powerfully by the "environment," especially economic upturns and downturns. It was to a lesser extent affected by "political drama," but even here the most powerful political drama was the sort the President was least able to control. That is, events like Reagan's colon surgery or prostate surgery, the bombing of Libya, and the summit with Gorbachev had notable positive results for Reagan in the polls while events like the PATCO strike, the stock market crash, and Iran-Contra had notable negative consequences for Reagan's popularity. But "discretionary" political drama—television speeches and presidential travel—had very little impact. See Charles W. Ostrum, Jr., and Dennis M. Simon, "The Man in the Teflon Suit? The Environmental Connection, Political Drama, and Popular Support in the Reagan Presidency," *Public Opinion Quarterly* 53 (1989): 353–387.

52. Stephen J. Wayne, "Congressional Liaison in the Reagan White House: A Preliminary Assessment of the First Year," in *President and Congress: Assessing*

Reagan's First Year, ed. Norman Ornstein (Washington, D.C.: American Enterprise Institute, 1982), p. 55.

53. *New York Times*, February 22, 1982, p. A-17.

54. Widespread as this view is today, there have been some convincing dissenters for some time—we note especially Thomas Patterson and Robert McClure, *The Unseeing Eye: The Myth of Television Power in National Elections* (New York: G. P. Putnam's, 1976), and Jeff Greenfield, *The Real Campaign: How the Media Missed the Story of the 1980 Campaign* (New York: Summit Books, 1982).

55. See Blumenthal, "Marketing the President"; Herbers, "The President and the Press Corps," p. 96; and Hedrick Smith, *The Power Game*, pp. 316, 319.

56. Laurence Barrett, *Gambling With History: Reagan in the White House* (Harmondsworth: Penguin, 1984), p. 443.

57. *Time*, August 16, 1982, p. 44.

58. Mark Crispin Miller, "Virtù Inc.," *The New Republic*, April 7, 1982, p. 30.

59. *Time*, July 11, 1983, p. 10; *Newsweek*, March 22, 1982, p. 92; *Washington Post*, January 24, 1982, p. A-3; and Herbers, "The President and the Press Corps," p. 75.

60. Barrett, *Gambling with History*, p. 444.

61. *Los Angeles Times*, August 8, 1982, p. 1.

62. For a critique of polling, see Benjamin Ginsberg, *The Captive Public* (New York: Basic Books, 1986). We rely primarily on the Gallup polls here. Other polls arrived at similar results. The Roper poll was quite comparable to Gallup—see Roper, "Presidential Popularity." That article interestingly argues that Reagan's "personal" popularity as compared to his "job performance" rating had been misinterpreted—that it was likely that Reagan's job performance was regarded more highly than Reagan as a person in his first years in office.

The only poll results we know that give any credit to the myth of Reagan's popularity come from the University of Michigan National Election Studies of 1980 and 1982 as reported in Jack Citrin and Donald Philip Green, "Presidential Leadership and the Resurgence of Trust in Government," *British Journal of Political Science* 16 (1986): 431–453. In the 1980 survey, voters were asked to compare Carter and Reagan on several different dimensions of personality and character. Carter had the edge on four of the seven categories. The category where Reagan had the biggest lead was "strong leader." That certainly has some bearing on "popularity," although it is not the same thing.

63. *Time*, August 16, 1982, p. 44.

64. Stephen Hess, *The Washington Correspondents* (Washington: The Brookings Institution, 1981), p. 118.

65. *Newsweek*, May 25, 1981, p. 92.

7. Watergate and the Press

1. Larry Sabato, *Feeding Frenzy* (New York: Free Press, 1991), p. 61.

2. Karen Rothmyer, *Winning Pulitzers* (New York: Columbia University Press, 1991), p. 9.

3. Katherine Graham interviews, December 21, 1984, and September 4, 1985, Poynter Institute for Media Studies "NewsLeaders" series, St. Petersburg, Fla.

4. Ben Bagdikian, "The Fruits of Agnewism," *Columbia Journalism Review* 11 (January/February 1973): 9–21.

5. Katherine Graham interviews, December 21, 1984, and September 4, 1985.

6. Howard Bray, *The Pillars of the Post* (New York: Norton, 1980), pp. 125–126.

7. Katherine Graham interviews, December 21, 1984, and September 4, 1985.

8. Epstein's essay originally appeared in *Commentary* 58 (July 1974): 21–24; reprinted in Edward Jay Epstein, *Between Fact and Fiction: The Problem of Journalism* (New York: Vintage Books, 1975), pp. 19–33.

9. Katherine Graham, "The Activism of the Press," *Nieman Reports* (Spring 1974): 21–25.

10. Thomas Edsall, personal interview, February 13, 1991, La Jolla, Calif.

11. Sabato, *Feeding Frenzy,* pp. 86–93.

12. See, for instance, S. Robert Lichter, Stanley Rothman, and Linda S. Lichter, *The Media Elite: America's New Powerbrokers* (Bethesda, Md.: Adler & Adler, 1986).

13. Barry Sussman, *The Great Cover-Up: Nixon and the Scandal of Watergate* (New York: Crowell, 1974), pp. 130–131.

14. Ben Bagdikian, personal interview, August 5, 1990, Berkeley, Calif.

15. Sanford Unger, *The Papers and The Papers: An Account of the Legal and Political Battles over the Pentagon Papers* (New York: Columbia University Press, 1972, 1989), pp. 130–147.

16. Chalmers Roberts, *In the Shadow of Power: The Story of the Washington Post* (Cabin John, Md.: Seven Locks Press, 1989), p. 441.

17. Stephen E. Ambrose, *Nixon: The Education of a Politician 1913–1962* (New York: Simon & Schuster, 1987), p. 664.

18. Timothy Crouse, *The Boys on the Bus* (New York: Random House, 1973), but see Edith Efron, *The News Twisters* (Los Angeles: Nash Publications, 1971).

19. Michael A. Genovese, *The Nixon Presidency* (Westport, Conn.: Greenwood Press, 1990), p. 48.

20. Bagdikian, "The Fruits of Agnewism," pp. 9–21. As for network television coverage of Watergate, it appears generally to have been scrupulously neutral. See Marlene Schuler Daniels, "Carbon Copy News: A Content Analysis of Network Evening News Coverage of Watergate." M.A. diss., University of Wisconsin–Madison, 1976.

21. Godfrey Hodgson, *All Things to All Men: The False Promise of the Modern American Presidency* (New York: Simon & Schuster, 1980), pp. 193–194.

22. Leonard Downie, personal interview, February 28, 1991, Washington, D.C.

23. Quoted in Roberts, *In the Shadow of Power,* p. 495.

24. Maxwell E. McCombs, "Testing the Myths: A Statistical Review 1967–86," *Gannett Center Journal* (Spring 1988): 101–108.

25. When Ben Bagdikian commented on a draft of this chapter that included this paragraph, it reminded him that a senior editor at the *Atlantic* at the last minute removed a paragraph explaining that the influx of students into journalism did not start with Woodward and Bernstein; the editor, Bagdikian recalls, was "obsessed with" the impression that it all began with Watergate (personal communication, October 16, 1991).

26. Dina Rasor, an enterprising Washington journalist, recalls that as a teenager during Watergate, she came to view the press as the "defenders of truth, justice, and the American Way." Dina Rasor, *The Pentagon Underground* (New York: Times Books, 1985), p. 49.

27. Thomas Edsall, personal interview, February 13, 1991.

28. *San Diego Union*, January 6, 1990, p. A-17. Nessen spoke at a symposium entitled "The Presidency, The Press, and the People," organized by the University of California, San Diego, and later broadcast on PBS.

29. David S. Broder, *Behind the Front Page: A Candid Look at How the News Is Made* (New York: Simon & Schuster, 1987), p. 167.

30. Michael K. Deaver and Mickey Herskowitz, *Behind the Scenes* (New York: Morrow, 1987), p. 148.

31. Peter Kaye, "When the White House Speaks, the World Listens," *KPBS on Air*, January 1990, p. 16.

32. Leonard Downie, personal interview, February 28, 1991.

33. Gerald Warren, personal communication, November 13, 1991.

34. Ben Bradlee, personal interview, February 27, 1991, Washington, D.C.

35. Steven Brill, "Back on the Beat with Woodward and Bernstein," *Esquire*, December 1983, p. 503.

36. William Goldman, *Adventures in the Screen Trade* (New York: Warner Books, 1983), pp. 115–116.

37. CBS Morning News, April 5, 1976.

38. Nat Hentoff, "Woodstein in the Movies," *Columbia Journalism Review* (May-June 1976): 46.

39. Vincent Canby, "Two Exhilarating Thrillers, Plotted by Hitchcock and Nixon," *New York Times*, April 11, 1976, p. II-1.

40. Barbara Stubbs Cohen, personal interview, February 25, 1991, Washington, D.C. (Cohen speaks anachronistically of computers; in 1972 reporters pounded furiously on typewriters.)

41. Bob Woodward and Carl Bernstein, *The Final Days* (New York: Simon & Schuster, 1976).

42. CBS Morning News, April 5, 1976.

43. William B. Arthur, *The Courier-Journal* (Louisville), March 21, 1974.

44. *New York Times*, December 2, 1974, p. A-29.

45. *New York Times*, May 4, 1976, p. 14.

46. John Osborne, "The Woodstein Flap," *The New Republic*, April 24, 1976, p. 8. Thomas Powers predicted in *Commonweal* that *The Final Days* would outlast its critics, as did Peter Prescott in *Newsweek*. See Thomas Powers, "The Nixon Finale," *Commonweal*, May 7, 1976, pp. 307–309, and Peter Prescott, "Instant History," *Newsweek*, May 3, 1976, pp. 89–90.

47. James Fallows, "The New Celebrities of Washington," *New York Review of Books*, June 12, 1986, p. 42.

48. In a recent brochure from a Washington speakers' bureau advertising a stable of "history makers, trailblazers, entrepreneurs, explorers, news breakers, pioneers, discoverers, educators, experts," nearly half of the speakers listed are journalists (eighteen of forty-two speakers are known primarily as journalists). Cosby Bureau International, 1991.

49. The best evidence on the status of Washington journalists comes from studies by Stephen Hess in *The Washington Reporters* (Washington, D.C.: The Brookings Institution, 1981), pp. 158–165; and *Live from Capitol Hill! Studies of Congress and the Media* (Washington, D.C.: The Brookings Institution, 1991), pp. 110–130. Hess's surveys do not indicate any marked rise in educational attainment in the past generation among Washington journalists. He did not gather data on income. Anecdotal evidence suggests skyrocketing incomes, at least

among an elite of Washington reporters. See Jacob Weisberg, "The Buckrakers," *The New Republic,* January 27, 1986, pp. 16–18; and Carol Matlack, "Crossing the Line?" *National Journal,* March 25, 1989, pp. 724–729.

50. Ben Bradlee, personal interview, February 27, 1991.

51. This is a topic that has been written about extensively. See in particular Jonathan Schell, *Time of Illusion* (New York: Knopf, 1976); William Safire, *Before the Fall: An Inside View of the Pre-Watergate White House* (Garden City, N.Y.: Doubleday, 1975); Genovese, *The Nixon Presidency;* William Porter, *Assault on the Media: The Nixon Years* (Ann Arbor: University of Michigan Press, 1976); Thomas Whiteside, "Shaking the Tree," *The New Yorker,* March 17, 1975, pp. 41–91.

52. Safire, *Before the Fall,* p. 341.

53. See Schell, *Time of Illusion,* pp. 24, 55.

54. Sig Mickelson, *The Electric Mirror: Politics in an Age of Television* (New York: Dodd, Mead, 1972), p. 4, finds this a turning point in government-television relations.

55. Charles Peters, "Why the White House Press Didn't Get the Watergate Story," *Washington Monthly,* July/August 1973; reprinted in *Watergate: Its Effects on the American Political System,* ed. David Saffell (Cambridge, Mass.: Winthrop Publishers, 1974), p. 31.

56. Safire, *Before the Fall,* p. 351.

57. The Kraft case has a particularly detailed history. See David Wise, *The American Police State: The Government Against the People* (New York: Random House, 1976), pp. 3–30, and also Joseph Kraft, "Reflections on a Personal Wiretap," *Washington Post,* June 12, 1973, p. 21.

58. Genovese, *The Nixon Presidency,* p. 54.

59. Daniel Schorr, *Clearing the Air* (Boston: Houghton Mifflin, 1977), pp. 30–34, 53–57.

60. Herbert G. Klein, *Making It Perfectly Clear* (New York: Doubleday, 1980), p. 109; the Haldeman memo was written on February 4, 1970.

61. Klein, *Making It Perfectly Clear,* p. 125; Larry Higby's letter is dated September 16, 1970.

62. George W. Johnson, *The Nixon Presidential Press Conferences* (New York: Earl M. Coleman Enterprises, 1978), pp. 369, 373. Nixon repeats this line in a video display at the Richard Nixon Library and Birthplace; his hostility to the press remained implacable.

63. Harry S. Ashmore, "Nixon's Regime Gave News Media Identity Separate from Public's," *Phoenix Gazette,* December 10, 1973. Ashmore attributes this view to Lisagor and endorses it.

64. Safire, *Before the Fall,* pp. 343, 351.

65. See Sabato, *Feeding Frenzy,* p. 45.

66. Theodore White, *The Making of the President, 1960* (New York: Atheneum, 1961).

67. American Society of Newspaper Editors, *Problems of Journalism* (Washington, D.C., 1983), p. 114.

68. See Michael Schudson, *Discovering the News* (New York: Basic Books, 1978), pp. 189–190.

69. Barry Sussman, personal interview, January 1991, Washington, D.C.

70. Stephen Hess, personal interview, January 1991, Washington, D.C.

71. *Washington Post*, August 5, 1977, p. A-21.

72. Ben Bradlee, personal interview, February 27, 1991.

73. "Carter and the Press: One Good Month," interview with Jack Nelson, *Washington Journalism Review* 13 (January/February 1991): 17.

74. James Deakin, *Straight Stuff: The Reporters, the White House, and the Truth* (New York: Morrow, 1984), p. 295.

75. Jody Powell, *The Other Side of the Story* (New York: Morrow, 1984), p. 173.

76. For reviews of *Absence of Malice* that comment on *All the President's Men*, see David Ansen, "Wayward Press," *Newsweek*, November 23, 1981, p. 125; Richard Schickel, "Lethal Leaks," *Time*, November 23, 1981, p. 98; and Stanley Kauffmann, "The Facts of Some Matters," *The New Republic*, December 23, 1981, pp. 24–25. Discussions of how journalists responded to *Absence of Malice* also include comments on *All the President's Men* in the *New York Times*, November 15, 1981, p. II-1, and in the *Washington Post*, November 18, 1981, p. B-1.

77. "Bernstein Chides News for Its Over-Confidence," *Harvard Crimson*, March 21, 1989.

78. *Washington Post*, August 8, 1984, p. A-12.

79. Bob Woodward and Scott Armstrong, *The Brethren* (New York: Simon & Schuster, 1979); Bob Woodward, *Wired: The Short Life and Fast Times of John Belushi* (New York: Simon & Schuster, 1984); Woodward, *Veil: The Secret Wars of the CIA, 1981–1987* (New York: Simon & Schuster, 1987); Woodward, *The Commanders* (New York: Simon & Schuster, 1991).

80. Steven Brill, "Inside the Jury Room at the *Washington Post* Libel Trial," *American Lawyer* 4 (November 1982): 1, 89–93.

81. This account of the courtroom and jury room follows Brill, "Inside the Jury Room."

82. *William P. Tavoulareas v. Washington Post*, 817 F.2d 762 (D.C. Cir. 1987); Kenneth Starr, p. 795–797; George MacKinnon, p. 834.

83. Tom Rosenstiel, personal communication, January 16, 1991, Washington, D.C.

84. Justin Kaplan, *Lincoln Steffens* (New York: Simon & Schuster, 1974), pp. 145–146.

8. National News Culture

1. Hedrick Smith, *The Power Game* (New York: Ballantine, 1988), p. 20.

2. Godfrey Hodgson, *America in Our Time* (Garden City, N.Y.: Doubleday, 1976), p. 152.

3. Kenneth C. Clark, "Networks Form Group to Pitch Themselves," *San Diego Union*, April 7, 1990, p. E11.

4. *Newsweek*, October 17, 1988, p. 94.

5. Alan Green, *Gavel to Gavel: A Guide to the Television Proceedings of Congress* (Washington, D.C.: Benton Foundation, 1986).

6. Marc Fisher, "All Things Reconsidered," *Washington Post National Weekly Edition*, October 30–November 5, 1989, p. 6.

7. David Shaw, *Journalism Today* (New York: Harper's College Press, 1977), p. 195.

8. Larry King, "Talk Radio: An Interview with Larry King," *Gannett Center Journal* 3 (Spring 1989): 17–24.

9. Sanford J. Ungar, *The Papers and the Papers* (New York: Columbia University Press, 1989), p. 107.

10. Quoted in Ellis Cose, *The Press* (New York: William Morrow, 1989), p. 58.

11. Peter Prichard, *The Making of McPaper: The Inside Story of USA Today* (Kansas City: Andrews, McMeel, and Parker, 1987), p. 311.

12. John C. Busterna, "Trends in Daily Newspaper Ownership," *Journalism Quarterly* 65 (Winter 1988): 833; and Ben Bagdikian, *The Media Monopoly* (Boston: Beacon Press, 1989).

13. Kay Mills, *A Place in the News: From the Women's Pages to the Front Page* (New York: Dodd, Mead, 1989), p. 149.

14. Ibid., p. 1. See also Marlene Sanders and Marcia Rock, *Waiting for Prime Time: The Women of Television News* (Urbana: University of Illinois Press, 1988).

15. Mills, *A Place in the News*, pp. 247, 251.

16. Herbert J. Gans, *Deciding What's News: A Study of CBS Evening News, NBC Nightly News, Newsweek, and Time* (New York: Vintage, 1979), pp. 42–52.

17. Smith, *The Power Game*, p. 29.

18. Stephen Hess, *The Washington Reporters* (Washington, D.C.: Brookings Institution, 1981), p. 13.

19. Brigitte Darnay, ed., *Newsletters in Print*, 4th ed. (Detroit: Gale Research, 1988).

20. Jeffrey Abramson, F. Christopher Arterton, and Gary Orren, *The Electronic Commonwealth* (New York: Basic Books, 1988), pp. 92–93.

21. Smith, *The Power Game*, p. 149.

22. Barnaby F. Feder, "The Business of Earth Day," *New York Times*, November 12, 1989, p. F4.

23. Connie Koenenn and Bob Sipchen, "Too Hip for Her Own Good?" *Los Angeles Times*, March 30, 1990, p. E1. See also, on media metacoverage, Todd Gitlin, "Blips, Bites, and Savvy Talk," *Dissent* (Winter 1990): 18–26.

24. From an interview conducted by America Rodriguez as part of a research project with Helene Keyssar. I am grateful to America Rodriguez for research assistance on this chapter.

25. Kathryn C. Montgomery, *Target: Prime Time* (New York: Oxford University Press, 1989), p. 31.

26. Adam Hochschild, "And That's The Way It Was . . ." *Mother Jones* (May 1981): 5.

27. "Trial Losers Blame Verdict on 'L.A. Law' Episode," *San Diego Union*, December 25, 1989, p. A5. See also Alan Waldman, "Hear Ye, Hear Ye! 'L.A. Law's' in Session," *TV Guide*, March 10, 1990, p. 7.

28. Leo Bogart, *Press and Public*, 2nd ed. (Hillsdale, N.J.: Lawrence Erlbaum, 1989), p. 337.

29. Ibid., p. 339. See also James Curran, "The Impact of TV on the Audience for National Newspapers, 1945–68," in *Media Sociology: A Reader*, ed. Jeremy Tunstall (Urbana: University of Illinois Press, 1970), pp. 104–131, for a detailed argument that newspaper consumption rose substantially during the first decades of the growth of television in Britain.

30. Reed Irvine, *Media Mischief and Misdeeds* (Chicago: Regnery Gateway, 1984), p. 9.

31. "Are You on the Nightline Guest List?" *Extra!* (January/February 1989): 2–15.

32. Peter Dreier, "Capitalists vs. the Media: An Analysis of an Ideological

Mobilization among Business Leaders," *Media, Culture and Society* 4 (April 1982): 111–132.

33. Leo Bogart, "The Case of the 30-Second Commercial," *Journal of Advertising Research* 23 (February/March 1983): 11–18. In 1965, 77 percent of network commercials were a minute long and there were no 30-second commercials; by 1970 25 percent of commercials were 30 seconds long, 95 percent by 1980. In the last few years, commercials have grown shorter still; in 1988 37 percent of all network commercials were 15 seconds long, compared to 5 percent in 1984, while the share allocated to the 30-second commercial has dropped from 89 percent to 60 percent. See *Television and Video Almanac 1989* (New York: Quigley Publishing, 1989), p. 23A. As Bogart shows, advertisers should not be pleased. In 1965, 20 percent of viewers could identify either the brand or at least the product line of the "last" commercial they saw before receiving a phone call from a market researcher; in 1981 only 9 percent could do the same.

34. Raymond Serafin, "Why GM Wants 'Pod Protection,' " *Advertising Age* (December 4, 1989): 25.

35. Key Lehman Schlozman and John T. Tierney, *Organized Interests and American Democracy* (New York: Harper & Row, 1986). On corporate lobbying, see David Vogel, *Fluctuating Fortunes* (New York: Basic Books, 1989).

36. This body of work is reviewed in Michael Schudson, "The Sociology of News Production Revisited," in *Mass Media and Society*, ed. James Curran and Michael Gurevitch (London: Edward Arnold, 1991), pp. 141–159.

37. Thomas Patterson, *Out of Order* (New York: Alfred A. Knopf, 1993), p. 20.

38. Mayer N. Zald and John D. McCarthy, *Social Movements in an Organizational Society* (New Brunswick, N.J.: Transaction Books, 1987).

39. U.S. Bureau of the Census, *Statistical Abstract of the United States 1990* (Washington, D.C.: U.S. Government Printing Office, 1990), p. 133.

40. Ibid., p. 227.

41. Ibid.

42. Lewis Coser, Charles Kadushin, and Walter Powell, *Books: The Culture and Commerce of Publishing* (New York: Basic Books, 1982), p. 349; Robert Baensch, "Consolidation in Publishing and Allied Industries," *Book Research Quarterly* 4 (Winter 1988): 10; U.S. Bureau of the Census, Statistical Abstract of the United States: 1993 (113th ed.) (Washington, D.C.: Government Printing Office, 1993); *Publishers Weekly*, April 11, 1994, p. 10.

43. Baensch, "Consolidation in Publishing," p. 13.

44. Daniel Hallin, "Whose Campaign Is It Anyway?" *Columbia Journalism Review* (November-December 1990); and Kiku Adatto, "Sound Bite Democracy: Network Evening News Presidential Campaign Coverage, 1968 and 1988," Research Paper R-2 (Cambridge, Mass.: Joan Shorenstein Barone Center, John F. Kennedy School of Government, Harvard University, 1990).

45. Lawrence C. Stedman and Carl F. Kaestle, "The Test Score Decline Is Over: Now What?" *Phi Delta Kappan* (November 1985): 204.

9. Was There Ever a Public Sphere?

1. Christopher Lasch, "A Response to Joel Feinberg," *Tikkun* 3 (1988): 43.

2. George Anastaplo, "Education, Television, and Political Discourse in America," *Center Magazine*, July-August 1986, p. 21.

3. *New York Times*, January 31, 1988, p. IV-5.

4. Walter Dean Burnham, "Theory and Voting Research," in Burnham, *The Current Crisis in American Politics* (New York: Oxford University Press, 1982), p. 83.

5. Ibid., pp. 84–86.

6. Lawrence Levine, *Highbrow/Lowbrow: The Emergence of Cultural Hierarchy in America* (Cambridge, Mass.: Harvard University Press, 1988).

7. Other dimensions of the public sphere would focus on the extent to which a legal or constitutional framework exists to preserve rational-critical discussion and citizen participation; the degree to which public-mindedness is encouraged in the ethnic and value system of public servants; the extent to which relative economic equality prevails or to which a political system prevents the undue influence of the wealthy; the extent to which social life (family, church, and private associations) is imbued with a democratic, rather than deferential, spirit that would socialize individuals into readiness for public participation.

8. Peter Hohendahl, "Critical Theory, Public Sphere, and Culture: Jürgen Habermas and His Critics," *New German Critique* 6 (1979): 92.

9. Jane Mansbridge, *Beyond Adversary Democracy* (New York: Basic Books, 1980), pp. 130–131.

10. Robert Zemsky, *Merchants, Farmers, and River Gods: An Essay on Eighteenth-Century American Politics* (Boston: Gambit, 1971), p. 37.

11. J. Morgan Kousser, "Suffrage," in *Encyclopedia of American Political History*, vol. 3, ed. Jack Greene (New York: Charles Scribner's, 1984).

12. Ronald Formisano, *The Transformation of Political Culture: Massachusetts Parties, 1790s–1840s* (New York: Oxford University Press, 1983), p. 30.

13. Ibid., p. 27.

14. Ibid., p. 17.

15. William Gienapp, " 'Politics Seems to Enter into Everything': Political Culture in the North, 1840–1860," in *Essays on American Antebellum Politics, 1840–1860*, ed. Stephen E. Maizlish and John J. Kushma (College Station, Texas: Texas A&M Press, 1982), p. 15.

16. Walter Dean Burnham, *The Current Crisis in American Politics* (New York: Oxford University Press, 1982), p. 129.

17. David Hall, "The Uses of Literacy in New England, 1600–1850," in *Printing and Society in Early America*, ed. David Hall (Worcester: American Antiquarian Society, 1983), pp. 27–28.

18. Harry S. Stout, *The New England Soul* (New York: Oxford University Press, 1986), p. 87.

19. From 1790 to 1830 evangelical Christianity became a powerful force for a democratic culture. In 1776 or 1787, however, the democratic revolution in the churches had not matured. See Nathan O. Hatch, *The Democratization of American Christianity* (New Haven: Yale University Press, 1989).

20. Quoted in Eric Foner, *Tom Paine and Revolutionary America* (New York: Oxford University Press, 1976), p. 83.

21. Harvey Graff, *The Literacy Myth* (New York: Academic Press, 1979).

22. Lawrence C. Stedman and Carl F. Kaestle, "Literacy and Reading Performance in the United States, from 1880 to the Present," *Reading Research Quarterly* 22 (1987): 8–46.

23. James Lemert, "New Context and the Elimination of Mobilizing Information: An Experiment," *Journalism Quarterly* (1984): 243–249, 259.

24. Quoted in Michael Schudson, *Discovering the News: A Social History of American Newspapers* (New York: Basic Books, 1978), p. 21. For a discussion of the model of journalism as the center of an association of readers, see David Nord, "Tocqueville, Garrison, and the Perfection of Journalism," *Journalism History* 13 (1986): 56–63.

25. Stephen Botein, " 'Meer Mechanics' and an Open Press: The Business and Political Strategies of Colonial American Printers," *Perspectives in American History* 9 (1975): 127–228.

26. Zemsky, *Merchants, Farmers, and River Gods*, pp. 239–241.

27. Ibid., p. 252.

28. Thomas Leonard, *The Power of the Press: The Birth of American Political Reporting* (New York: Oxford University Press, 1986), p. 70.

29. Richard Hofstadter, *The Idea of a Party System* (Berkeley: University of California Press, 1972).

30. Ballard Campbell, *Representative Democracy: Public Policy and Midwestern Legislatures in the Late Nineteenth Century* (Cambridge, Mass.: Harvard University Press, 1980), p. 92.

31. Michael McGerr, *The Decline of Popular Politics* (New York: Oxford University Press, 1986), p. 21.

32. Maurice Duverger, *Political Parties* (London: Methuen, 1954), p. 378.

33. Ibid., p. 380.

34. Gienapp, " 'Politics Seems to Enter into Everything,' " p. 33.

35. Ibid., p. 35.

36. Ibid.

37. Ibid., p. 40.

38. Stanley Kelley, Jr., *Political Campaigning: Problems in Creating an Informed Electorate* (Washington, D.C.: The Brookings Institution, 1960), p. 3.

39. McGerr, *The Decline of Popular Politics*, p. 31.

40. Ibid., p. 32.

41. Benjamin Ginsberg, *The Captive Public* (New York: Basic Books, 1986).

42. Gary Nash, "The Transformation of Urban Politics, 1700–1765," *Journal of American History* 60 (1973): 605–632.

10. The News Media and the Democratic Process

1. Lane Davis, "The Cost of Realism: Contemporary Restatements of Democracy," *Western Political Quarterly* 17 (1964): 37–46. See also a definition of democracy that sits somewhere between the most grandiose versions of classical views and the most mechanical versions of realism in Robert A. Dahl, "Liberal Democracy in the United States," in *A Prospect of Liberal Democracy*, ed. William S. Livingston (Austin: University of Texas Press, 1979), pp. 57–72. Dahl takes "political equality," "effective participation," and "adequate understanding" as necessary criteria for setting the rules of political decision making if a democratic ideal is to be enacted.

2. Walter Lippmann, *Public Opinion* (New York: Harcourt Brace, 1922), pp. 342–345, 379–397.

3. Walter Lippmann, *The Phantom Public* (New York: Harcourt, Brace, 1925), pp. 61–62.

4. Ibid., pp. 78, 109.

5. David S. Broder, *The Party's Over* (New York: Harper & Row, 1972).

6. Gerald N. Pomper, "The Decline of Partisan Politics," in *The Impact of the Electoral Process*, ed. Louis Maisel and Joseph Cooper (Beverly Hills, Calif.: Sage Publications, 1977), p. 14.

7. James Gazlay, "State of Parties," *Western Tiller*, September 26, 1826. The *Western Tiller* was an early Jacksonian newspaper in Cincinnati, Ohio.

8. Pomper, "The Decline of Partisan Politics," p. 15.

9. Ibid., p. 27. Studies published since this chapter was originally written suggest the strength of the trend toward independence has been exaggerated, although the direction of the change is not in doubt. See Bruce E. Keith et al., *The Myth of the Independent Voter* (Berkeley: University of California Press, 1992).

10. Ibid., p. 36. See also Samuel P. Huntington, "The United States," in Michel J. Crozier, Samuel P. Huntington, and Joji Watanuki, *The Crisis of Democracy* (New York: Trilateral Commission, New York University Press, 1975), pp. 85–91.

11. Huntington, "The United States," pp. 64, 115.

12. Charles E. Lindblom, *Politics and Markets* (New York: Basic Books, 1977), p. 356. For the data on PACs and other campaign contributions, see Larry Makinson, *Open Secrets: The Dollar Power of PACs in Congress* (Washington, D.C.: CQ Inc., 1990), pp. 18, 42, and Frank J. Sorauf, *Inside Campaign Finance* (New Haven: Yale University Press, 1992), pp. 71, 88, 100, 108.

13. Lindblom, *Politics and Markets,* p. 218.

14. Peter Clarke and Susan Evans, *Covering Campaigns: Journalism in Congressional Elections* (Palo Alto, Calif.: Stanford University Press, 1983).

15. Clarke and Evans offer a more extensive set of recommendations, which inspired my own.

16. Clarke and Evans, *Covering Campaigns.* See also Clarke and Evans, "All in a Day's Work: Reporters Covering Congressional Campaigns," *Journal of Communication* 30 (1980): 112–121.

17. David Burnham, from Aspen Institute conference on the Governed, the Governors, and the News Media, 1979. Burnham's practice is very common among investigative journalists. For a rich and nuanced account of how investigative reporters use dominant moral values in their work, see Theodore L. Glasser and James S. Ettema, "Investigative Journalism and the Moral Order," *Critical Studies in Mass Communication* 6 (1989): 1–20.

18. Broder, *The Party's Over*, p. 222.

19. Richard L. Rubin, *Press, Party, and Presidency* (New York: W. W. Norton, 1981), pp. 192–195.

20. Huntington, "The United States," p. 114.

21. Ronald Inglehart, *The Silent Revolution* (Princeton, N.J.: Princeton University Press, 1977).

22. Albert O. Hirschman, *Shifting Involvements: Private Interests and Public Action* (Princeton, N.J.: Princeton University Press, 1982), pp. 103–111.

Credits

Chapter 1 Originally published in *Proceedings of the American Antiquarian Society,* vol. 100, pt. 2 (1991): 421–444; reprinted with the permission of the American Antiquarian Society.

Chapter 2 Reprinted by permission of *Daedalus,* the Journal of the American Academy of Arts and Sciences, from the issue entitled "Print Culture and Video Culture," vol. 111, no. 4 (Fall 1982).

Chapter 3 Originally published in *Media, Culture & Society,* vol. 16 (October 1994).

Chapter 4 Originally published in *Media, Myths, and Narratives,* ed. James W. Carey (Newbury Park, Calif.: Sage Publications, 1988), pp. 228–245.

Chapter 5 Originally published in TIKKUN Magazine, A Bi-Monthly Jewish Critique of Politcs, Culture, and Society, vol. 6, no. 1 (March/April 1991).

Chapter 6 Also published in *Public Opinion and the Communication of Consent,* ed. Theodore Glasser and Charles Salmon (New York: Guilford Press, 1995).

Chapter 7 Originally published in Michael Schudson, *Watergate in American Memory* (New York: Basic Books, a division of HarperCollins Publishers, 1992), pp. 103–126.

Chapter 8 Originally published in *America at Century's End,* ed. Alan Wolfe (Berkeley: University of California Press, 1991), pp. 265–282. Copyright 1991 by The Regents of the University of California; reprinted by permission of the University of California Press.

Chapter 9 Originally published in *Habermas and the Public Sphere,* ed. Craig Calhoun (Cambridge, Mass.: MIT Press, 1992), pp. 143–163.

Chapter 10 Originally published in 1983 by the Aspen Institute as a Wye Resource Paper. Reprinted with permission from The Aspen Institute, Queenstown, Maryland.

Index

democracy and, 20, 24, 26–30, 31, 33,
204–205, 211–214, 216; influence on
public opinion, 21–22, 121, 122–123;
visibility of, 24–25; effects on commu-
nity, 40–42, 50; term "the media," 156,
171; control of, 170, 183–184; satura-
tion, 170, 186–187; as social practice,
170; ethnic/linguistic, 177; religious,
177; schizophrenic view of, 211–212,
223; reform proposals, 219–220
Mellon, Andrew W., 83
Meyer, Richard E., 139
Miller, Mark Crispin, 138
Minneapolis Star, 141
Mitchell, John, 165
Mondale, Walter, 24, 121, 122, 178
Morgan, Thomas, 87
Morning Post (London), 78
Mother Jones, 175, 180
Moyers, Bill, 6
Muckraking, 97, 101, 104, 108, 142,
164–165, 217. *See also* Reporting,
investigative
Munsey's Magazine, 85
Murrow, Edward R., 6, 39, 172

Nader, Ralph, 184
Narration, 15, 41, 54–55, 65, 118; politi-
cal, 53, 65, 71
Nation, The, 76, 184
National Conservative Political Action
Committee, 136
National Journal, 125
National News Council, 153
National Press Club, 176
National Public Radio, 173
NBC, 127
Nelson, Gaylord, 178
Neoconservatism, 135–136
Nessen, Ron, 150, 159
New-England Courant, 45
New Republic, The, 132, 138, 154
New Right, 135–136
News, 26, 38–39, 171; as culture, 3–8,
14, 15–18, 21, 31, 176–179; informa-
tion and, 3, 69–70, 171; modes of
explanation, 14–15; local, 15; effects of,
16–25; vs. direct messages, 20; organi-
zation of, 21, 25, 206; events, 25, 49,
56; and social movements, 27–28;
social construction of, 38, 49, 65–66,
230n19; literary conventions of, 54–59,
70–71; novelty of, 48, 55, 56, 59, 95;
time frame for, 55, 91; political, 65–66;

format, 67–68, 215–216; objectivity of,
70, 108; as entertainment, 171, 179;
nationalization of, 172–179; services,
174–175; right vs. left interpretation of,
182–185; foreign, 198; institutions,
216; cultural study of, 229n27. *See also*
Bias in news reporting
Newsday, 158
News letters, 177, 197
News media in foreign countries, 31, 76,
181, 182, 198, 227n4
Newspapers, 16, 31, 114; local, 3, 13; foreign news in, 13, 45, 46–47; alternative, 29–30; letters to the editor, 30,
50–51; government subsidies to, 30;
ordinariness of, 37, 50; history of, 37–
52, 72, 197–198; circulation, 43–44,
175, 182; local, 43–44, 45, 50–51; metropolitan, 43, 44, 66, 175; associational, 44, 50; as printed record, 47, 48;
influence on public opinion, 50; corporate, 67; readership, 67, 181; partisan,
72, 84, 190; foreign, 76, 181, 198;
illustrations, 88–89; sources, 136;
home-delivery of, 174, 175, 182;
national, 174; regional, 174; chains,
175–176; daily, 175; op ed page, 176;
election coverage by, 214–215
Newspaper formats, 13, 14, 16, 215–216;
leads, 13, 16, 49, 55, 59, 60, 61, 67,
69, 83, 91, 92; sports section, 13, 26;
headlines, 16, 60; columns, 51
News stories, 55, 59; features, 13; human
interest, 13, 86; descriptive, 59, 68,
109; political, 60–61, 68; form and content, 64, 66; direct quotations in, 77
Newsweek, 175; coverage of Reagan, 126,
127, 128, 130, 131–132, 134; coverage
of Carter, 133
New York Evening Post, 98, 105
New York Evening Sun, 87–88
New York Herald, 44
New York Journal, 231n53
New York Times, 4, 6, 16, 17, 28, 48, 97,
115, 175, 176, 188, 190, 236n4; coverage of Reagan, 11, 125, 127, 128, 129;
and State of the Union messages, 57–
58, 60, 61, 62–63; front-page stories,
63; interviews, 84, 85; op-ed page, 119,
127; television critics in, 120; publication of the Pentagon Papers, 142, 146,
174; coverage of Watergate, 144; on
Nixon's Vietnam policy, 146; review of

216; participation in politics, 192, 193–203

Public Broadcasting System, 154, 173

Public knowledge, 16, 19–21, 33

Publick Occurrences, 44–45

Public opinion, 49, 106, 139; influence of media on, 21–22, 121, 122–123; influence of television on, 22–24, 131, 137, 138, 154, 155, 172, 173, 174, 176, 181, 215; role in democracy, 32, 206; Congress and, 135; image of the President and, 138, 140; polls, 140, 213–214, 222

Public sphere, 106, 107, 110, 171, 188, 193, 203, 254n7; decline of, 189–190; participation in, 192; political, 192; press and, 197–201

Publishers, 2, 12, 16

Publishing (book), 185–186

Pulitzer, Joseph, 5, 39, 231n53

Pulitzer Prize, 142–143, 161, 165, 217

Radio, 62, 117, 120, 173–174

Ralph, Julian, 81, 91

Rather, Dan, 6, 92

Rational-critical discourse, 192, 195, 198, 202, 203

Rayburn, Sam, 53

Raymond, Henry, 55

Reagan, Ronald, 121, 132–133; Louisiana flood photo op, 10–11, 16, 229n24; popularity in press/approval ratings, 16–17, 125–130, 136–140, 244n13, 246n51, 247n62; -Gorbachev summit, 109, 246n51; manipulation of press and television, 115, 116, 118–120, 122–123, 137–138; job approval ratings, 119, 125–126, 127–128, 247n62; relations with Congress, 123, 132, 134, 136, 137; as the Great Communicator, 124–125, 126, 130, 131, 137, 138, 139–141, 244n7; speeches, 124, 130, 136, 140; Iran-Contra scandal, 125, 246n51; low poll ratings, 127–130; assassination attempt against, 128, 130; economic/budget policy, 128, 130, 134, 135, 137, 244n13; relations with news media and press conferences, 130–132, 138, 140–141, 150–151; in 1980 election, 133, 134, 137, 185, 244n13; in 1984 election, 133; New Right and, 135–136, 137; tax policy, 137, 244n13; direct relations with the public, 140, 159

Redford, Robert, 149, 151–152, 153, 157

Religion, 136, 177, 190, 254n19

Reporters, 2, 66, 91, 92, 157, 174; and sources, 3, 48–49, 74–93, 104; political, 6–7, 10, 31, 66, 70; social background of, 6–8; objectivity of, 9–10, 56, 61, 108, 110, 171; foreign, 48; authority of, 49, 65–67, 92; analysis and interpretation of the news by, 56, 59, 61, 62, 63, 64, 66, 68, 69, 91–92; role and responsibilities of, 65, 107, 109; autonomy of, 67, 68, 76, 91; salaries, 67, 150, 154, 177; women, 86, 150, 176; defined, 94–97, 104, 105–106; feelings of, 98–101; knowledge of, 101–106; desires of, 106–110; television news, 138; education levels of, 154, 176, 249n49. *See also* Newspapers; Press

Reporting, investigative, 16, 72–73, 150, 157–165, 217, 256n17. *See also* Muckraking

Republican Information Network, 178

Republican National Committee, 178

Republican party, 113, 134, 145, 185, 199

Reston, James, 118–119, 127, 132

Richardson, Francis A., 73, 77

Riesman, David, 65–66

Right, political, 6, 21, 27, 119, 135–137, 183, 185, 228n12, 244n13

Riis, Jacob, 104

Ritual model of news, 41–42

Robinson, Max, 176

Robinson, Michael, 9, 27, 185

Rogers, Will, 44

Rolling Stone, 175

Roosevelt, Eleanor, 62, 86

Roosevelt, Franklin D., 62, 86, 121, 124, 125, 132, 153, 236n4

Roosevelt, Theodore, 53, 64, 65, 84, 108, 165

Rosenstiel, Thomas, 163–164

Rosenthal, Abe, 146

Rothman, Stanley, 6, 7

Rubin, Richard, 218

Russo, Anthony, 174

Sabato, Larry, 145

Safire, William, 154–155

Salisbury, Harrison: autobiography, 94, 95–96, 97, 102–103, 110; in Russia, 96, 100, 103, 107, 108, 110; style of journalism, 97, 100–101, 110; on being